GALW

with Ollie Turner

www.**HERO**BOOKS.digital

HEROBOOKS

PUBLISHED BY HERO BOOKS
1 WOODVILLE GREEN
LUCAN
CO. DUBLIN
IRELAND

Hero Books is an imprint of Umbrella Publishing
First Published 2020
Copyright © Ollie Turner 2020
All rights reserved

A CIP record for this book is available from the British Library

ISBN 9781910827284

Cover design and formatting: jessica@viitaladesign.com
Ebook formatting: www.ebooklaunch.com
Photographs: Inpho and Ollie Turner

★ DEDICATION ★

To the memory of Tony Keady (1963-2017)...
One of the Greats

Here you go Paul,
Best Wishes,
Liam

HEROBOOKS

P: 00 353 (0)87 2867084
E: submissions@herobooks.digital
www.herobooks.digital

★ CONTENTS ★

★ ACKNOWLEDGEMENTS ★

'HURLER.'

That was how he answered the phone to me.

'How's things, Tony?' was my reply.

That became the routine almost every day for the month between the 2012 All-Ireland semi-final win over Cork and the upcoming final against Kilkenny.

Tony Keady, two-time All-Ireland winner and 1988 Hurler of the Year had written a song for the All-Ireland final and he wanted me to record him singing it in the studios of my work place, Galway Bay fm.

'Sure, come in to the station and we will have a listen to it, Tony.'

The first thing that struck me was his smile and his aura. He had never set foot in Galway Bay fm in his life, yet he strode in with the confident air of a man on a mission. Tony had it in his head for a few years to record the song *Galway Heroes* and by the time he got around to ringing me in 2012, he had changed the names of the Galway players in the song about 10 times as one lad retired and another took his place.

We had the best fun imaginable as we organised a local band, *Vinnie Mongan and Restless* to accompany him. I was supposed to be the 'producer' but, in reality, I sat at the back of the recording studio and marvelled at the sheer honesty and passion of one of Galway's greatest ever hurlers as he tried to stir the Galway public to get behind their team for the upcoming final against Kilkenny.

The song worked a treat and achieved everything Tony hoped it would. It was never about *him*, but he didn't mind if he was the vehicle that drove the people of Galway to get behind their team.

That honesty and passion is symptomatic of so many lads that pulled on the Galway jersey over the decades. There is a reason why Galway hurling is unique and I hope by the end of this book you get a sense of why that is so.

This entire project was a privilege as I listened to Jimmy Hegarty and Ned Dervan talk about rarely winning a game in their careers with Galway in the late 1950s and 60s. Yet, they are every bit as important as the men that came after them in 1975 and '80, because they kept the spirit of Galway alive in the face of massive adversity. The highs and lows of the 1980s are laid bare, the emergence of Galway as a major force in minor and under-21 is detailed too, while the extraordinary success of Galway sides in the All-Ireland Club Championship is chronicled from the breakthrough of Castlegar to the dominance of Sarsfields, Athenry and Portumna.

One word appears in several chapters and you will struggle to find it in any Irish-English dictionary, or even Google translate.

The word is *Báireóirí*, a word derived from Cúl Báire, the Irish for goalkeeper.

Báireóirí na Gaillimhe is a fraternity of over 300 former hurlers from the last six decades that was launched in 2015 and they are 'keepers' of the Galway hurling tradition.

I had the great fortune to be in the company of these men on a number of occasions and the bond they have is special. It is a bond, not just with their teammates, but with men from different generations who have one thing in common... the Galway jersey.

To all the lads and their families who gave of their time to allow me to tell their story, I say thank you. To my own family, Therese, Rachel, Emma and Laura, thanks for being so supportive. To Liam Hayes and the team at Hero Books, thank you for the opportunity to go down memory lane and relive some of the great sporting stories of our time.

In the words of Leo Moran and Padraig Stevens...
My heart is in Maroon and White
I'll stick with what I know
It's Maroon and White forever
No matter where I go

Ollie Turner
October, 2020

JIMMY HEGARTY

LIMERICK 2-13, GALWAY 2-7
Munster SHC Quarter-Final
Cusack Park, Ennis
MAY 27, 1962

Two outstanding hurlers and two great opponents. Jimmy Hegarty (right) with Tipperary legend Jimmy Finn

★ **GALWAY:** J Hegarty; P Burke, J Murray, T Conway; J Duggan, N Dervan, J Conroy (0-1); J Salmon (0-1), S Gohery; M Regan, M Cullinane (0-3), PJ Lally; J Gillane (2-0), J Conway, T Sweeney (0-2).

★ **LIMERICK:** J Hogan; T Bluett, JJ Bresnan, Jack Quaid; A O'Brien, K Long, S Quaid (0-1); P Hartnett (0-3), PJ Keane; M Rainsford (0-4), T McGarry (0-1), L Hogan (0-1); E Carey (2-1), O O'Neill (0-2), Jim Quaid.

THE ACTION

LIMERICK ADVANCED TO a Munster semi-final meeting with Tipperary after a comfortable six-point win over Galway in front of 12,000 spectators at a sunny Cusack Park. Indeed, Limerick's winning margin would have been far greater but for the spectacular goalkeeping of Galway's Jimmy Hegarty, who gave one of the great individual displays of all time and saved his side from being annihilated.

Backed by the breeze, Limerick started in whirlwind fashion with an Eamonn Carey goal after just two minutes, and thanks to further points from Martin Rainsford, the free taking of Pat Hartnett and a second Carey goal, the winners led by 2-7 to 0-2 at the break.

Two Mickey Cullinane points and a sideline cut from Joe Salmon reduced the lead at the start of the second-half, but it took two brilliant reflex saves from Hegarty to deny Limerick the goals that would have ended the game as a contest.

Joe Gillane worked his way through for a great Galway goal midway through the second-half to bring it back to 2-10 to 1-6, but Limerick responded with points from a Liam Hogan free and Rainsford. Galway ended the scoring with a consolation goal from Joe Gillane, his second, but it was Limerick who deservedly advanced on a day when Hegarty's performance in the Galway goal will live long in the memory.

★★★★★

66

I WAS BORN at No 2. Daly's Place in Woodquay. There was only ourselves and the Smiths, so it was the smallest place in Woodquay and my earliest memories were of playing on the streets when there were only three cars in Galway – a taxi and two others.

That was 70 years ago and I can tell you times were tough.

The Cullinanes were very good neighbours to us and even though their father was a Castlegar man and I was with Liam Mellows, he would always make sure I had a hurley, even if it meant taking one off one of his own sons.

Woodquay produced some great hurling people at that time… like the Hughes' and Mickey Elwood. They were just great people.

I remember seeing a hurley in the shop window of Ned Walsh's priced at seven shillings and six pence, which my mother Lena didn't have, so she gave him half a crown and Ned said to pay the balance whenever she had it, which she did. It was always great to have a new hurl, but I suppose I would be lucky if it lasted two or three matches, especially as I used to always play outfield in the 'plots', down by the riverside.

When I was around 12, I got my appendix out and was very sore and couldn't run so the men that were over Liam Mellows at the time, Jimmy Duggan and Sean Turk from College Road, asked me to stand in goal. The 'goals' at the time were two rocks, but soon I was stopping one or two balls and started to enjoy myself, especially when I saw the great Sean Duggan going down to training.

Sean was one of the greatest goalkeepers of all time and he was the Galway goalie during the 1940s and 50s, which inspired me to eventually make the Galway minor panel in 1957.

I played in the All-Ireland semi-final that year against Tipperary, when the great Jimmy Doyle beat us on his own. I had never been in Croke Park before that game and I recall I was the last Galway player out of the dressing-room.

We played reasonably well that day, but there was no marking Jimmy Doyle and we lost by seven or eight points, although I considered it a great thing for a young lad like myself to have played in Croke Park. According to the papers I was the only city lad on that Galway minor team, because Gabriel Egan was from

Castlegar, which at the time was considered out the country. The Egans were all great hurlers, including Paddy and John Joe... the whole lot of them.

The following year, 1958, Galway got a bye to the All-Ireland senior-final where we lost to Tipperary and Mike Sweeney was in goal. I went to England to try and make a few bob but instead of finding work and sending money home to my mother, it ended up the other way around and she had to send money over to me.

I found it really hard to get a job and before long I was homesick, so after nine months in London I returned home. I did play junior with the Emerald hurling club while I was over there and they were very decent to me, but when I couldn't find work and pay the rent I had to go home.

To be honest, I was delighted to be heading back and the day I left was like an All-Ireland final with all the people on the platform waving me off!

The following year, 1959, Galway entered the Munster championship for the first time and I came on against Waterford for Paddy Fahy from Craughwell in the second-half. That was a great Waterford team and they won by 7-11 to 0-8 before going on to win the All-Ireland.

It was tough being a goalkeeper in those times.

The forwards could come in on top of you before the ball and the only protection you got was from your full-back line. I got the best that Galway could put in front of me and I loved having Pakie Burke from Turloughmore at full-back.

Pakie was tough, but he had to be because of the men that were playing on him. We got another big beating from Waterford the following year, but in 1961 I got my first start for the Galway seniors when we beat Clare in what turned out to be the only match we won in the whole time we spent in Munster.

We won that day by 2-13 to 0-7 and I have great memories of the game, but we were soon brought back down to earth by Tipperary in the Munster semi-final. That Tipp team were, in my estimation, one of the greatest teams of all time and they gave us an awful beating... 7-12 to 5-6.

There was nothing I could do about it and the lads in front of me did their best too, but what could you do about the likes of Liam Devaney, Donie Nealon, Theo English, Jimmy Doyle and 'Hell's Kitchen' in the full-back line... Kieran Carey, Mick Maher and John Doyle.

I actually played with Kieran Carey when I moved to Roscrea for a while to work. I was driving around lads who were working on a farm, but I only stayed for a couple of months. In fairness, Roscrea preferred another local goalkeeper, which was understandable, so when I wasn't playing I didn't stay very long.

In 1962 we were drawn to play Limerick in the first round of the Munster championship in Ennis. It was the fourth year of Galway playing in Munster, and I wasn't too bothered about any debate going on about whether we should be in the province or not. I know we would probably have been better off in Leinster at the time because it wasn't as strong, but I was just happy to be playing.

Limerick were known as the 'greyhounds' because they were so fast and while they might not have been in the same class as the great Tipp team, they were still a very good side. I was warned in the run up to the game by plenty of 'experts' in town that the Galway backs were not up to it and certain players shouldn't be on the team.

I was told the Limerick forwards would be in on top of me, but I can honestly say the reason I'm remembered to this day for my performance in that game was down to the backs in front of me. Yet, we had a terrible start.

After only three minutes Limerick got a goal.

There must have been 10 of them around me in the goals when I got knocked over and the ball ended up in the net.

All that came into my mind was the fear of another cricket score.

The backs kept working hard though and although we were 2-7 to 0-2 down at half-time, it could have been a lot worse. Our first-half scores came from Tim Sweeney, a brilliant hurler from Fohenagh who should have been on the Galway team long before he was picked.

I made a few saves in that first-half, but it was easy enough once I got a bit of cover when the shots were coming in. At midfield for us that day was Joe Salmon, one of the greatest centrefield players of all time, and any time I pucked out the ball to Joe it was nearly always the overhead pull to send the ball forward.

We had the best centre-back in the country in Ned Dervan, and yet at that time you had Galway selectors picking Ned at full-back sometimes, and Pakie Burke at corner-back. It was crazy stuff.

The following year Ned proved it in Croke Park when he didn't give Tom Cheasty from Waterford a look at the ball. The same selectors wanted to play me corner-forward a few years after that… when they wanted to get rid of me!

The second-half that day in Ennis got a bit better and we put a bit of respectability on the scoreboard with a couple of goals, but we were determined not to let any more goals in at the back so even though it was disappointing to lose, we had restored a bit of pride after conceding the seven goals to Tipp the year before.

I was delighted to get a great write-up in the *Connacht Tribune* the following week from Frank O'Dea, while the day after the match Peadar O'Brien wrote in the *Irish Press… Indeed it was the magic of goalkeeper Jimmy Hegarty that saved Galway from being swamped. He stopped shots from every angle, but even he could do nothing with the two that beat him.*

Meanwhile, Donal Carroll wrote in the *Irish Independent* on the same day… *It was well indeed that young Jimmy Hegarty's goalkeeping was as colourful as the sun cap he wore throughout and backing his anticipation with tremendous courage, he prevented an avalanche of scores.*

Legendary Limerick hurler Mickey Cross was said to remark, 'That young fellow stopped Limerick winning by 10 goals. He'd stop taws.' In case you don't know what taws are, they are the miniature marbles you see on ball frames at school!

All I ever wanted was to play in the same position as Sean Duggan, Tony Reddan and Ollie Walsh, so when some newspapers started comparing me to those goalkeeping legends the following day I was delighted. For me, the satisfaction of playing for Galway was coming up against great players from other counties.

I played against Christy Ring once, in a Railway Cup game against Munster in Ballinasloe about three months before the Limerick game in February 1962. He got three goals on me that day, and I can still see him flicking the first goal past me one-handed from a dropping ball. I went to grab it but he had it gone past me before I knew it.

The sliotar at that time was extremely heavy, and Noel Lane once asked me if I was playing today in Croke Park with the lighter ball where would my puck outs land? I told him O'Connell Street!

Apart from Ring, I played against the aforementioned Tom Cheasty, Paddy Barry of Cork, Clare's best ever hurler Jimmy Smith, Dermot Kelly and Tom McGarry of Limerick, as well as Ned Wheeler and the Rackard brothers from Wexford.

People seem to think I only played one good game for Galway, but we came up against a brilliant Waterford team in the league semi-final the following year. Their six forwards were the best in Ireland... Frankie Walsh, Tom Cheasty, Mick Flannery, Seamus Power, John Barron and Philly Grimes.

I was genuinely expecting to concede three or four goals, but at half-time in that game in Croke Park my cousin Walter had his transistor radio with him and he heard Michael O'Hehir remark that, 'Great goalies must grow on trees in Galway'.

We ended up losing that game by 0-9 to 0-7 and Waterford went on to beat Tipperary in the 'Home Final' and then New York to win the league title for the first time. I was very upset at losing that game and was crying coming off the field when one of our mentors, Fr Lee put his arm around me and said look up at the scoreboard...

'There is nothing to cry about after that performance.'

There was a lot of club rivalry in Galway in those days.

Fohenagh had a great team with Tim Sweeney, Fr Nicholas Murray and goalkeeper Frankie Madden. Bobby Madden of Turloughmore was another great goalie at the time, while the man who took over from me as Galway goalkeeper in 1965 was Peter Cosgrove from Oranmore Maree.

I didn't think I should have been dropped that year but when Peter put in a brilliant display against Clare in the first round of the Munster championship, I didn't mind as much because I was being replaced by someone who was better than me. Yet I knew that one man in particular was trying to get rid of me off the Galway panel.

One evening I arrived late for a training match because I was thumbing a lift to get there, and the game was at half-time when I arrived.

This individual called me 'Hegarty', while everyone else was called by their first name. He threw a number 18 jersey at me and said he might throw me in corner-forward at some stage in the second-half.

I never got a game that evening so I threw the jersey at him and told him what to do with it. So that was that.

I have no regrets. I played with the best and against the best.

In 1982, Liam Mellows presented me with a gold watch for 25 years of service. I didn't play with the club for a couple of years over a misunderstanding at half-time in a match in Pearse Stadium. I got upset over a comment that was made and walked out of the dressing-room.

Jimmy Duggan and his brother 'Mogan' came in after me to try and get me to change my mind, but I kept going.

A couple of weeks later Mellows were playing in Athenry and I was expecting to be called for but it never happened. I never asked to join Castlegar, but I was on my way to the cinema one night when I met Paddy Egan and he invited me to come and play with them, rather than not play at all.

I was honoured to be asked, so I played with Castlegar for two years and won a county league until Mr Fahy, who had a chemist shop in Shop Street, asked me back to Mellows. It was the first time someone from Liam Mellows had spoken to me about going back and I was delighted to do so.

In 1970 we won the county championship with a great team that included Tom Ryan and Seamus Hogan from Tipperary, the Duggan brothers, Paddy Ryan, Willie Concannon, Pat Harrington, Jim Bishop. I could name them all. We beat a good Killimordaly team by four goals in the final that year.

Officially, I always say my career finished in 1983.

Liam Mellows went on a trip to London and when the regular goalie didn't show up for a challenge game, I stood in goal. It wasn't the only time in my career I had to go between the posts at the last minute.

Towards the end of my playing days I suffered a lot with a bad back, and for a time I had Plaster of Paris all around my back and chest area to try and heal it. During that time I was umpiring a junior game between Liam Mellows and Rahoon in St Mary's College, but Mellows only had 10 players at the start so I stood in goal.

I could hardly move, but at one stage one of the Rahoon lads ran straight through and lashed the ball at me. It rebounded off my chest and went about 40 yards out the field!

I would have done anything for Liam Mellows.

I was so glad to see the club winning their first Galway championship in 47 years back in 2017. I would hardly know any of the young players now, bar the Elwoods and the Hughes' but they are a credit to this great club. I don't go out much now, but when the Báireóiri lads called out to me I got a new lease of life.

First in the door was another great Galway goalie, Seamus Shinners, who is one of the nicest people you could ever meet, along with Iggy Clarke, Noel Lane, Sean Silke, Vincent Mullins, Tony Raftery, John Connolly and Ted Duffy.

There are lots of other lads involved that have been so good to me. They are like the big family that I never had. Here are men with All-Ireland medals treating me, that didn't win anything, the same as themselves.

Then again, I always tell them they never played against Christy Ring or the Rackards! I have my own museum here in the house with all of the articles written about me. Martin Breheny of the *Irish Independent* did a piece on 'unsung heroes' a few years back and I featured in the All-Ireland final programme in 1987.

I celebrated my 80th birthday earlier this year and I got a lot of letters and cards, including one from Pat Hartigan, who won five successive All Stars with Limerick in the early 70s. It was very kind of Pat to write… *Jimmy, I wish to congratulate you on the great service you gave to Galway hurling for many years. Who will ever forget '62? You were one of the all-time greats when it was most difficult and dangerous to be a goalkeeper. As a full-back myself, Jimmy, my life would be very easy having a goalie like you behind me.*

After that Limerick game I could never repeat anything like that again.

I always say I'm only human… I let in a few soft ones as well.

NED DERVAN

WATERFORD 0-9, GALWAY 0-7
NHL Semi-Final
Croke Park
APRIL 7, 1963

Galway hero Ned Dervan recalls the county's long, tough march through Munster in the 1960s

★ **GALWAY:** J Hegarty; S McGill, P Burke, T Conway; J Duggan, **N Dervan**, J Lyons; J Salmon, J Conroy (0-2); M Curtin (0-2), T Sweeney (0-1), Mickey Cullinane (0-1); M Regan (0-1), J Gohery, Michael Cullinane. Subs: PJ Qualter for Michael Cullinane, M Connaughton for Conroy, S Conroy for Connaughton.

★ **WATERFORD:** P Flynn; T Cunningham, A Flynn, J Byrne; L Guinan, M Óg Morrissey, J Irish; J Condon, J Meaney; M Flannelly, T Cheasty (0-3), F Walshe (0-2); S Power, J Barron (0-1), P Grimes (0-3). Sub: J McGrath for Meaney.

THE ACTION

FAVOURITES WATERFORD FINALLY broke the spirit of gallant Galway in a dour National League semi-final in Croke Park, thanks to late points from Phil Grimes and Tom Cheasty.

Galway led from the second to the 52nd minute, thanks mainly to a superb defensive display which kept the highly regarded Waterford unit at bay. Central to this was the performance of centre-back Ned Dervan, who kept ace marksman Tom Cheasty scoreless, until the latter moved into full-forward in the closing minutes to help turn the tide.

Galway, backed by the wind, led by 0-5 to 0-2 at half-time with Joe Salmon in inspired form at midfield for the westerners, but three great chances to extend their lead were missed at the start of the second-half and this would prove costly.

Waterford began to dominate and were level with 13 minutes to go through a Frankie Walshe point. Cheasty edged his side in front for the first time in the game a minute later, but Galway responded with the levelling point from Mickey Cullinane with only two minutes left.

As the game entered its final seconds, Phil Grimes popped up with the lead point for Waterford and Cheasty lofted over the insurance point with virtually the last puck of the game.

★★★★★

66

IN 1956, TYNAGH were playing Ballymacward in a minor game and I was marking Nicholas Murray, who went on to become a priest and a hurling legend with Fohenagh. Obviously, whatever county minor selector was there thought that I had played particularly well, so I was called in for a trial and ended up playing at centre-forward.

At that time, Kilkenny and Tipperary were the two outstanding minor teams and we were drawn to play Kilkenny in the All-Ireland minor semi-final of 1956.

Not too many balls came my way in the forwards, so I remember being brought back at one stage to wing back and that was the kind of introduction to minor hurling we got at the time. We lost 4-8 to 2-4 that day, and the following year when I went to the trial game I was told I was big enough to fill the only position that was left, which was full-back!

In 1957, we played defending champions Tipperary in the All-Ireland semi-final. That was Jimmy Doyle's team and he scored 2-5 on the day as we were beaten 4-12 to 3-7. In 1958, I played junior hurling for Galway against Roscommon and was then brought into the senior panel ahead of the All-Ireland final.

That time Galway went directly into the All-Ireland final every third year, so in 1958 we were straight through to meet Tipperary.

Fintan Spillane got injured just after half-time and I was brought in at corner-back for the rest of the game. That was my first time playing senior for Galway and it was one month before my 19th birthday. We lost that final by 4-9 to 2-5, but it was a game that should have been a lot closer.

Tipp got their four goals in the first-half, including two from the middle of the field, but then Fergie Benson went in goal from wing back at half-time and we came much more into the game in the second-half. At that time we had a few army lads playing with Galway, like Joe Young, Billy O'Neill and Jim Fives; then throw in the brilliant Joe Salmon and you could see Galway had a fair team to challenge for honours.

Shortly after that we won the Oireachtas tournament which was contested by Tipperary, Kilkenny, Wexford and Galway. Even though Tipp were All-Ireland champions, we beat Kilkenny in the semi-final and hammered Wexford 5-16 to 2-4 in the final and it turned out to be the only major senior medal I won with Galway.

There was a lot of debate about Galway going directly into the All-Ireland final in 1958, and rightly so, but that Oireachtas win over Wexford probably had a bearing on them objecting to Galway going into Leinster the following year.

It was a good Wexford team at the time that still had the Rackards and Morrisseys from the team that had won the All-Ireland in 1956, but our fitness and training for the All-Ireland final definitely stood to us when it came to taking them on only a few weeks later in November.

As it turned out, we ended up playing in the Munster championship from 1959 to '69 and that proved to be a disaster. Munster hurling was incredibly strong at the time, with Tipperary, Limerick, Waterford and Cork all top class teams.

We found it easier to beat Kilkenny those years than any of the top four Munster teams because of the style of hurling that they played. I think some of the Munster counties felt sorry for Galway that we weren't getting any championship matches every year, but in truth we weren't seen as a threat to them.

We only won one match in the Munster championship in that decade and that was against Clare in 1961. That first year we played in Munster, Waterford went on to win the All-Ireland. They were a brilliant team and were all pretty much still together when we got a crack at them in the National League semi-final in 1963.

In the late 1950s and early 60s, Tom Cheasty of Waterford was recognised as the outstanding player in Ireland. He was their main playmaker at centre-forward, so when I was picked to mark him in the 1963 league semi-final, it seemed a big ask for someone who was more used to playing at corner-back or full-back for the county.

Yet, everything went right for me that day and Tom didn't score until the Waterford mentors switched him into full-forward.

I really enjoyed centre-back if the truth be told.

It was where I played with the club and I felt less *restricted* than in the full-back line because I liked to hurl. Your job in the full-back line was, more often than not, to stop your man from hurling.

We had Pakie Burke from Turloughmore back there and he was immense.

That physical strength was typical of the great Turlough team that won six county championships in-a-row during the 1960s. Yet the story of how I came to be centre-back for Galway in that 1963 league semi-final was most unusual.

Mike Sweeney from Loughrea was a huge presence at centre-back for Galway in those years but a bizarre set of circumstances meant he was in America and unable to play. Loughrea were due to play Fohenagh in the East Board final that year but Loughrea refused to play unless the match was taken out of Duggan Park in Ballinasloe, which they felt favoured Fohenagh.

The East Board officials refused to bend to Loughrea's request to play the match elsewhere, so when Loughrea refused to fulfil the fixture, the club and all their players were suspended. That meant their two county senior stars, Mike Sweeney and Fergie Benson, were unavailable to play for Galway.

Mike left for the U.S. and Fergie never played for Galway again. It was a huge price to pay for a club trying to stand up to the county board.

Galway had some really good teams during that era, but were always missing one ingredient to get over the line to win a major title. In 1963, we beat Antrim, Westmeath and Dublin to qualify for the league semi-final against Waterford.

Apart from Tom Cheasty, they had household names like Frankie Walsh and Philly Grimes, so we knew it would take our best efforts to keep them at bay. We played with the wind in the first-half and tore into them. By half-time, we had restricted them to just 0-2, while we had 0-5 on the board.

Jimmy Duggan, Joe Lyons and myself seemed to be controlling the game in the half-back line and I vividly remember at one stage intercepting a pass from Cheasty and soloing up the length of the field until I took a shot that the Waterford goalie saved.

That was a scenario that I definitely wasn't used to!

The Galway crowd were really behind us at this stage and it was amazing how we always seemed to get a huge crowd to follow us when we played in Croke Park. I think there was an awful lot of people from Galway living in Dublin at the time that used to come to our games, even when Galway weren't going terribly well.

Our goalie Jimmy Hegarty had a great game that day as well. It was an open game of hurling and that suited Jimmy's style. If Jimmy was playing today, he would be an All Star for certain. Our other big star that day was Joe Salmon.

His speciality was the overhead pull, but when it came to picking a ball at speed and running with it, there was no one better than Joe. He could drive the heavy ball 70 or 80 yards, which very few players could do and his physical build gave him a huge advantage. He was the type of man who could just as easily have become a top class footballer. But above all else, Joe was a pure gentleman.

He was the kind of person that would come around and talk to us when we first came into the panel; he was constantly praising us and giving us every encouragement. He made us feel we were important. He was our best player and everyone looked up to him.

Waterford knew if they could stop Joe Salmon they would go a long way towards stopping Galway. In a previous meeting of the sides in 1957, one of the Waterford lads drew a dirty belt on Joe, so two of our lads ran in to defend him and got sent off. He meant that much to the Galway lads.

It was very much the same story for me and Tom Cheasty.

We were still in control of the game until the last few minutes when Cheasty went into the full-forward line and scored two points in quick succession. Before we knew it, a game we could have won had gone from us and we ended up losing by two points.

My last game for Galway came in early 1966.

I played in the opening round of the National League but I had recently married Ber Lynch from Duniry and had taken over the running of the farm, so I made the decision that it was time to pack it in.

I was 26 years of age.

Then again, I suppose I had been playing from 1958 to '66 and it was a long spell without much success and anyone would get tired of it. It wasn't just being beaten. On many occasions we were badly beaten.

My only medal from the Oireachtas Cup win in 1958 now sits proudly on the wall alongside the 1923 All Ireland winner's medal belonging to my father Jack, who was a sub on the Galway team that won our first senior All-Ireland. My uncle Mick was corner-back on that team and was also picked on the Galway hurling Team of the Millennium.

The other medal in the collection represents the Galway Senior Hurling Championship success of the great Tynagh team that went unbeaten during the 1920s. Tynagh won all five senior championships that were completed in the decade, but only got one medal to represent those wins, as money was so scarce with the Galway County Board!

Later on, when I started playing with Tynagh, we were competing at junior level until we won that championship in 1971 and went senior. Playing junior didn't make any difference to my chances of playing for Galway.

Once I got on to the minor team in 1956, I was on the radar for the county team from then on. There were four of us on the Tynagh team those days. My brother Michael was also on the Galway panel but tragically was killed in an accident in Dublin in 1971. He would have had a few runs with the county. Another brother, Jimmy played county intermediate, and Bill was on a Galway team that won an All-Ireland junior title.

Our front lawn was the hurling pitch when we were growing up. You could have had 30 or 40 lads playing hurling on a Sunday in front of our house because there was no pitch in Tynagh until the mid-50s. My two lads, Ian and Eamon played for Galway as well, keeping up a long family connection to Galway teams, while I have two daughters, Bernadette, who lives nearby in Tynagh and Martha, who is married in Macroom in Cork.

I have 11 grandchildren, ranging in age from 10 years old to 29.

Even to this day, people remind me of that league semi-final and the great battle with Tom Cheasty. Not long after that game, Mike Sweeney returned from America after his suspension was over and he reverted to centre-back for Galway, while I went back to the corner.

I admit myself that Mike was a better centre-back than me.

I saw him one day in Ballinasloe against Tipperary running after Donie Nealon, who was heading for the Galway goal on a solo run. Mike put the hurl in over Donie's shoulder and robbed him, turned and belted the ball the length of the field and out into the green beyond the pitch.

He had an unbelievable belt of a ball.

God knows what he would do if he was playing with the current ball! But there were many other great players I came up against. I came up against Liam Devaney of Tipperary in a league game one day and he begged me not to use the knee because he had a boil on his backside and he was in agony!

I played on Christy Ring on a couple of occasions. He was a great hurler but the couple of times I played against him in Railway Cup and tournament games I was described as *dangerously venturesome* in the papers because I was more inclined to try and keep the ball away from him than go man-marking.

I remember he pulled on one ball I was going for and caught me on the hand.

There was an obvious mark and some blood drawn, so he was quick to remind me to, 'Look after that, boy!' I played on Jimmy Smith the day we beat Clare in our only Munster championship victory in 1961. These are the games and little incidents that I recall when I look back on those bygone days.

My entire Galway senior championship career spanned eight years, but only nine matches. The Clare game was the only match I ever won.

Even at club level, it was knockout.

You lost the first match and you were gone for the year. The main reason for this in Galway was there were four divisional boards and nearly every parish had at least two teams. There were loads of games to try and get played. You had Eyrecourt, Meelick and Clonfert in one parish, while Athenry also had teams in Newcastle and Cussaun. It was just the way it was.

I was invited back by Fr Solan to join the Galway team after I stepped away in 1966; he had taken over the team. He had also married myself and Ber, so I think he felt he would convince me to go back. But I had made up my kind to concentrate on club hurling, which I stayed at until I was nearly 40 years of age.

There was just no enjoyment in the county scene when you felt so demoralised after losing year in, year out. So many great Galway hurlers played all those years with little or no reward. I mention Joe Salmon again.

If he was with any other county in Ireland he would have multiple All-Ireland medals.

When it came to how I played the game, I have no regrets.

I was very much a 'clean' hurler. I was never booked or sent off in my life. Fr Solan once remarked to me that it was a pity there wasn't a bit more of a 'devil' in me, but I didn't believe in going out to injure anyone deliberately.

Both my lads, Ian and Eamon were great club hurlers and Eamon, in particular, had great ability if you could get it out of him. He loves a challenge and whether its hurling, rallying or golf, once he has reached the pinnacle he will move on to the next challenge. Ian's youngest lad, John is now playing under-16 and they got to the county final against a great Turloughmore team this year (2020).

Our parish team is now Tynagh-Abbey Duniry, an amalgamation that is working really well in recent years. There was no team in Abbey Duniry when I was playing, so we had lads like Michael Broderick, father of Galway star Kevin, playing for Tynagh. So too did Johnny Kelly, who played in goals for Galway on a number of occasions. There was never any great rivalry between us because Abbey Duniry only really became a force in the 1990s with a brilliant team led by Mattie Kenny. They were most unfortunate not to win at least one county senior title.

The amalgamation started at underage and then when those young lads came of age, it was natural that they would play together at senior level. There is still a great awareness of the history of hurling in the parish and even my own grandchildren have become aware of grandad's time playing with Galway in the 1950s and 60s.

The past hurlers group known as the Báireóirí has helped greatly in this regard by organising reunions with players that I might not have met in over 50 years.

We get together now from time to time to look back on our time playing with Galway and get great satisfaction from the lads that thank us for laying the foundations for the glory days that would eventually come in the 1980s.

ANDY FENTON

GALWAY 2-9, DUBLIN 1-10
All Ireland Under-21 HC Final
Limerick
SEPTEMBER 10, 1972

Winning Galway's first ever All-Ireland under-21 title after withstanding a strong second-half fightback from Dublin still lives with Andy Fenton

★ **GALWAY:** E Campbell; L Glynn, G Kelly, L Shields; I Clarke, F Donoghue, T Brehony; G Glynn (0-1), F Burke; M Coen, **A Fenton (1-0)**, M Donoghue; M Barrett (0-1), T Donoghue, G Holland (1-4). Subs: PJ Molloy (0-3) for Coen, J Duggan for Barrett.

★ **DUBLIN:** M Holden; M Leonard, N Quinn, V Lambe; G Ryan, J Brennan, E Rheinisch; PJ Holden (0-2), M Greally; P Lee (0-2), V Holden, J Kealy (0-3); C Henebry, B Sweeney (1-0), J Whelan (0-2). Subs: G O'Connell (0-1) for Greally, B Donovan for Lee.

THE ACTION

GALWAY MADE HURLING history in Limerick by winning their first ever All-Ireland under-21 title after withstanding a strong second-half comeback from Dublin. Despite playing with a strong wind in the first-half, Galway only led by 2-3 to 1-0 at the break, and a total of 13 wides looked like it might come back to haunt them when their six-point lead was eventually whittled down to one by the end of the third quarter.

Andy Fenton gave the winners a huge boost early on with a goal in the fourth minute and this was followed soon after by a second Galway goal from the impressive Gerry Holland. Dublin responded a minute later with their only score of the half, a Brian Sweeney goal, but a succession of Galway wides meant their six-point lead looked precarious.

Dublin made immediate inroads into the Galway lead at the start of the second-half with points from Jim Kealy, Pascal Lee and Jim Whelan, and even after PJ Molloy had pointed to give the Westerners some breathing space, the Dubs came again with three further points to get within one.

The winners responded with three great points of their own from Gerry Holland, super-sub PJ Molloy and Gerry Glynn to retake control of an absorbing final, but they were made to sweat for the remaining minutes as Dublin piled on the pressure and came within a whisker of snatching victory with a last gasp goal.

★ ★ ★ ★ ★

"

WHEN YOU LOOK back at the renaissance of Galway hurling in the 1970s, you need to appreciate there was a concerted effort made to improve things at underage level in the middle of the 60s with the setting up of the Juvenile Hurling Board, Coiste Iomána na nÓg. The way they encouraged hurling was to ensure that everybody had a stick to play with, something that wasn't that easy to guarantee in the mid-60s.

I can still recall Fr Jack Solan, who was a big driver of that, coming to our school, opening the bonnet of the car and dropping off an armful of hurleys. Before that it was nearly impossible to get a hurley. It turned out our parish Clontuskert got to a county final that year only to lose out to Turloughmore by a couple of points.

That was the start of it. After that came county under-14 and under-16 teams, which all led up to a county minor team in 1970 reaching the All-Ireland final.

We beat Wexford in the semi-final that year in Athlone, the first semi-final a Galway minor team had won in 12 years – and our senior team should have won that day as well, only to get pipped by Wexford by two points.

In the minor final we played a very strong Cork team and even though we got a great start and were a goal and a point up early on, in the end we were well beaten. It was an experience though that stood to us and a lot of lads came out of that team… Iggy Clarke, Joe McDonagh, Gerry Holland and myself. Ciaran Fitzgerald, who went to become a legendary rugby player for Ireland, was on that team as well.

That group were kept together deliberately, with a few additions, for the 1972 under-21 championship.

A good few of us were going to college in Maynooth at the time and we were involved with the Galway senior team for the National League that year. In the last game of the 1972 league in March, we were due to play Laois in a promotion game in Portlaoise but at the last minute it was switched to Abbeyleix.

The winners would go up to Division 1 so there was probably a bit of gamesmanship involved in the game being moved. There was a gale force wind and Laois had the advantage of it in the first-half.

To say the half didn't go well for us was an understatement because at half-time we trailed by 4-5 to 1-0. We got a right rollicking at the break.

To go in 14 points down to Laois in a big promotion game was a huge embarrassment, so we were told to go out in the second-half and try and get a few goals. So we did.

Laois still thought they had it won when they led by two points with time almost up, when Mickey Donoghue scored our final goal to win the game 7-0 to 4-8! It has to be some sort of record for a team to win a game with a scoreline like that.

I certainly never heard of it before, or since.

Things began to get a lot more professional in terms of training and preparation around that time. The pint of milk and a sandwich after training went, and we were brought for a bit of grub.

The lads bought into it and we had some great mentors, people like Frank Fahy who is now living in Tuam, Pat Robinson from Tynagh, Michael Kelly from Ballinderreen and Tommy Fahy from Craughwell.

Another unique aspect of our preparations for that under-21 championship was our full-forward Tom Donoghue was about to graduate as a PE Teacher from Strawberry Hill College in London, so he took all the physical training, while the four mentors looked after the hurling.

In comparison to today, the amount of training was not as intense, but we did a fair bit ahead of our first game against Tipperary in the All-Ireland semi-final in Nenagh on August 15. In those times that date was a very significant church holiday where everybody took the day off and there were significant traffic problems getting to the game.

The team was picked and our corner-back Frank Fahy from Tommy Larkins and our full-back Kieran Maher from Loughrea didn't make it to the match on time. Iggy Clarke as well was delayed so there was some commotion in the dressing-room beforehand trying to pick a team.

It was like an underage club game with lads looking out the dressing-room door to see if the others were coming or not. Liam Shields and Gerry Kelly were drafted in... and out we went. Tipp were hot favourites that day as they had careered through Munster but even though our pre-match preparations were far from ideal it turned out to be a belter of a game, one of the best games I ever played in.

We matched Tipp all over the field until a key incident during the second-half became a major talking point.

That time, there were no neutral officials with the match referee so the competing teams provided two umpires and a linesman each. Tony Qualter from Turloughmore was one of our umpires and he was at the end Galway were attacking in the second-half when a major shemozzle occurred in the small square.

There was little or no protection offered to goalies at that time, so when the ball bobbled around the goal-line every man was fair game. Quick as a flash Tony had the green flag in the air and despite Tipperary protests, he stood his ground and the goal was allowed.

I have no doubt in my own mind it was a goal but it became a big talking point afterwards when we won by 2-11 to 1-11 to qualify for the All-Ireland final for the first time ever. It was a great achievement, given that Tipp, Cork and Wexford were the only counties to have ever won the under-21 championship since it started in 1964, and our big support in Nenagh that evening knew it was a famous win.

The two lads that came in at the last minute to start the semi-final kept their places for the final against Dublin and I was picked again at centre-forward. My favourite position was centre-back, where I played on the minor team two years previously, but Frank Donoghue was a tremendous No 6 and like so many lads going to college at the time, he could have made a far bigger impact in the senior championship in the years that followed.

You would go a long way to find a better half-back line at under-21 level in any era than Iggy Clarke, Frank Donoghue and Tony Brehony, while behind them we had a goalie and full-back line to match anything else in the country.

Dublin had beaten Offaly in the Leinster final and Antrim comfortably in the All-Ireland semi-final and they were a talented group powered by the Holden brothers, Mick, PJ and Vinny. Mick, who sadly died too young, was in goals and would be familiar to a lot of people for the very successful football career he had afterwards; and we knew from the Leinster final that Dublin had a tactic of bringing him out of goals and into the full-forward line if a game was getting tight in the second-half.

We were anticipating a similar move in the All-Ireland final if we were leading, so we were instructed to delay his 'route' up the field.

I remember Tom Donoghue putting his arms around him to give him a hug and we all gave a hand to make sure Mick's trip from the goals to the forwards took around three minutes! Mick was a fine hurler and he hit the post with one shot late in the game which could well have won the match.

The game was in Limerick on September 10 and a good crowd came to see a novel pairing in action that had never been in a final before. There was a big wind blowing and we had it in the first-half and led by six points at half-time, when we should have been 10 or 12 points in front.

We should have had the game won at half-time but we hadn't and Dublin came at us in the second-half and reduced the lead down to a single point. I got a goal myself in the first-half and Gerry Holland, our scorer-in-chief, got the other but even though we were hurling very well, we were hitting too many wides.

The big move we made was bringing on PJ Molloy, and he scored three points from play which proved the difference in the end along with Gerry Holland's scores. It was backs to the wall in the closing stages and our goalie Eamon Campbell, who we knew as Ned, made a couple of great saves to keep us in front.

Ned is another man who could have had a long career with the Galway seniors but he went to Chicago not long after that, and is still there today.

Another great hurler lost to emigration.

At midfield, Frank Burke was a real powerhouse hurler and he was perfectly complimented by Gerry Glynn, who was a beautiful, elegant player and a brilliant striker of the ball who had scored five points in the semi-final win over Tipperary. Up front we also had Mick Coen from Ballinderreen, Michael Donoghue from Kilchreest, the late Marty Barrett, who scored a point in the final and Tom Donoghue from Killimordaly, who later won an All-Ireland senior championship with Offaly in 1981.

Tom was teaching PE in Tullamore and lives in Durrow between Kilbeggan and Tullamore but he ended up corner-back on the Offaly team in 1981 despite never having played in the backs as far as I can recall when he was with Galway.

We had another great Galway legend in the subs that year in Joe McDonagh, alongside Jimmy Duggan from Carnmore, so there was no doubt we had a strong and determined panel that was definitely good enough to achieve something special. The proof was in how many of those Galway lads went on to play senior in the years to follow.

After the final whistle it didn't take us long to realise how special that win actually was because we were the first team to bring back an All-Ireland hurling title to Galway in nearly 50 years. There was hardly any swapping of jerseys after a final those times either.

I know I still have my jersey at home, even if it is gone a shade of pink now after all the years! The under-21 hurling trophy was called the Cross of Cashel, which was a statuette rather than a cup, so the publicans were delighted because they didn't have to fill it.

Our first stop on the homecoming was in Woodford on the way back from Limerick and we eventually ended up in Kiltormer, having coming down through Gurtymadden, Mullagh and other places.

We didn't get to the west of the county until a few days later and there was a big function organised for us in one of the hotels in Galway. There was no team bus either, it was all cars; so myself and the Kiltormer lads, Ned and Donie would have gone with Pat Robinson to training and matches.

That was the thing about 1972, when you said goodbye to the lads on a Sunday evening you didn't see or hear from them again until the next night at training. There was little or no means of communication.

As it happened, the under-21 football team were in the All-Ireland final against Kerry a few weeks later and they were also looking to win an under-21 title for the first time. When I was younger I went to all the senior football games with my father and our local parish priest Fr John Kelly, who was a big football fan like most Galway people.

I was lifted over the turnstiles for the three in-a-row final and I wasn't a small lad in 1966! The big thing about our under-21 win was it raised the profile of hurling in the county. A hurling board was formed, separate to the county board, and that did help in promoting and organising the game in the county.

Gerry Cloherty was a major innovator at the time and if I was to pick out one other man, it is Frank Fahy who always made sure we had the best of everything, including hurleys. At a recent function I asked Frank how he always had a car boot full of the very popular Randall hurleys from Wexford and he told me that he always paid a bit more than the asking price to make sure he was looked after. There is no doubt Frank was a revolutionary figure in the game in Galway.

After the under-21 win I went back to Maynooth where we won the Fitzgibbon Cup in both 1973 and '74. We had a great team, with a half-back line of Iggy Clarke, Sean Silke and Sean Stack, and all our challenge games were against senior county teams.

My time in Maynooth was a wonderful experience and I went on to complete my teaching degree. I actually taught for six months as a substitute teacher for my father in Clontuskert after he had a bad car accident. I didn't like it and I knew then that teaching was not for me so I went down the business route and spent over 40 years with the one company, where I ended up as a senior director, so I have no regrets when it comes to my professional career.

I married Anne Monaghan from Ballinakill in 1977 and we have four children, Deirdre, Cathal, Aoife and Enda. I now enjoy a happy life in retirement and I am kept busy with nine wonderful grandchildren.

We had a 25th anniversary reunion for the under-21 panel in 1997 and as recently as 2019 the Galway past hurlers group, the Báireóirí honoured the lads at their annual dinner in the Loughrea Hotel.

I meet quite a few of the lads on a regular basis and others whenever we have an organised get together. I had a great friendship with the late Marty Barrett, who was a teacher in later years in St Peter's in Wexford, and my wife Anne and I and the kids used to love travelling down to Wexford to what became our favourite holiday destination.

The Báireóirí have brought a lot of those lads together and it is unfortunate that great men like Joe McDonagh and others are no longer with us. I think the reason we won that All-Ireland is that the great bond that existed between all those lads then is still very much in evidence now.

IGGY CLARKE

GALWAY 4-9, TIPPERARY 4-6
NHL Final
Gaelic Grounds, Limerick
MAY 25, 1975

Iggy Clarke formed a brilliant half-back line in 1975 with Joe McDonagh and Sean Silke

★ **GALWAY:** M Conneely; N McInerney, J Clarke, P Lally; J McDonagh, S Silke (0-1), **I Clarke (0-1)**; S Murphy, Joe Connolly (1-0); G Coone, F Burke (0-2), PJ Molloy (0-3); M Barrett (2-0), PJ Qualter (1-0), P Fahy (0-2).

★ **TIPPERARY:** J Duggan; L King, J Keogh, J Bergin; T O'Connor, N O'Dwyer, J Dunlea; J Kehoe, S Hogan; F Loughnane (0-1), T Butler (1-0), F Murphy; P Quinlan (1-1), R Ryan (1-1), J Flanagan (1-3).

THE ACTION

GALWAY HURLERS BRIDGED a 24-year gap to win the National League title for just the third time after a sensational late surge saw the underdogs overcome a much fancied Tipperary. The celebrations afterwards suggested this was a huge moment in Galway hurling history as a national senior title was finally heading west.

Indeed Galway can take much satisfaction from having beaten Cork, Kilkenny and Tipperary to win the title, but it was the manner in which the Tribesmen snatched victory from the jaws of defeat in the final that will live longest in the memory.

A jittery Galway trailed at half-time by 3-4 to 2-3, despite a stunning early goal from John Connolly which gave them the perfect start. Pat Quinlan answered with a Tipp goal on 15 minutes, but Marty Barrett responded with a similar score for Galway from an overhead shot.

Trailing by four points, Tipp finished the half stronger and goals from Roger Ryan and a John Flanagan penalty swung the tie firmly in the Munster men's favour.

Galway upped the ante in the second-half. Another Barrett goal, as well as a fine long range Sean Silke point, had the side's level just 10 minutes in. Tipp regained the initiative, however, and after Tommy Butler ran through to score a simple goal, Pat Quinlan pointed to put his side four ahead with seven minutes to go.

From somewhere, Galway found the strength to come back again and after Frank Burke and PJ Molloy had pointed to cut the gap to two points with three minutes to go, the key moment arrived. Cork referee Frank Murphy awarded Galway a 21-yard free.

It looked like an opportunity for a certain point, but John Connolly had different ideas and the Galway captain blasted for goal. As the ball rebounded off a wall of defenders, PJ Qualter flashed the rebound to the net for a match winning goal.

★★★★★

66

ONE OF THE most important games in Galway hurling history was the 1972 All-Ireland under-21 final when I was lucky enough to be captain. I say lucky because in the semi-final that year we were playing Tipperary in Nenagh and I was late getting to the match.

The bridge in Portumna was up, so that delayed me even further and I remember saying to my brother Tom, who was driving, that the only thing I could do was tog out in the car. That's exactly what I did.

But by the time I got to the dressing-room the management had picked another team and I remember Frank Fahy, who was the manager at the time, saw me coming in the door and said, 'Clarke is here... give him a jersey!'

It was the 15th of August and I went out and played a fantastic game, and then retained my place for the final, which we won against Dublin. I consider myself lucky because had I missed the start of that game and not gone on to play in the final, I might not have been heard of again and not progressed on to that senior team in 1975.

That under-21 victory was very significant for Galway.

It was our first All-Ireland championship victory of any kind since 1923 and our first national win since Galway won the National League in 1951. I was part of the minor team that got to the final in 1970 but we lost out to Cork, so this was the first win of significance in years. Another aspect of that under-21 win was important – lads like Joe McDonagh, PJ Molloy, Frank Burke and myself graduated on to the senior panel that year and started blending in with the older and more established players like John Connolly, PJ Qualter, Padraig Fahy and Sean Murphy.

A bit of hope began to emerge, although we did hit one of our lowest points ever in 1973 when we lost to London in Ballinasloe in the All-Ireland quarter-final. After that, we pulled ourselves together and I remember lads like Sean Silke and John Connolly, who would normally have gone to America to play and work for the summer, returning early because they saw these young lads coming through and a team starting to take shape.

We were in Division 2 for the National League in 1974/75 and after beating

Kildare at home, we played Wicklow in Baltinglass. The Galway footballers played beforehand in a double-header and I was surprised when both teams went to the hotel afterwards and the hurlers got steak and onions while the footballers got chicken.

We had idolised the three in-a-row footballers in the 1960s and the lads that came after that, when hurling at that time in Galway was second class.

Yet, here we were being treated better than they were and I think a lot of it had to do with the ethos of Frank Fahy, who had taken over as senior manager after our under-21 win; he made sure the players were looked after well. He was famous at the time for getting us the Randall hurleys from Wexford and we loved them.

He made sure we had the best of equipment and were looked after with meals. Frank showed initiative and creativity, and he had a different approach to management which we were delighted with.

After winning in Wicklow, our next away game was against Antrim in February of 1975 and I will never forget going through Belfast at the height of the Troubles. We were all nervous passing these army checkpoints with soldiers holding machine guns and I will never forget our bus driver that weekend was a lovely man from the north, who drove us to Corrigan Park from the Four Seasons Hotel in Monaghan.

A week later we heard on the news that he had been found shot dead in the boot of a car after an attack of some sort.

We ended up top of Division 2 after our five group games, which I think was our aim, and when we heard we would be playing Cork in the quarter-finals we just felt it was a free shot and we would have a go. I used to always enjoy playing against Cork because they were very pure in their hurling and it was nearly always a free-flowing game.

We hit our best form against Cork and won by two points in Limerick, then we played Kilkenny in the semi-final. Frank Burke at one stage got a ball in midfield and just tore up the field before scoring a fantastic goal and lifting all our spirits. We won that game by three points and after two great performances I think we got on a roll.

Our manager Inky Flaherty always told us to believe in ourselves as a team and that way of thinking definitely evolved that year, but it was still like a fairytale to think we had just beaten Cork and Kilkenny.

A huge amount of Galway people followed us at that time and we saw ourselves very much as down to earth lads who interacted with the supporters quite naturally. The Connollys had a great link with the Gaeltacht and the crowd that used to come to our games from Connemara and Mayo was unbelievable.

At some stage after we had qualified for the league final I remember thinking that we would now be on television and this was a whole different profile altogether, just like the footballers. I had looked at the football team in the 60s and thought they were mighty men because they were on television, and here it was now happening to us.

There were newspapers and media outlets looking to interview us; it was unheard of, so there was definitely a great sense of excitement about something new happening in Galway and we were privileged to be part of it.

We were all nervous before that league final against Tipperary.

I was due to mark Francis Loughnane, who was top scorer in the league, and my brother Joe was at full-back and he was due to mark Roger Ryan, so there was a family nervousness before that game! Even though we had beaten Cork and Kilkenny we were still heavy underdogs because Tipp were well established.

Myself, Joe McDonagh and Sean Silke always had a chat together as a half-back line before a match and we said no matter who Tipp play in the half-forward line we would cover for each other like an accordion.

Early on, John Connolly scored a goal for us and a dog ran out on the pitch as if it was celebrating with Galway! Tipp got three goals in that first-half though and we were disappointed in ourselves and knew we were capable of much better.

Inky and John Connolly both spoke and everyone agreed we had to just go for it in the second-half and express ourselves.

We went back out with a different attitude and even though Roger Ryan got a goal which set us back, we showed our determination and loyalty to one another by clawing our way back again. There were a lot of natural leaders on that team like Niall McInerney, John Connolly and PJ Qualter, and the few of us coming from the under-21 set up a couple of years previously had an energy and winning mentality that all added up to us believing in ourselves when it mattered.

Tipp were a bit shocked at our determination in those last few minutes, but I also think we had a bit of luck. John Connolly stood over that late free with seven or eight Tipp men on the goal-line and when it was blocked out, PJ Qualter reacted first and flicked it along the ground and into the net.

Even before that goal, if Tipp had scored even half of their chances I don't think we would have been in a position to win the game. It wasn't like us to rally at that stage and I'd imagine there were a lot of Galway people in the stand who thought that this was another big chance gone west. I'd say that was in John's mind when he decided to go for goal with that free.

We were going for that game, come hell or high water, and I'd say PJ knew that too because he was right alongside him.

A ball broke around centrefield immediately afterwards and I intercepted it, tore off down the field and scored a point. It was pure defiance and I'd say there was only about a minute left at stage. We were two points up now and were not going to let another one slip away. Padraig Fahy added the last score and the full-time whistle was an incredible moment.

Looking back on the TV coverage, Mick Dunne was commentating and you could hear the excitement in his voice at the end of the match. Mick always had great time for Galway, he liked interviewing us and I suppose he enjoyed a new team coming out of nowhere to win it.

Mick's excitement was symbolic of all the neutral GAA people who wanted Galway hurling to emerge as a force. After the game we went back to the hotel and John Connolly was interviewed in Irish by Micheál O'Muircheartaigh; then I knew we had really arrived!

We had a celebration tour a few days later and I will never forget the team bus with the league trophy going through Bohermore in Galway, where Inky Flaherty was living at the time – the excitement of the people that was unleashed that day.

John Connolly turned to me and said, 'What will it be like when we win the All Ireland?'

Part of our celebrations involved a trip to An Poitín Stil in Inverin, again because of the Connemara connection to the Connollys. We were having a great reception there when Joe and I got a phone message to say our grandmother had been killed in a car accident at the age of 100.

The Poitín Stil holds many memories for me, not just for that wonderful reception, but the fact that my late brother Tony, who died in 1977, did a lot of the carpentry work there. My brother Joe used to work with him there during the summer holidays to make a bit of money for going to college so it is a place of great significance to me thinking back to that time.

Expectations were now through the roof in Galway for the championship and after we beat Westmeath in a quarter-final, we played Cork in the semi-final.

It was a cracker of a game with both sides playing free-flowing hurling and it was like a whirlwind that year when suddenly we found ourselves in an All-Ireland final.

That final against Kilkenny was another story.

They were such an experienced team and we just weren't ready for the intensity of it all, but when you consider where we came from when losing to London in 1973 to becoming league champions and getting to an All-Ireland final two years later, it was unbelievable progress. When you think back to the foundations of Galway's success that time, we had the minor team of 1970, the under-21 win of 1972 and quite a few of the Galway lads were playing Fitzgibbon at that time as well.

You had Joe McDonagh, Frank Burke and Joe Connolly in UCG, and Andy Fenton, Sean Silke, Joe and myself in Maynooth.

A lot of people in Galway were getting excited at the time, believing we should all be coming down for training but we said there was no point driving down for four hours to Galway to train and then fours back, when we could be training away ourselves in Maynooth.

That's exactly what we did, and we ended up winning the Fitzgibbon in 1973 and '74 and were fitter than any of them! The one memory I have of that '73 final in Pearse Stadium against UCG was being sent off for the only time in my career.

I was marking Mattie Murphy, who went on to become Galway minor and senior manager, and about 10 minutes into the second-half we were leading by around seven or eight points when I let the hurl back.

Mattie went down and made the most of it I suppose, because the referee John Maloney took my name and then pointed to the line. I was straight off and sitting on the sideline watching our lead slip away.

I got so nervous I drank a full bottle of Lucozade straight back as UCG got back within a point of us. The Galway crowd were roaring them on at this stage and I thought I was going to be devastated if we lost because of my sending off.

Luckily we rallied and won by two points so it all worked out in the end.

The following year we retained the title in Ballycastle against UCD and with four or five lads coming out of that double success, I think it all helped to contribute to the build-up that eventually led to the famous league win in 1975.

99

SEAN SILKE

GALWAY 4-15, CORK 2-19
All Ireland SHC Semi-Final
Croke Park
AUGUST 17, 1975

The National League victory in 1975, Sean Silke believes, brought the extra bit of steel Galway needed

★ **GALWAY:** M Conneely; N McInerney, J Clarke, P Lally; J McDonagh, **S Silke**, I Clarke; J Connolly (1-1), S Murphy; G Coone (1-3), F Burke (1-0), PJ Molloy (0-3); M Barrett, PJ Qualter (0-2), Padraig Fahy (1-3). Sub: M Connolly (0-3) for Barrett (36).

★ **CORK:** M Coleman; T Maher, P McDonnell, B Murphy; T O'Brien, M O'Doherty, C Roche (1-5); P Hegarty, G McCarthy (0-3); J Barry Murphy (1-1), W Walsh (0-1), D Allen (0-1); C McCarthy (0-2), R Cummins (0-1), S O'Leary (0-4). Subs: D Burns for O'Brien (36), J Horgan for O'Doherty (39), E O'Donoghue (0-1) for Walsh (58).

THE ACTION

DESPITE BEATING CORK, Kilkenny and Tipperary en route to winning only their third ever National League title in May, Galway were written off by many heading into the 1975 All-Ireland semi-final.

Their opponents Cork had just toppled Limerick in the Munster final and were confident of extending their record of never having lost to Galway in 19 senior championship meetings. For the Tribesmen, the clash was seen as an opportunity to announce the arrival of a new contender – a chance to right the wrongs of decades of frustration.

Led by inspirational captain John Connolly, Galway had emerged from the wreckage of a disastrous decade in the Munster championship in the 1960s by blooding a whole host of exciting new talent from the All-Ireland winning under-21 team of 1972.

Players like Iggy Clarke, PJ Molloy and Marty Barrett injected new life to the Galway cause and they were joined by a swashbuckling centre-back from Meelick Eyrecourt, who had just won back-to-back Fitzgibbon Cup medals with St Patrick's College, Maynooth.

His name was Sean Silke.

★★★★★

❝

AFTER THE LEAGUE final win, the celebrations went on for a bit, but I remember I was in the midst of doing college exams starting on the Monday so my involvement in the revelry was limited.

There were a lot of people who were emotional because it was 17 years since Galway had competed in anything of significance. Along the way, we had taken out some of the big guns. We beat Cork in the quarter-final and that was a great game, a typical game of two halves. We were playing with a gale in the first-half and led by 2-8 to no score when Cork got a point.

Now we were facing the gale in the second-half. There is no doubt, that day I think was the arrival of the bit of steel that Galway needed.

We were playing a Cork team that was expected to win. They had all the big names and they were keen to bury us, but we were resolute and we fought like tigers. The entire second-half was played in our half of the field so whenever we got the ball, all we could do was run with it as far as possible.

We were in the zone throughout that second-half once we realised we could beat them. And we did. In the league semi-final we defeated Kilkenny, a major skin, on a day when Padraig Fahy gave an exhibition.

Then, we battled hard to defeat Tipperary in the final.

In the championship the good money was on Limerick to come out of Munster as they had played in the two previous All-Ireland finals. I remember going to watch the final against Cork in Limerick to experience the atmosphere and see what it was all about.

The Munster final was a great occasion but it was one-way traffic as Cork got three goals and won by nine points. The Cork centre-forward Willie Walsh was playing very well and after getting one of the goals, I turned to my brother Michael and said, 'Oh Good Jesus!' But Michael is a shrewd analyst of the game.

'Don't worry… you'll manage that fella alright… just play from the front,' he told me.

Cork, like ourselves, are passionate but we felt they would let us hurl and if our forwards could stop their backs clearing the ball that would be a big plus.

We knew we had good forwards, headed up by PJ Qualter and Frank Burke.

Marty Barrett inside was an opportunist, Gerry Coone and PJ Molloy likewise. Padraig Fahy was one of the unsung heroes of Galway hurling. We were ready for Cork and our game plan was simple… attack from the start, and keep attacking.

On the morning of the game, I casually came home from early Mass and had a very large breakfast before heading off to Ballinasloe to get the train. We met up at the Aisling Hotel before the game and then off to Croke Park by bus, quietly confident this would finally be our day.

Right from the off we threw caution to the wind and, quick as a flash, goals from Frank Burke and John Connolly had us 2-2 to 0-0 ahead inside the first seven or eight minutes.

Even after that, every time Cork got a score we seemed to be able to come back and nail them with one of our own. Half-time provided a welcome break. The intense pace and heat left many with weary legs.

We were ahead by seven points, but we weren't being told to consolidate; instead we were told to keep going, keep scoring, keep it moving because the one thing we didn't want to do was pull the handbrake and get caught.

We knew that Cork only needed a couple of chances because they had great forwards and were strong throughout the team. We had to be ruthless.

Galway supporters are just extraordinary.

I suppose they had seen their team beaten so often and there were a lot of pessimists who didn't believe that Galway could deliver on a big day. In the All-Ireland final in 1953 and '58 Galway came up short, and there were other years they could have … should have, might have won.

I thought in 1975 there was a new resolve and a fresh approach.

We began to realise that we were just as good hurlers as a lot of the players in other counties. We had no medals to show for it but we were evolving and we were confident in our own ability. We were able to make decisions on the field.

That time, players played in their set positions, but lads like Iggy Clarke and Joe McDonagh had no fear of speeding up the field, while John Connolly had an engine that meant he could keep going all day. The weight of history might have been against us but I think for too long we had been defined as losers who accepted defeat on the big day and that wasn't a true representation of the way we as individuals felt as confident players and young men.

During the second-half, Ray Cummins came out to centre-forward as pickings were poor inside on Joe Clarke, and he caused me huge problems because he was taller than anybody I had ever hurled on before.

All of a sudden, instead of being seven points up, the margin came down to a couple… and then to one. The next thing we got a fairly standard 21-yard free and Cork lined their goal. Maybe they were rattled, but Gerry Coone's free dipped under the bar and the net shook for a goal.

It was a very welcome tonic and a huge lift.

Cork came down the field. They got a point and in the next attack Jimmy Barry Murphy soloed in and was ready to let fly when Iggy Clarke hooked him.

That was immense.

The difference in the second-half was John Connolly. He was really in his prime in the mid-70s and he was captain and leader of the team, always encouraging lads and very dominant in the middle. Alongside him, Sean Murphy was exceptional and had his best ever game for Galway.

Joe Clarke was the essence of coolness, out-hurling a series of Cork forwards who had given such terrific displays in Munster. Alongside him both Niall McInerney and Pat Lally were invincible.

No matter what was thrown at them they got it out one way or another, and once they got it out towards Joe McDonagh and Iggy… they were off on their horses. They sent great ball into the forwards and at vital times in the second-half we got scores that hurt Cork.

With a few minutes to go we began to realise for definite that this was doable, but Cork had a habit in the past of stealing games in the last couple of minutes and we were a bit concerned about what might even happen in injury time.

Mick Spain from Offaly was the referee. We were hoping he would blow it up.

There was a passion and a frenzy towards the finish to make sure that we blocked out Cork and Joe Clarke threw himself at a shot, while Big Mike Conneely in goals was superb throughout.

It took a few minutes at the end to realise the significance of our victory, that instead of being a spectator at the All-Ireland final, that year we were going to be participating in it. In some ways, people were saying coming into the semi-final that we were in bonus territory but I think we were where we should have been because we were good enough to be in All-Irelands in the early 1970s but for whatever reason our team didn't click or blend together.

That year we were very fit, we had a brilliant trainer in Inky Flaherty; we had good hurlers and I think on the day things happened.

And they happened very quickly.

Napoleon once said that the best general he ever had was General Luck … and I think that we had luck on our side that day.

After the game we got a bus back to the Aisling Hotel for a bite to eat and it was only when we got into the hotel that the significance of what we had done began to hit home.

Inside there were a lot of supporters, but I remember meeting Sean Meade, Seamus Leydon and the Keenan brothers from the Galway football three in-a-row team. I had never met anyone of that sporting significance in my life.

They reassured me that we had taken out a big name and we needed to take confidence from it and go on and win the final. Some time later, I visited Maynooth College where I met up with a great friend from Béal na Bláth in Cork and he would be known as an unbelievably passionate Cork supporter, like all Rebels.

He was crying that night when I met him; he cried the next day and for a few days after that. He in some ways reflected the huge disappointment that Cork people felt, that they almost felt entitled to win.

This was Cork's first semi-final loss, a further cue that things were changing.

Cassius Clay once said that he got his strength from the people, and I think we got a lot of encouragement from our supporters after that – some of it was realistic and some wasn't. But I always think that John Connolly's contribution to Galway hurling at that time was not unlike Cassius Clay's contribution to the way boxing evolved.

He shaped our generation of players and many since.

It was at that time that I began to believe that the key thing was… 'The ball is king'. If you get the ball, your opponent can do nothing.

I knew I was reasonably fast so I could get out in front and get possession, and there were times in that first-half when I told myself … *I'm enjoying this.*

We were spreading the ball wide and making Cork do the running, rather than a military style of play up and down the middle. As a set of backs, we were very secure in our own skin. I think we tuned into each other well and we knew when Iggy or Joe went for a ball we intuitively knew the outcome.

Back in 1975 one of the big hit records was Glen Campbell's *Rhinestone Cowboy* and in some ways we were all cowboys.

We were all trying out something new but we had a great passion and we loved hurling. We began to look at lads like John Connolly, Padraig Fahy, PJ Qualter and some of the older brigade who had served Galway well and we knew if we could do our bit, that they had done it previously and would do it again.

And they did. I think the fact that we understood each other so well was one of the big factors in that victory.

All of that era was a building process because it took Galway a little bit longer than other teams to become successful. We had teams capable enough after 1975 to win an All-Ireland. The following year, 1976 we lost a semi-final to Wexford after a replay in a great game.

We were always hurting about the way it happened and some of the refereeing decisions. We felt that if we had got to Croke Park to play Cork, who came along and won three in-a-row from 1976 to '78, we were definitely good enough to beat them.

Joe McDonagh and Frank Burke, in the drawn game against Wexford in 1976 in Páirc Uí Chaoimh, illuminated the place. Iggy gave an exhibition the second day. It was just a pity the All-Ireland win was postponed until 1980 because there were teams before us who wore that jersey and although collectively they might not have been as good a team, individually some of them were better hurlers.

The fact that so many of the hurlers in the 1970s were playing right throughout the year in college was a huge advantage and we regularly met some of these players like Kieran Purcell and Pat Delaney, and some of the Cork lads, by either playing alongside them or against them in Fitzgibbon or Combined Universities matches.

We got to know them, and realise that they were human, too and even though some of them had greater achievements than we had, fundamentally we were comparable hurlers. We began to believe that, and to realise that Seanie O'Leary might be a good hurler but Padraig Fahy or PJ Molloy were equally as good.

I think there is a very important human component to it all though and in the aftermath of all those matches the hair was let down and we were able to enjoy ourselves. We had a lot of good singers like Niall, John Connolly, Frank Burke and his hit *Ernie*, Sean Murphy and his *Suitcase* song, PJ Qualter and, of course, Joe McDonagh, who entertained everyone after the All-Ireland final defeat to Kilkenny in 1975.

The Kilkenny lads had just won the two in-a-row for the first time in over 40 years and that was being celebrated in a tamer manner than it would have been had we won it. There was almost a 'business as usual' theme.

When we were watching the match on the Monday, a singsong started close to the bar and the next thing McDonagh took the microphone and started to do a Micheál O'Muircheartaigh commentary in Welsh – as he had picked up the language while doing his Post Graduate over in Wales.

Joe was an extraordinary kind of person with the gifts he had for music, for singing, for knowing people's names, and I think he definitely helped to heal the wound of losing the All-Ireland final in 1975.

All the time though there was a quiet resolution that we needed to get back there and we *needed* to win an All-Ireland because we really believed that we were good enough.

Most of us could never imagine life without hurling, it was our passion and will likely remain so. It has helped bring out the best in us by nurturing a determination to learn and improve by giving us feelings of competence and autonomy.

Sport in general also helped us form lifelong friendships among fellow players and also among the opposition. It was our constant companion on life's journey and while it definitely tested our endurance to the limit, it magnified us with skills in the areas of team-work, and character building, and it enhanced our self-esteem.

Finally, sport and especially hurling taught us about life's values and anointed each of us with that unique sense of engagement and, most especially, belonging to something bigger than ourselves.

99

JOE CONNOLLY

UCG 1–14, MAYNOOTH 1–12
Fitzgibbon Cup Final
St Mary's Park, Leixlip
MARCH 6, 1977

The 1977 Fitzgibbon Cup victory was a deeply personal day for Joe Connolly

★ **UCG:** B Kenny (Clare); H O'Donovan (Cork), T Cloonan (Galway), C Hayes (Galway); N McInerney (Galway), P Fleury (Offaly), P Leahy (Galway); J McDonagh (Galway 1-1), F Holohan (Kilkenny); P Costello (Galway), M Quilty (Limerick), G Fahy (Galway 0-1); J Spooner (Tipperary 0-3), **J Connolly (Galway 0-8)**, C Farrell (Galway). Subs: A Barrett (Galway) for Costello, S Flaherty (Galway 0-1) for Quilty.

★ **MAYNOOTH:** F Crowley (Cork); A Kelly (Galway), J Clarke (Galway), A McNamara (Limerick); S Clarke (Offaly), I Clarke (Galway), C Woods (Clare 1-0 free); A Brennan (Galway 0-1), S Stack (Clare); N Foynes (Laois), F O'Driscoll (Cork 0-8), R Marnell (Kilkenny 0-1); T Ryan (Tipperary), G O'Driscoll (Cork 0-2), L Everard (Tipperary). Subs: W Allen (Dublin) for Foynes, H Goff (Carlow) for Allen.

THE ACTION

UCG WON THE Fitzgibbon Cup for the first time since 1970 with a thoroughly deserved two-point win over host college Maynooth. The win was a personal triumph for All Stars Joe McDonagh and Niall McInerney, with McDonagh winning his first Fitzgibbon medal at the seventh attempt and McInerney adding to the medal he won seven years previously. The Galway college, who qualified for the final the day before with a 2-12 to 1-6 win over UCC, led by 0-9 to 0-7 at half-time thanks to the accuracy from play and from frees of full-forward Joe Connolly, and three fine efforts from Jody Spooner. Maynooth relied almost exclusively on the free taking of Fachtna O'Driscoll, who landed six of his side's points.

The key score came early in the second-half as a McDonagh shot from 50 yards flew into the net off goalkeeper Finbarr Crowley's hand to give UCG a handy five point lead. Maynooth controlled the next 15 minutes of play as they landed four points in-a-row, but a crucial missed free by O'Driscoll, which would have levelled the match, proved costly. A fine point from Ger Fahy and three more Joe Connolly frees restored the five-point cushion for the Galway lads and despite Con Woods crashing home a late free to the net in the final minute, time ran out on Maynooth.

★★★★★

"

I WAS CAPTAIN of the UCG fresher team in 1975 after I started doing Arts and we won, and it's amazing how a culture of loyalty and friendship can be sustained, because in 2015 a few of us organised a 40-year reunion of that fresher team that won the All-Ireland championship and 22 lads from the panel showed up.

Even at fresher level we had something going as a group, although I missed the Fitzgibbon that year with a bad leg injury. The following year I played my first Fitzgibbon down in Cork – we played Maynooth in the semi-final.

We travelled down in Paddy Leahy's Morris Minor and it was definitely missing one gear, if not two! We eventually got there anyway but my abiding memory of that game, to my embarrassment, is that it was the only time in a match that I gave up before the end.

What came stupidly into my head with about 10 minutes to go was the thought that… *We're going to have a great night tonight.*

The Fitzgibbon weekends were fantastic craic, and wild nights were guaranteed.

I didn't do what I could have done and *should* have done in the last 10 minutes of that match and we lost by six points in the end. Cyril Farrell was captain that year and I remember Pat Fleury crying in the dressing-room afterwards.

The following year Pat and myself were made captain and vice-captain and I know that on a personal level, I was determined to make up for the year before and ensure that was something that would never happen again in my lifetime.

In 1977 Joe McDonagh was doing a Masters, which was a rare enough thing at the time, and Jody Spooner was back doing the H-Dip and they were starting out in their seventh Fitzgibbon campaign, which was a huge deal at the time.

Joe was also a great footballer and I remember one game where he was full-back marking Gay McManus in an inter-faculty final at Fahy's Field with thousands of people at it. It was a real clash of the titans.

A lot of lads would credit Joe for them becoming UCG hurlers because he was like a chief scout and saw his job as making sure any young hurler who came into the college would join the club and be introduced to other lads. That was crucial because some fellas were more academically driven – like our wing back Paddy Leahy from Loughrea, Sean Flaherty from Abbeyknockmoy and Sean

Burke from Limerick, who were all studying to be doctors.

It wasn't that common that medics would play hurling because of the danger to their hands, and all the lectures and tutorials they would have to attend, but Joe made sure that they all played. Niall McInerney and Tom Cloonan were both on the 1970 team and they were both teachers and were married with kids.

As far as I can make out, I don't think you needed the H-Dip in the early 70s but it either became compulsory or was worth more to them because the two lads came back for two more years and were delighted to be able to hurl again for UCG, even if they couldn't train as often as the rest of us.

There were three army lads on the team – Hugh O'Donovan from Cork, Martin Quilty from Limerick and Pat Costello from Aughrim, outside Ballinasloe, who was a lovely wing forward. They were the lads who provided the transport from UCG to Fahy's Field, along with Jody Spooner whose family had a garage in Roscrea.

The college facilities at the time were terrible. So before Christmas we used to go to the 'Bish' gym on Wednesday nights for circuit training. A few hundred yards away was Glynn's pub on Mary Street and after every Wednesday night training session we would end up there for another session of a different kind!

We used to have rollicking nights in there that often went on until 4am with the most magnificent sing songs. It was that kind of era though and I remember a great friend of mine from our St Mary's College days, Denis Hurney from Turloughmore, who sadly died in his mid-50s, went into first year with me to UCG and we both failed it miserably.

I think we passed one subject between the two of us.

I decided to do first year again and not even bother with the repeats, while Denis left to go working with Galway County Council. In the following years, Denis used to take his holidays in half days to go up to Fahy's Field training with us, so he could still be a part of it. He used to have his dinner in the college and then drive us in his blue mini to training and drop me off in Ballybrit on his way home to Turloughmore.

We had a good team and had already won the league under our manager Eamonn Cody before we were due to play UCC in the Fitzgibbon semi-final. Eamonn is an older brother of Kilkenny legend Brian, but long before Brian came on the scene I had a huge regard for Eamonn as a hurling man.

He was great for a quiet word in your ear and he was a master at instilling good habits. Eamonn was studying archaeology at the time and he had played Fitzgibbon for the college and always wore glasses, but he was a tremendous influence on our hurling careers.

Then we had Tony 'Horse' Regan with the team as well as trainer, so the whole set up was top class. Tony 'Doc' Finan was chairman of the club at the time and a real legend, for whom we all had a great affection and respect. He was a tremendous organiser and the heart and soul of the UCG club for decades.

Sadly, Tony passed away the week after the 2005 All-Ireland final and is greatly missed. There were a few other universities like Trinity and Queens that competed in Fitzgibbon but inevitably the last four would nearly always be UCC, UCD, Maynooth and ourselves.

Ahead of the UCC game we made one positional change by putting in Martin Quilty at centre-forward, an army officer who was about six feet six inches tall. As it happens, he is an uncle of the Irish rugby legend Paul O'Connell and you would know it if you saw the way he demolished one poor UCC lad with a shoulder in that game! Another tough cookie we had on the team was Tom Cloonan at full-back.

At one stage a high ball came in between Tom and the Cork full-forward. The next thing the Cork lad hit the ground and there was no getting up. I was out near the dugouts at the time in the half-forward line and I saw this Cork sub getting ready to go on.

Now you can imagine this lad... over six feet tall, but only 10 and a half stone... skinny legs, left hand on top going in to mark Tom Cloonan. He was about half way to Tom when the Cork full-forward groggily got to his feet and decided he was going to play on.

You never saw a lad to turn and sprint off as quick in all your life as that 'sub', and I remember him saying to the other subs as he sat back down... 'Thanks be to Christ for that!'

At one stage in the second-half a row broke out and the referee Jimmy Rankin from Laois went in to break it up but ended up getting a broken nose. The game was held up for 12 minutes while Jimmy got treatment, but we went on to win it quite comfortably in the end.

The following day we were due to meet Maynooth in the final.

They were down around 10 or 12 points in the other semi-final at one stage to UCD but came back and won by a goal. They were the host college and had been in the last four finals, winning the first two with Sean Silke in the team and losing in 1975 and '76.

We were staying in the Skylon Hotel in Dublin and travelled out to Leixlip the next day. The Sigerson Cup football weekend was in Galway the week before and a couple of weeks before that the Sigerson programme was available around the college.

I remember reading the programme before we travelled to the Fitzgibbon, and there was an article by Mick Raftery, a teacher in Castlegar National School who was corner-back on the Galway football teams that won the All-Ireland titles in 1934 and '38. Mick was a fantastic gaeilgeóir – all he ever spoke was Irish – and he wrote a piece about Sigersons in the 1930s and his record of winning eight titles.

The Tuesday before at training in Fahy's Field, a few of the lads mentioned the Sigerson programme and Mick Raftery's article about a chant that the UCG team in the 30s had. I knew it off by heart:

> *Yerra Waddy, Yerra Waddy, Yup, Yup, Yup.*
> *Hora, Hora, Yup, Yup, Yup.*
> *Ha ha ha, hee hee hee.*
> *Yerra Waddy, Yerra Waddy, U.C.G.*

In the dressing-room before the final, Farrell turned to me and asked me again about the war cry from the Sigerson lads of the 30s. By the time it was said for the third time, everybody had picked up on it and we roared it as loud as we could as we got ready to run out on the field.

This was the first time ever that we had done this as a team, and talk about getting us ready for battle! We nearly took the door off the hinges.

The game got under way and, in fairness, that was a superb Maynooth team. They had Joe and Iggy Clarke, Con Woods and Sean Stack, top players at the time. The frees went well for me that day and Joe McDonagh's goal was a killer blow for them at the start of the second-half. My clearest memories, however, are the celebrations afterwards.

Fitzgibbon and Sigerson final nights were notorious, where the four semi-final teams would come together and if there was a shield or plate competition there could be four more, all together in a hotel for a night of mayhem.

It had to be stopped eventually because things would regularly get out of hand. I remember a few of the Queens lads would try and start up their chant…

Q.U.B… Q.U.B…

But then we would launch into…

Yerra Waddy… Yerra Waddy.

Yup, Yup, Yup.

It was untouchable.

We ended up back at the Skylon Hotel in Dublin and there were hundreds from Galway that had come up for the final who ended up coming back with us. That time there was a round table beside reception and I can still see around 100 sleeping bags coming down the stairs the next morning.

In the end, the hotel didn't even bat an eyelid, there were so many staying there that night! We stopped in The Roost in Maynooth on the way home on the Monday for more celebrations and a sing song, and my other clear memory of that day was when four car loads of lads landed in to my mother, Mary's house in Ballybrit from nowhere.

Like all great Irish women did at the time, she managed to feed 20 lads without any prior warning and a lot of the lads to this day refer to that feed. We had the Fitzgibbon Cup with us and it was a huge trophy, much bigger than the Sigerson, and my mother and father Pat were delighted.

Anyone who has ever played Sigerson or Fitzgibbon knows that it is generally a small group of players and mentors involved, and the bond that is created lasts to this day. I still meet a lot of those lads and it is amazing how so many of them did well in life and left a mark on the world in different ways.

It was a great one to win, because most lads only get a few chances.

Of course, we think of the lads that are gone like Joe, Denis and Gerry P Fahy from Gort, a beautiful hurler who played basketball for Connacht. In the very first game Galway played in 1980, a challenge against Limerick in Loughrea, Gerry was playing and fell into a ground stroke and picked up a terrible injury.

Masses were said for him at the time and while he recovered somewhat he never really hurled again. Gerry lived in Limerick and died a few years later in his forties but he was a much loved and respected man.

There was a strong Galway contingent on that Fitzgibbon team and so many lads went on to make a big impact with the county. Joe McDonagh was captain in the All-Ireland final in 1979 and went on to become President of the GAA, I was captain in 1980, Conor Hayes went on to captain two All-Ireland winning teams in 1987 and '88 and, of course, Cyril Farrell went on to manage Galway to win three All-Ireland senior titles in the 80s.

Then you had Pat Fleury captaining Offaly to win an All-Ireland in 1985, Frank Holohan was captain of Kilkenny the following year when Galway beat them in the semi-final, having won three club All-Irelands with Ballyhale.

So, you had a lot of lads from that team making a big impact and to this day, thankfully, I am in regular contact with a lot of them. I think of so many great players who tried for years and bled to win a Fitzgibbon but were never as lucky as I was in my era.

I had great players around me and when I look back on it, I would put that Fitzgibbon win awful high up in my career list of achievements, having satisfied a savage hunger to win it.

PJ MOLLOY

CORK 3-14, GALWAY 1-15
All-Ireland SHC Semi-Final
Croke Park
AUGUST 7, 1977

PJ Molloy's silken touch allowed him to score at will in the 1977 All-Ireland semi-final against Cork

★ **GALWAY:** F Larkin; N McInerney, J Clarke, A Fenton; J McDonagh, S Silke, I Clarke (0-2); M Connolly (0-1), F Burke; V Mullins (0-1), John Connolly (1-3), **PJ Molloy (0-7)**; M Curtin (0-1), PJ Qualter, P Fahy Subs: T Cahalan for Qualter, Joe Connolly for Mullins, T Donoghue for Cahalan.

★ **CORK:** M Coleman; M Murphy, M O'Doherty, J Horgan (0-1); D McCurtin (0-2), J Crowley, D Coughlan; T Cashman (0-1), T Crowley (0-3); M Malone, J Barry Murphy (1-0), G McCarthy (0-2); C McCarthy (1-2), R Cummins (0-1), S O'Leary (1-2).

THE ACTION

DEFENDING ALL-IRELAND champions Cork finally saw off a determined challenge from Galway, thanks to a strong final quarter in which they outscored their opponents by 1-8 to 0-3.

Fifteen minutes into the second-half, Galway looked like they would repeat their shock win over Cork from two years earlier when they led by 1-12 to 2-6, but when Sean O'Leary scrambled home the equalising goal moments later, the tide turned.

The fact that Galway were in such a strong position at that stage was practically all down to one man, PJ Molloy, who had an inspired game in the half-forward line and scored at will almost every time he touched the ball.

If Molloy was Galway's stand-out player, next best was midfielder Michael Connolly who put in a Trojan effort throughout, but Cork had too many weapons in the final 20 minutes and deservedly qualified for a meeting with Wexford in the final.

Galway raced into a 0-3 to 0-0 lead before Cork struck for two goals in a minute from Jimmy Barry Murphy and Charlie McCarthy. PJ Molloy brought Galway right back into the game with five splendid points in-a-row and when John Connolly blasted home a trademark '21' to the net just before half-time, the Tribesmen had an interval lead of 1-9 to 2-4.

An injury to full forward PJ Qualter midway through the first-half certainly didn't help Galway's cause and his loss was sorely felt in the second-half.

★ ★ ★ ★ ★

"

MY FIRST INVOLVEMENT with Galway was in 1970 when I was part of both the minor hurling and football panels at the start of the year. I was only on the football panel for a while and was dropped.

In fairness, I wasn't good enough to be on that team that went on and won the All-Ireland, but I trained with them in Tuam in the early part of the year and marked Paddy Joe Burke from Annaghdown at wing forward. After I was dropped off the football panel before the start of the Connacht championship, I was called into the hurling panel as they were getting ready for a semi-final against Wexford.

Athenry had won the minor championship in Galway in 1969 and I was minor again the following year. That Wexford game was in Athlone and I was picked up by Bobby Gardiner outside Newcastle Church, after a neighbour of mine repaired my broken hurl that morning with a metal strip cut from a tin of peas and the tube of a bike!

We beat Wexford that day.

The seniors would have won, too, had Frank Coffey's shot in the last minute gone inches inside the post rather than just outside. I know Wexford got a good beating from Cork in the senior final on the day Eddie O'Brien scored the three goals with his hand, while we were well beaten in the end by a Cork team that was a lot more streetwise than we were.

We went up the night before that final and stayed in the Aisling Hotel, and I was rooming with a cousin of mine, Mixie Donoghue, who was a Killimordaly man. I could hardly sleep with the noise of wind in the room and eventually woke up around 6.30am.

I couldn't contain my disappointment at the conditions that lay ahead for an All-Ireland final on our first big day out in Croke Park so I woke Mixie and told him there was a storm.

It turned out it was the air conditioning that was on full blast!

We had no air conditioning in a thatched house in Athenry that time I can tell you. Mixie got a goal early in the game but after a good start the game went away from us.

In 1971, Wexford beat us in the under-21 semi-final and I was playing midfield when we lost to them in Ballinasloe. Cork won the under-21 that year as well for the fourth year in-a-row, a record that still stands, but '72 was our year and finally we made the big breakthrough.

Beating Tipp in their own back yard in Nenagh that year in the semi-final was a big thing and regardless of what we had done at minor level two years previously, we still had the element of surprise when it came to playing the big counties.

We beat a good Dublin team that featured the Holden brothers in the final, but it was a final that I have largely forgotten, because I was dropped for it.

I had played in the semi-final against Tipp and then went down to Rathmore in Kerry on a week's holiday with my future wife Pauline, who had a sister living and married there. I trained every day that week in a place called Gneevgullia, which is where Kerry footballer Ambrose O'Donovan comes from, but after I got back I was dropped for the final.

I was very disappointed to say the least, so much so I wasn't even going to go to the final. On the morning of the match I was down fencing in Monivea when Bobby Gardiner came down and dragged me along to the game.

I came on as a sub in the first-half and ended up scoring three points in that final but I was still miffed afterwards and headed straight home without going for the meal. I know it was immaturity on my part and management were entitled to make their decision, but I was home to hear the report on radio at 6.40pm.

There were plenty of celebrations after that under-21 win, but not long after tragedy struck when our corner-back Liam Shields from Ballinderreen drowned in a boating accident. That left a massive cloud of grief over the function that was held to honour the team at the end of the year.

I was a sub on the senior team in 1972 when Kilkenny gave us an awful beating in Croke Park, but the under-21 win soon after lifted the spirits in the county and things slowly began to change. Normally at senior training when you were in the dressing-rooms you tended to sit beside the lad from your own club.

You'd never see a Castlegar lad sitting beside a Turloughmore lad, or a Carnmore man next to an Athenry man. We weren't inclined to integrate too well.

John Connolly, in fairness to him, changed all that.

He was a great leader and when the likes of John and PJ Qualter and Padraic

Fahy started to stay around during the summer months to train with Galway – because they could see new talent coming through – we knew the good days were not too far away. 1973 though, was a disaster.

Pauline and I were in Ballyconneely and we drove all the way to Ballinasloe to watch Galway get beaten by London in the All-Ireland quarter-final, and I didn't get a run. After that it was the end of the road for a number of the older players who had been around for a while; good lads who had given a lot to Galway, but after the low point of losing to London there had to be a shake up.

1974 wasn't a bad championship when you think of it. Kilkenny beat us in the semi-final but we put up a big score of 3-17, so when we moved on to '75 there was a better structure about everything we did. We got on a great run in the league and beat the big three, Cork, Kilkenny and Tipperary to win it out.

There was a great spirit at that time in the panel, we had bonded well together. Then we went on and beat Cork in the All-Ireland semi-final and it was a result that finished Justin McCarthy as manager. He was a great coach but he never got a chance with another team down there after that.

Cork came back and won the next three All-Irelands but we beat them again in 1979 so there are plenty of lads in Cork that will still tell you to this day that only for Galway they would have won the five in-a-row! After losing the 1975 final to Kilkenny, we lost in a semi-final replay to Wexford the following year, where a John Quigley goal was allowed even though it was scored after the referee's whistle had gone.

That had a big bearing on the game and it was a sickening defeat to take. Only for that, we would have been up against Cork again in the 1976 final and even though I'm sure they would have been ready for us, who knows what might have happened?

Going into the 1977 championship there was both expectation and motivation.

At club level we reached the county final and even though we lost to Kiltormer, at 25 years of age you don't think it's the end of the world because you have other priorities. I had been in America with the 1976 All Stars as a replacement and, for some reason, I trained very hard ahead of the start of the championship.

It was probably down to the lads I was chatting to on that trip, who were telling me the kind of training they were doing, especially on their own. That year

I would run the bog roads near our house every morning and evening, and I regret that I didn't continue doing it in the years after 1977 because it's only when you retire that you realise the condition that lads are in now and the big advantage that the Corks and Kilkennys had on us at the time.

Inky Flaherty was still manager but he decided to bring in Babs Keating from Tipperary as coach to try something different. Babs was in great shape that time and he trained every evening with us; his confidence levels were very high and he kept telling us we were every bit as good as a lad from any other county.

He was a big influence that year and would go on to manage Galway two years later when he came back to guide us to an All-Ireland final. We beat Laois by 10 points in a quarter-final before renewing rivalry with Cork in the All-Ireland semi-final in August. Cork had all the star names, the McCarthys, the Cummins, Jimmy Barry Murphy, Seanie O'Leary, Martin Doherty, John Horgan, Brian Murphy and John Crowley.

They were a good team, had won the All-Ireland the year before and I'd say they took us a lot more seriously than in 1975 when we had the element of surprise. For some reason though, everything I touched that day turned to gold.

Even before we left the Aisling Hotel to go to Croke Park, I was bulling to get out on the field. It was one of those games when I just had to put out my hand and the ball would stick to it. I suppose I was marking an inexperienced player in Dermot McCurtin, who was playing in his first championship season, while Denis Coughlan came over on me for a while as well.

We had a terrible start when we lost PJ Qualter early on to a nasty head injury.

It was a pure accident because he fell as Martin Doherty was pulling on the ball. We missed PJ's vision and goal-poaching ability. We were still well in the game at half-time though and I was really enjoying every time I got on the ball because it seemed to go over the bar. Even though I had one of my best ever games, there was still an awful sense of disappointment when the game got away from us in the last few minutes.

We had a very good side and were just unfortunate to come up against a fine Cork outfit. This was the third championship in-a-row where we had lost a good chance of winning an All-Ireland and the pressure was really starting to mount now on the players to deliver the holy grail.

From then until the glorious day in 1980 it became an obsession.

After that semi-final in 1977, Jimmy Barry Murphy had a lot of kind words to say about me in the national press. I met Jimmy years later when he was managing Cork and I was in charge of Athenry seniors, and we went down to play them in a challenge in Páirc Uí Chaoimh. He was a very modest man who carried huge respect from everyone but he had to fight his corner to get what he wanted for the players given the grip that certain people had on the county board purse strings down there.

I remember him telling me that all the Athenry lads would be fed after that challenge game, even if it meant sending some of the Cork lads home because he was told they were going to be strict on numbers for the meal. That's when Donal O'Grady got involved and they took on the Cork County Board, who had a lot more wealth than a lot of other counties.

It's funny, because back in 1977, Jimmy Barry Murphy and Brian Murphy had to get permission to play in that semi-final against us after the county board had suspended the Cork football panel in a row over Adidas gear – so even 20 years later the tension between players and officials in Cork was there.

The other big thing to happen to me at the end of 1977 was winning an All Star – I was the only Galway man that year on either the hurling or football teams.

It's funny to look back on that Carroll's All Star poster now because for some unknown reason I had grown a beard by the end of that year and next thing a photographer arrived down from Dublin to take my photo before the All Star banquet.

That day I was with Paddy Coleman, a brother of Michael the hurler, and he was buying a machine off me when I got word that the photographer was at the house. I made my excuses to Paddy and told him I would be back in a couple of minutes.

I ran back to the house and shaved off the beard, got the photo taken, and ran back to Paddy who didn't know what to make of me coming back clean shaven to finish off the deal! In later years so many Galway players went on to win All Stars, but at the time I was only the seventh player from Galway to win one since it started in 1971 so it was a pretty big deal.

We were gone on the All Stars trip to the USA the following Spring for three weeks and we played games in Chicago and Boston before heading to Los

Angeles and San Francisco, and finished up back in New York.

One thing I remember about that trip in 1978 was how good the Dublin football lads were to be around. They were the nicest of fellas and great company … Kevin Moran, Jimmy Keaveney, every one of them.

Cyril Farrell got involved in the training of the team in 1979 under Babs and took over himself in 1980. We trained savage hard that year, mostly in Fahy's Field. We were probably lucky to avoid Kilkenny that year as well because Offaly had won Leinster for the first time, so we had to beat them and Limerick to finally get the All-Ireland title the whole county craved.

A lot of people were very disappointed after losing to Offaly in the 1981 final, but that was a good Offaly team and even though the next couple of years weren't great, the success of the minors and under-21s in 1983 kept a lot of us going – and I would have kept hurling until I was 40 at that stage. There was certainly no thought of packing it in.

Of all the games we lost, the 1985 final against Offaly is the one I most regret.

That was one we should have won. In 1986 I was nearly finished, but I came on in the All-Ireland semi-final against Kilkenny and scored a point in a match we won well. All the young players like Finnerty, Keady, McInerney, Cooney and Naughton were really starting to come of age. We were staying in the Grand Hotel in Malahide the night before the All-Ireland final against Cork when the match programmes were handed out, and I noticed I wasn't even listed in the Galway panel.

I was very upset, but I didn't make a big deal of it and the management ended up switching jerseys between the subs – and I came on again in the final and scored 1-1.

Tomas Mulcahy created havoc that day and it was revenge for Cork for the semi-final the year before. By early 1987 I was left off the Galway panel for the National League and I thought that was that, but the club got on a good run in the Galway championship and I was delighted to get the call from Cyril to go back in before the All-Ireland semi-final against Tipperary.

I came on in that game and set up a goal and a point, and came on again for the last 15 minutes of the final against Kilkenny, so to get a second All-Ireland medal, having started out 16 years before that, was very satisfying.

In 1988 we played Offaly in a league quarter-final in Croke Park and after they beat us by a point, I said I had enough and decided to pack it in.

Phelim Murphy came in to me a few times to see would I come back but I was 36 years-old and had enough of it.

By that stage Athenry were getting ready for an All-Ireland club final on St Patrick's Day against Midleton, after we ended 1987 with our first ever county senior championship title. As far as I was concerned, I hadn't done the club justice in the county final in 1977.

I had broken a couple of fingers in the semi-final against Ballinderreen and the county final was delayed because of that, but I felt I had let the lads down that year and wanted to make up for it when we eventually got back to the final 10 years later.

Everyone likes to win a county final with their club so when we did in 1987, I felt a sense of relief at having completed a journey.

NOEL LANE

KILKENNY 2-12, GALWAY 1-8
All-Ireland SHC Final
Croke Park
SEPTEMBER 2, 1979

Noel Lane scored the Goal of the Year in the tough loss to Kilkenny in the 1979 All-Ireland final

★ **GALWAY:** S Shinnors; N McInerney, C Hayes, A Fenton; J McDonagh, S Silke, I Clarke; John Connolly, S Mahon (0-1); B Forde, F Burke, Joe Connolly (0-2); PJ Molloy (0-3), **N Lane (1-0)**, F Gantley (0-2). Subs: S Linnane for Forde, M Whelan for Burke.

★ **KILKENNY:** N Skehan; P Larkin, P Prendergast, J Henderson; R Reid, G Henderson, N Brennan; J Hennessy (0-1), F Cummins; G Fennelly, W Fitzpatrick (0-1), L O'Brien (1-7); M Brennan (1-1), M Crotty (0-1), M Ruth. Subs: K Fennelly (0-1) for Crotty, D O'Hara for Prendergast.

THE ACTION

GALWAY'S HOPES OF landing an elusive All-Ireland title were dashed by Kilkenny after the Westerners failed to score in the final 20 minutes following a truly brilliant goal by Noel Lane which looked to have turned the game in their favour.

Playing with the advantage of the driving wind and rain in the first-half, Galway were well on top, but 11 wides meant the sides were level at 0-4 each when a mis-hit Liam O'Brien '65' evaded defenders and goalkeeper alike to end up in the net and give Kilkenny the lead.

The excellent Joe Connolly cut the deficit to two points before half-time and even though Kilkenny got the opening score of the second-half, Galway were level when Steve Mahon lofted over a superb score, followed by two Finbar Gantley frees to make it 1-5 to 0-8. Kilkenny edged in front with a Liam 'Chunky' O'Brien point, but then in the 14th minute came Lane's Goal of the Year as he fielded a long ball in front of Paddy Prendergast, turned and unleashed a brilliant shot into the top right hand corner of the net past a startled Noel Skehan to put Galway in front 1-8 to 1-6.

Unfortunately for Galway they would not score again, as Kilkenny hit three points in-a-row to regain control. Galway were thrown a lifeline seven minutes from time when Joe Connolly was upended in the square for a penalty, but his brother John's effort was saved by Skehan and with it went Galway's hopes of winning.

★ ★ ★ ★ ★

66

THE LANES ARE a family synonymous with the Ballinderreen, Craughwell and Clarinbridge areas. My father and his two brothers played for Clarinbridge in the 1939 county final against Castlegar, before he got a place over in Lavally Connor where he married and started a family.

My father always encouraged me from a young age to fight for every ball and give as good as I got. I went to school in Ballyglass and had a great mentor there called Tom O'Doherty, a Limerick man, who coached us on the basic skills of hurling.

Growing up where I live, we learned how to walk, we learned how to talk and we learned how to hurl. There was nothing else.

We live in the middle of a real hurling stronghold in South Galway, with Ardrahan, Craughwell, Clarinbridge, Ballinderreen and Kinvara all in close proximity. There was a great South Board Championship going back to the 1950s and 60s with intense rivalry between the teams and, as a young lad, I'd listen to some of the team talks before the games and think it was like the movie *Braveheart*. The captain outlining exactly what he expected his men to do to the opposition!

Our house was a lot closer to Ardrahan than Ballinderreen, and seeing as we went to school in Ballyglass there was a lot of pressure put on my brothers and myself to play for Ardrahan when we were young, but a man called Martin Joe O'Connor used to pick us up for training and matches and he made sure we played for Ballinderreen.

I captained Ballyglass National School to a county final and being made captain was a great reassurance of my ability at a young age. My first time going up to Ballinderreen was at under-12 and that was the first time I met Joe McDonagh, Tom Quinn, Liam Shiels, Walty Murphy, and Martin and Michael Coen amongst others; the lads I would spend my life hurling with.

Even at that time, Joe McDonagh showing his leadership qualities. He came down the road to meet me as I stood shyly beside my bike, and he introduced me to the other lads. He was always an idol of mine since that moment.

I played with Ballinderreen up along the underage ranks and won a South

Board under-21 title and, by then, I had realised that I could hold my own against players from other clubs. It was around then that the dream of playing for Galway began to take hold.

In 1970, I went to see Galway play Wexford in the All-Ireland semi-final in Athlone with a couple of my first cousins. Joe McDonagh was centre-forward and scored a goal for the Galway minor team that beat Wexford beforehand, but the senior game really sowed the seeds for my aspirations to play for the county as I watched the Galway lads lead until late on when Wexford came back to win by two points.

I was just turning 18 in 1972 when five Ballinderreen lads were part of the Galway team that won the All-Ireland under-21 title and the following year I was on the Our Lady's Gort team that reached a colleges All-Ireland final only to lose out to St Peter's of Wexford in a replay. Sean Devlin was a great coach and trainer on that college team and was a huge influence to me.

I made the Galway under-21 panel later that year but I was now based in Kinnitty Castle in Offaly as a trainee forester and didn't make the team as I lost out to Jimmy Cooney for the wing back position. We were well beaten by Kilkenny in that semi-final so I never got to play underage for Galway. Coming from a farming background and with a brother already in the forestry industry, I decided to take the exams and see what came out of it. I was already in agricultural college at the time and stayed on to complete my exams there to have as a safety valve.

I made my senior debut for Ballinderreen around 1974, having lined out in the Offaly championship with the newly affiliated Forestry team the year before. We regularly played the Kinnitty team that included Johnny Flaherty, Pat Delaney, the Corrigans and Ger Coughlan... with no referee and no lines on the pitch.

There was blue murder half the time but it hardened me up for senior hurling.

There was no place to hide. Ballinderreen had a very strong team at the time with a few older lads like Micheál McTigue, Stephen Gill, Eamon Fahy, John Coen and John Faul linking up with the younger lads like Joe McDonagh, Michael Coen, John Costello, Pat Gill and myself. We lost the county semi-final to Athenry in 1977 but the following year we got to the final against our near neighbours Ardrahan in what was one of the highlights of my career.

We were probably the better team in the first county final, which ended in a draw.

We were four points up with only a couple of minutes left when they came back with a goal and a point to level it. We drew again in the replay after a controversial finish when Ardrahan were given a '70' from what everyone seemed to think was a wide ball – and Michael Bond scored it to send the game to extra-time.

It was nearly dark at this stage and a lot of our lads didn't want to go back out for extra-time but we had some officers that wanted to be compliant with the county board so we went out and lost by four points. That was the only senior county final we got to and it wasn't until 1998 that I won my only adult county medal with the club when we won the County Junior B championship with Joe McDonagh as captain.

I treasure that win as much as any other success during my career, club or county. Winning with the club is very special and it was great to get that win and at 44, I got Man of the Match for good measure.

After I qualified as a forester and left Kinnity, my first appointment as an assistant forester was in Aughrim in Wicklow in 1977. I was staying in the Ardee House Hotel with several other young forestry graduates. One evening, out of the blue, one of the lads ran upstairs to me with a copy of the *Irish Press* that carried the Galway hurling team to play Clare in the National League the following Sunday. I was named at corner-forward.

That was the first I had heard of being selected to make my debut in a Galway jersey! We got to the league quarter-finals in April 1978 in my debut season and even though I scored four goals against Limerick, we were well beaten. Later on that year in the championship we were beaten by seven points by Kilkenny in the All-Ireland semi-final and it was worrying because it seemed like we were slipping back again after great progress in recent years.

In 1979, Babs Keating was back as coach, with Cyril Farrell in the backroom team and we had a lot of younger lads like Bernard Forde, Sylvie Linnane, Steve Mahon and Jimmy Cooney and myself coming through. It was also starting to come into being that the Galway team was picked on how you were playing and not who you were.

There was far more team spirit and even though we got destroyed by Tipperary in the league final, we came back to beat Laois in the quarter-finals of the championship and then produced a memorable performance in the All-Ireland semi-final to stop Cork in their quest for four in-a-row.

I was marking one of the all-time great full-backs, Martin O 'Doherty that day and I remember not caring one bit who I was on. It was the same kind of attitude the whole team had, and whatever way we were prepared for that game I knew we were going to win. Finbar Gantley and I got a goal each as we won by 2-14 to 1-13 and qualified for the final against Kilkenny.

There was a lot of hype surrounding the final in 1979.

My great club mate Joe McDonagh was captain and I really wanted to win for him, as he was a born leader. The word around the country was that Galway had finally arrived and the Kilkenny team was not a patch on great Kilkenny teams of the past. Surely this was to be our time!

Of course, the closer we got to the match, the more we realised that there is no such thing as a bad Kilkenny team so I'm not one hundred percent sure we were mentally right going into that final. The wet day certainly didn't help us and the tougher the game and the conditions got, the more Kilkenny liked it.

They were a big physical team with the Hendersons, Dick O'Hara, Chunky O'Brien and Frank Cummins and unfortunately, we let it come down to a physical battle that day when we were the better team for long periods of the game. We had a lot of wides in the first-half and they got a soft enough goal, even though Seamus Shinners had a great game in goals apart from one lapse towards the end of each half.

The reason we lost the All-Ireland final that day was we only scored 1-8 and I think it was very unfair of certain Galway supporters to pin the blame on Seamus.

We were very good at looking for scapegoats in Galway when it came to losing big matches over the years and the easy target was our goalie, whose puck outs were brilliant – he also made some great saves that day. We just didn't play well as a unit and ended up reverting to playing as individuals, which was so disappointing on the biggest day of the year.

Personally, I felt really good that day. Babs had spent a lot of time with me in the build up and had given a lot of personal attention to both Conor Hayes and myself as full-back and full-forward to outline what he expected of us. He gave me great confidence and I believed that I would wreak havoc if I got the right supply.

Midway through the second-half I eventually got my chance as I caught a high ball on the Cusack Stand side, shipped a couple of tackles and unleashed a shot to the net to put us two points up.

Everybody believed at that stage we would go on and win the game, but straight away Kilkenny got a couple of soft frees to pull level and after they went ahead, we seemed to lose all our shape and we didn't score again.

We had our chances right throughout the game but unfortunately it all fizzled out by the end. At the end of the year, I was awarded an RTE Goal of the Year trophy for the one I got in the final, but the main thing I took from the goals I got, both in the semi-final against Cork and the one against Kilkenny, was that I could do it against the big teams on the big day and that it would stand to me when we would come back to Croke Park again in future years.

I don't really go with the old adage that you have to 'lose one to win one', but playing in the final in 1979 and experiencing the pain of losing stood to us in 1980. Babs might have gone, but he had laid the coaching foundations and Cyril was now the boss on his own. Maybe now looking back, with the benefit of hindsight, having two people in charge could have led to confusion and disharmony, but in '80 Cyril picked two able warriors to be with him in Bernie O'Connor and Phelim Murphy.

Of course, the fact that it was Offaly and Limerick in the semi-final and final made it easier for us psychologically, as we knew we had the beating of both those teams. Still, we only just got past what would turn out to be a great Offaly team by two points and it took a late interception from Conor Hayes in the final against Limerick or we might have been caught, but it was a great relief to get over the line and finally win an All-Ireland.

The fact that Joe Mc and Iggy Clarke were missing for the final in 1980 was also a huge motivating factor, but we had good lads to come in and Seamus Coen did a great job in place of Iggy, who in my opinion was one of the greatest wing backs of all time. He ticked all the boxes and to see him at Mass on the morning of the All-Ireland with his arm in a sling, having broken his collar bone in the semi-final win over Offaly, was enough to get the entire team to make a pact that there was no way we were going to let this one slip.

I had my own bit of drama running out onto the pitch for the All-Ireland final as Bernie Forde caught me with a swing of his hurl just over the eye. I had to get five or six stitches as a result, but our doctor Mary McInerney was worried and said I might have to go to hospital.

I told her if she wanted to bring the eye to the hospital she could, but I wasn't going! The whole incident actually took away all the nerves that Bernie and I had, and as it turned out he had the game of his life and scored 1-5.

'Big Mike' Conneely had a fairytale day in the final as well and he made some miraculous saves, but it was only just reward for the hard work he put into it over the years. PJ Molloy would often puck 150 balls at him… left, right and centre before training and Mike would come off the field with hardly any skin left on his knees. He was truly outstanding that day.

I had been on a number of All Star trips as a 'replacement' up to the time I won my two awards in 1983 and '84. Those All Stars came in what were the lull years for Galway but going on those trips to the U.S. gave players like myself a sense that we were equal to players from the likes of Cork, Tipperary and Kilkenny, who had won so many All-Irelands between them.

I was lucky to be one of the four or five lads who straddled the two successful hurling eras in Galway, firstly from 1975 to '81 and then from 1985 to '90. In the first era, I was one of the young lads without a care in the world, but in the second era, I became one of the older lads who couldn't sleep the night before a big game!

In 1985, I was a 'young' 30 year-old, but I knew there was a great bunch of young players coming through from the All-Ireland winning minor and under-21 teams of 1983 and it would take a year or two for us to get back to the top again. Cyril Farrell was back in charge and there was a very good set up where there was harmony in the county. We could have won in 1985 and '86, but didn't and being captain and having a poor final in '86 made me think that Cyril would pull me aside and tell me my time was up. He ended up doing the exact opposite, calling to my home and telling me I was going to be a huge part of the Galway squad for the next couple of years which gave me huge encouragement to keep going.

In 1987, I was on the bench and came on in the semi-final against Tipp and got a goal; and came on again against Kilkenny in the final and also got a goal, so that buried the disappointment of the previous year. In 1988, I was hurling really well and scored 1-4 from play against Offaly in the semi-final.

I felt the younger players were looking up to me as one of the more experienced lads on the team. Then on the Tuesday before the final at training in Ballinasloe, a few of us were pucking the ball around when Farrell came to within 20 metres of me and said out loud that Michael Coleman was in and I wouldn't be starting in the final. He was probably wise not to have come any closer because I had a hurl in my hand and I was very annoyed. I was angry and felt an enormous sense of injustice at being left out.

I finished out the training session and attended the player's meeting afterwards but had little or no interest in it. I had a couple of pints on my way home and it took a day or two before I came to the realisation that this was not about Noel Lane, but about Galway hurling doing two in-a-row.

I went out on the Sunday in the final with the attitude that if I got a chance I would prove them wrong and that's exactly how it transpired. I had no problem with Michael Coleman starting as I believed he should have been on much sooner, but I should not have been the one to lose out.

If we had lost that final, I would have been very unhappy, but as it turned out management were proved right and Michael Coleman would prove that day and for years afterwards that he was one of the finest hurlers we ever produced. They felt they wanted to have as strong a team finishing that final as possible and that if the game was tight, I might be the trump card that Galway needed.

Looking back on it now, the whole controversy played right into our barrow and probably affected Tipperary who I'm sure felt Galway were in turmoil. Seeing the Galway supporters on O'Connell Street after we won it made it all worthwhile though.

I married my wife Carmel in the summer of 1980 and our first child Aoife arrived the following year. Mark and Patrick came later and, of course, they were and still are all mad into the hurling. We had been going out for a few years and had built up a great relationship with the other players' wives and girlfriends. Those ladies made huge sacrifices for us to be able to play the sport we loved and we still meet up from time to time at functions and get-togethers.

I was very lucky to have Carmel, not just on the good days when we won, but more importantly on the days we lost and I needed a comforting word at home. Throughout the 1980s I got involved with coaching, firstly with Clarinbridge in 1983 when they won the intermediate championship and then when I finished playing I managed the Galway minors and under-21s for two years each.

We didn't have much luck though as we lost All-Ireland finals in three of the four years when we came up against an excellent Cork team at both minor and under-21 during that time. I got the senior manager's job in 2001 and felt I had the right CV and could bring the players along with me.

I had John Connolly, Niall McInerney and Mike McNamara with me, and the one thing we identified as a weakness in Galway at that time was our mental toughness, particularly in the last five minutes of big games.

The plan worked and we had a great win over Kilkenny in the semi-final in 2001. Brian Cody has often acknowledged that it was a turning point in his management career as he vowed never to send out a team to be physically dominated like we did to them that day. In the final against Tipperary we were the better team throughout but were on the wrong side of a lot of key decisions by match officials. The following year after beating Cork in Thurles, we were pipped at the post by a late Colin Lynch point against Clare in the quarter-final.

Despite that defeat we were on an upward curve and I felt I was getting better at my job as manager but we never got the chance as in typical Galway fashion we were 'out'. I was bitter at the time and the players were really disappointed as they craved continuity. I, along with a superb backroom team, had invested a lot of time in our various roles and felt that being removed was not in the best interest of Galway hurling. Conor Hayes came in and things moved on.

I have played and worked in administration with my club Ballinderreen at all levels and continue to do so to the present day. I would love to have won that county senior final against Ardrahan in 1978.

Being on the line as a selector with my club's Junior A team in 2020 gave me as much satisfaction as ever and nothing will ever come close to that feeling. Winning a tight club game is magic and losing is as sore as ever. I was chairman of our camogie club for a number of years also and enjoyed great success with our camogie teams over that period.

For any county player, to win an All-Ireland is the ultimate.

Whether it's one, two, three or more, it doesn't matter, and I always feel sorry for players who don't get to achieve that. I was lucky enough to win three All-Irelands and I made a lot of friends and had great fun along the way.

You can't have any regrets with that.

99

JOHN CONNOLLY

CASTLEGAR 2-9, BLACKROCK 0-9
All Ireland Club SHC Semi-Final
Kenny Park, Athenry
MAY 25, 1980

Castlegar's victory over reigning All-Ireland club champions Blackrock was a day when all of Galway celebrated

★ **GALWAY:** T Grogan; T Murphy, P Connolly, John Coady; G Glynn, **J Connolly**, M Glynn (0-1); T Murphy, S Fahy; J Francis (0-1), Joe Connolly (2-2), P Connor; G Connolly (0-2), M Connolly (0-3), L Mulryan. Subs: P Burke for Mulryan, T Connolly for Connor.

★ **BLACKROCK:** T Murphy; F Norberg, C O'Brien, J Horgan; D McCurtain (0-1), F Cummins (0-1), J O'Grady (0-1); A Creagh, P Moylan (0-1); D Collins (0-1), T Lyons, D Buckley (0-2); E O'Sullivan (0-1), R Cummins (0-1), E O'Donohgue. Subs: P Power for Collins, P O'Neill for Sullivan.

THE ACTION

AS CLUB CHAMPIONSHIP upsets go, this one is right up there. Galway's most successful club, Castlegar were taking on the reigning All-Ireland club champions Blackrock, a side that included no fewer than seven members of the Cork team that had won the National League title the Sunday before.

The foundation for Castlegar's victory lay in their supreme levels of fitness and for this the credit must go to trainer Tony 'Horse' Regan.

The Castlegar defence also revelled in the familiar surrounds of Athenry. Ted Murphy and Padraic Connolly totally outplayed Ray Cummins and Eamon O'Donoghue, while John Coady, Gerry Glynn, John Connolly and Mícheál Glynn all shone throughout.

Up front, Michael Connolly pointed after just four minutes with his first touch of a ball since Castlegar won the Galway final in December, while he and brother Joe landed further scores to edge an 0-4 to 0-3 advantage at the end of the first quarter.

Then came the crucial first goal as Mícheál Glynn broke up a Blackrock attack and his long clearance was picked up by Michael Connolly who handpassed over the last defender to Joe Connolly. He duly slotted home for a tonic score. Castlegar maintained their dominance until the interval when they led 1-6 to 0-5.

The all-important second goal came eight minutes into the second-half as John Connolly launched a huge 100-yard free into the Blackrock square and as the ball broke, Joe Connolly was on hand to poach his second goal of a memorable afternoon. Jimmy Francis pointed soon after to give Castlegar a 2-7 to 0-7 lead with 15 minutes to go, before the Cork side exerted a period of huge pressure, culminating in a penalty awarded in the 49th minute. Much to the home side's delight, Frank Cummins' effort was touched over the bar by Castlegar goalie Tommy Grogan.

★★★★★

"

I'VE FORGOTTEN AN awful lot of the games I've played over the years but this one definitely sticks out. To beat a team like Blackrock was huge.

They had half of the Cork senior team that won the league the previous Sunday; the rest of them had all played for Cork at some level up along the line – and they had the great Kilkenny hurler Frank Cummins. The importance of it in my mind is the fact that it is the only scoreline I can remember from all the games I ever played… 2-9 to 0-9.

We weren't given much of a chance by anyone of beating Blackrock but we knew we had a great team ourselves. We had six great backs, a strong midfield pair and great attacking forwards. I wouldn't say we were confident of beating Blackrock that day but we knew they were going to have earn it.

Blackrock always thought it was a real 'stroke' on our behalf to have the match played in a 'bog' in Athenry and that we had narrowed in the sidelines to make the pitch even smaller! How it came about was we were entitled to home advantage for the semi-final and, at the time, Ballinasloe and Pearse Stadium were the two county pitches.

At a meeting to decide on the venue a couple of weeks before the game, our wing back Micheál Glynn suggested playing the game in Athenry where we had a played loads of times in the Galway championship. It would be new to the Cork lads and a big advantage to us. We all agreed with Micheál that it would indeed be a great 'stroke'.

The All-Ireland club championship was in its tenth year, and was starting to grow and become a big deal around that time. I had missed our first tilt at an All-Ireland semi-final in 1973 when we lost heavily to Glen Rovers, but in the years that followed it looked like Galway teams didn't believe that they could win it.

Cork clubs had taken over and won it nearly every year, and clubs from Tipp and Kilkenny had already won it, but a bit like the Galway senior team, it looked like there was a monkey on our back.

We had beaten Roscommon's Tremane by six or seven points in a Connacht final at the end of March but whatever it was about the All-Ireland semi-final, we were worked up for that day. Tony Regan, our trainer, had us motivated to the last and we were determined to have a real cut at it and go down fighting.

'Horse' had a great way with lads.

He knew how to train hard but also keep a fun element in it. While he was a football man himself, he knew what it took to win games and how important mental preparation was. There wasn't a lot of tactics involved at that time in any game, club or county. It was the back's job to stick like glue to his man, don't attack too much and when he got the ball… belt it up the field.

There was great skill though – high fielding, control of the ball, reading the play, that kind of stuff. Hurling 'cuteness' and acumen was brilliant in our team. It's only in recent years that tactics like man-marking came into it.

Athenry was jammed that day. A great crowd had come up from Cork to follow the 'Rockies' and there had to be 8,000 or 9,000 people there. Our supporters had no issues with going out to Kenny Park; they would have crawled out on their hands and knees to support their team but I don't think too many saw what was coming.

We matched them tit for tat all through the early stages of the game. The great Dermot McCurtain pointed a great sideline ball for them in the first few minutes but we never buckled and I remember Mícheál Glynn pointed an even better lineball late on for us. It was a great statement to make.

No matter what you can do today, we will better it.

Cutting a lineball over the bar that time was no joke because the ball was so much heavier. It was a rarity. The other telling moment of that game that forever sticks in my mind involved Ray Cummins, who was one of the best players that I ever saw playing. Ray was cutting in along the end-line during the first-half and heading for goals, when our corner-back Ted Murphy met him head on and sent him flying.

No free, only a wide ball. That fairly laid down a marker.

It's a shoulder that has gone down in folklore. Ted was our most iconic club player ever but to do what he did to the great Ray Cummins was unbelievable. Ray would see a fly coming over Galway bay but he didn't see Ted coming that day. It was all about timing.

Even to this day, mention 'Tedeen' anywhere in Galway and his name resonates with people who followed hurling at the time.

Midway through the first-half Joe got our first goal and it's true to say that a goal is always a great boost for a team to get. It's really worth more than three points psychologically, but to go in at half-time leading was huge.

Regan said to us, 'Lads… ye have this game won if ye keep going. They can't stay with ye'. My other memory of half-time involved the much loved Willie Fahy, who was probably one of the best left full-backs ever in Galway and was on the historic Connacht team that won the 1947 Railway Cup.

Willie was the loveliest, quietest man you could ever meet, but he charged into the dressing-room at half time.

'Ye have it lads… if ye stay cool!'

He was roaring. It was obvious Willie himself had lost his cool in all the excitement! But we went out for the second-half with real belief. I know Blackrock had the star names and maybe they felt they could just turn it on when they had to, but when we got our second goal at the start of the second-half we could sense it was going to be our day.

I remember I just bombed a free in towards the goal and a few seconds later heard the cheer. I hadn't a clue who had scored. It turned out it was Joe's second goal of the day. All I knew is we had 20 minutes to stop them scoring a goal and we would be okay. We held a six-point lead for most of the second-half but at no stage did we believe we had the game won until the final whistle.

Frank Cummins had a penalty with a few minutes to go but Tommy Grogan got a touch on it to flick it over the bar, and then Mícheál Glynn cut that masterful ball over the bar near the end for us. That final whistle though was the sweetest sound I ever heard!

The other abiding memory of that day was after the final whistle. There was always a great and healthy rivalry in Galway club hurling down through the years. When you think about it, that was what kept Galway teams going as we had no Connacht championship. We had great rivals at that time in Kiltormer, Ardrahan, Gort, Killimordaly, Turloughmore and other great teams.

There was nothing between any of us.

The amazing thing was when we came off the pitch, we had to push our way through the crowd and there were fellas from those clubs, arch enemies of ours, roaring us on and cheering us and clapping us to a man. That was fantastic to see because the Sunday before we would have been belting hell out of one another and here they were being so enthusiastic about us winning.

There was no doubt in our minds then that we were a Galway team, representing Galway. I was good friends with Frank Cummins since we were selected on the first All Star team together, and his wife Madeline and my wife Nuala also became good friends and remain so to this day. Frank was a Garda based in Blackrock and we hadn't seen each other since that All Star trip in 1971.

Nuala couldn't get over how quiet Madeline was after the game. Frank was devastated to lose as well because he was a real winner. They were stunned.

The big danger for us after winning the game was thinking we had won the All-Ireland when, in fact, we were out again the following Sunday in Navan in the final against Ballycastle. I can tell you there was a lot more drinking done at that time after a game than nowadays, but the reality check came on Monday after a great night of celebrations.

In fairness to 'Horse' Regan he got us right during the week because there were a few lads who would easily have continued the session into Tuesday or Wednesday – and this was our big shot at making history and becoming the first team from Connacht to win an All-Ireland club championship.

Preparations were far from ideal for a real 'banana skin' final against a Ballycastle team that had beaten Leinster champions Crumlin by 10 points. They were a team packed with quality hurlers like the Donnellys and I remember thinking after 10 minutes of the final that we were in big trouble as they came at us in waves.

We all thought the same thing before that final. If we beat Blackrock and then lose the final it will be a disaster. Luckily we came out the right side of the final by three points. Eddie Donnelly and I had been on a couple of All Star trips as well and after the game both teams dined together in Navan, which was most unusual and I got talking to Eddie for a while. He was obviously disappointed to lose a game they came so close to winning but what he said to me put both our lives and our clubs into perspective.

'John, you're going home to the west with the cup and stopping along the way to be met by bonfires. We are going to be stopped three or four times by the British Army.

'Our gear is going to taken off the bus and thrown around the road. We will go another 10 miles and the same thing will happen again.'

We were worlds apart. I almost convinced him to come to Galway that night! They were some club. They presented us with a framed harp made of silk threads and thumb tacks by a republican inmate in Long Kesh that day after the game in Navan. It hung in our clubhouse for years.

We eventually got back to Jackson's bar in Merlin for our own celebrations but just like the Blackrock game, our celebrations didn't last as long as we would have liked.

When you look back on it now it's hard to believe that we won an All-Ireland club title on June 1, when you consider the major fixture it has become on St Patricks Day, but that's the way it was at the time. Between us winning the Connacht final and playing the All-Ireland semi-final, the Galway club championship had already started for the following season.

We had already lost to Sarsfields in our first championship group game a couple of weeks before the Blackrock game, and the Sunday after that we played the All-Ireland final. The Sunday after that we were asked to play Rahoon in our next group game in Pearse Stadium... and the Sunday after that we played our final group game against Kiltormer, which we lost in controversial circumstances.

It was crazy stuff. Two weeks after being crowned All-Ireland champions we were out of the championship.

Kiltormer were great rivals and they were primed and ready for us. I often think we were daft to play them. There was a lot of rancour after that game and a few lads were called in to a disciplinary meeting the following week for words said to the referee.

This was now the middle of June and Galway's All-Ireland quarter-final against Kildare was fast approaching. In the end, everyone got off and the focus switched to the county team. What I would say is, our All-Ireland club success had a big impact on us winning the All-Ireland with Galway that September. You must remember that in 1979, Galway had lost the All-Ireland final, the National League final, the Oireachtas final and the Railway Cup final. You would think we were losers, but after we won the Railway Cup on St Patrick's Day in 1980 for the first time in 33 years, our All-Ireland club win came just over two months later. It was a huge confidence boost, and the fact that we could beat a club team like Blackrock with so many Cork lads had to have been a help when it came to what happened with the county team later in the summer.

What it was, of course, was the first. And the *first* is always the *first*.

Galway clubs have won 13 hurling and seven football All-Ireland Club championships but we were the first to do it. And I know there have been other great teams like Sarsfields, Portumna and Athenry, but they never beat a team like Blackrock as we did on that day.

99

MICHAEL CONNEELY

GALWAY 2-15, LIMERICK 3-9
All-Ireland SHC Final
Croke Park
SEPTEMBER 7, 1980

Mike Conneely comes to the aid of Niall McInerney as Galway end a 57-year wait to reclaim the Liam MacCarthy Cup

★ **GALWAY: M Conneely**; C Hayes, N McInerney, J Cooney; S Linnane, S Silke, S Coen; M Connolly, S Mahon; F Burke, Joe Connolly (0-4), PJ Molloy (1-0); B Forde (1-5), John Connolly (0-2), N Lane (0-3). Subs: F Gantley for M Connolly, J Ryan (0-1) for Molloy.

★ **LIMERICK:** T Quaid; D Murray, L Enright, Dom Punch; L O'Donoghue, M Carroll, S Foley; J Carroll, David Punch; P Fitzmaurice, J Flanagan, W Fitzmaurice; O O'Connor, J McKenna (1-1), E Cregan (2-7). Subs: B Carroll (0-1) for Flanagan, P Herbert for M Carroll, E Grimes for W Fitzmaurice.

THE ACTION

SCENES OF UNBRIDLED joy greeted the end of the 1980 All-Ireland final as Galway ended a 57-year wait to win the Liam MacCarthy Cup, and for only the second time ever. An attendance of 64,895 saw Galway get off to a perfect start when Bernie Forde kicked home an early goal, quickly followed by a second from PJ Molloy on 10 minutes.

A minute later, Limerick had a goal when ace marksman Eamonn Cregan palmed home, but Galway maintained their dominance on the scoreboard with Noel Lane adding some wonderful points to help his side lead by 2-7 to 1-5 at half-time.

That lead was stretched to seven points by the 44th minute, thanks to the continued brilliance of Forde, before full-forward Joe McKenna tore through the Galway defence to finally beat Mike Conneely and bring his side back into the game.

Conneely had already foiled McKenna and Cregan, and stopped certain goals earlier in the half, but when Cregan slammed home a 61st minute penalty, the gap was incredibly down to just two points.

Galway responded with a free from captain Joe Connolly and an insurance point from substitute John Ryan, as a success starved county celebrated the end of a famine.

★★★★★

"

IT WAS ALWAYS my dream to play for Galway and, once I achieved that, I always wanted to play in Croke Park but I sometimes think back to the time that I nearly packed in hurling in 1974.

At the time our club Sarsfields were junior and when I was growing up we usually got just one game in the year at minor and under-21.

My father and mother were originally from the Newbridge, Ballygar and Ballinamore Bridge area and, as a youngster, I wanted to be Mattie McDonagh from the Galway three in-a-row football team. The football in Sarsfields started up in 1972 and we got to a junior county semi-final and final in the first couple of years, with practically the same panel of players who also played hurling.

We even amalgamated with Loughrea to compete in the Galway Senior Football Championship in 1974 and we gave a great run to Fr Griffins in Athenry on a day that I played full-back. I was also playing rugby with Loughrea at the time and was really enjoying it, so when we were playing the first round of the junior hurling championship that year in Ballinasloe, I remember telling my cousin Seamus Doyle who was doing umpire that as soon as we were out of the championship, I was finished with hurling.

In the second-half of that game, I got a bang to the head but went on to have a great game and as a result, got a call the following Friday week to be in Tuam Stadium for a challenge match between Galway hurlers and Dublin on the same day as the Connacht football final. The regular Galway goalie Sean Kelly from Tynagh was in Cork at the time and it wasn't easy to make the journey home for training and matches, so when Sean didn't make it to Tuam, I got my first start.

I always tell young lads the reason I got to play for Galway was all the dreaming I did which made it a reality. Later that summer I played in the All-Ireland semi-final in Birr against Kilkenny and luckily not a lot of ball came my way.

The thing about getting picked to play for Galway was once you got a taste of it, you wanted more. What really stood to me was the training and the effort that I was putting in, helped greatly by PJ Molloy. I had heard of PJ from the under-21 winning team in 1972 and we used to go in to training an hour early to practice shots.

In fact, if I was working in Galway I would head out to Athenry at lunchtime and PJ would get the keys to Kenny Park and we would tog out. PJ was extremely competitive and had to make a game of it... so with a bag of balls he would take 10 shots at me to see how many goals he could get.

In 1975 we beat Cork and Kilkenny to qualify for the league final against all the odds. I remember the Cork game because I was up to my ankles in muck down in Limerick.

After the Kilkenny game I decided to buy a brand new pair of boots for the final against Tipperary. They were immaculate because I only put them on for the first time in the dressing-room before we ran out for the final.

Unfortunately, in the space of a few weeks the ground had gone as hard as concrete and I felt I was walking on stilts in the goals. That was an experience I will never forget!

The following year I got a belt under the eye in the puck around before the Oireachtas final and lost confidence for a while. Frank Larkin took over, but then I got back and, in 1979 Seamus Shinners came in.

Seamus was a great goalkeeper who had played with Tipperary. When it came to the 1980 championship, there were three of us battling for the goalkeeper's jersey... Seamus, Michael King and myself.

In the All-Ireland semi-final that year, I had a very poor game.

What I didn't tell Cyril Farrell was that I had broken a finger playing football in the lead up to the game, but I just bandaged it up and played on. It was a wet day and towards the end I put up my hand to grab a ball and it went into the net off the underside of the crossbar. Coming home on the bus I was extremely disappointed and, in truth, I didn't think I would be playing in the final. The following Sunday, I played with Sarsfields in the county final when we won the Galway championship for the first time ever. It was a huge relief to the three lads from the club on the Galway panel – Jimmy Cooney, Michael Mulkerrins and myself. It was the last time a Galway county final was played in August and we were given the Monday night off county training to celebrate, but went back at it again two days later.

It was back to doing the extra training with PJ Molloy in the run up to the final in 1980 and where PJ used to score eight out of 10 shots in the past, I had him down to scoring just two.

I was still nervous until the Wednesday before the final, when I realised that it was just going to be another game. I wasn't going to lose my job or get shot if things didn't work out, and I would still be coming back home to New Inn so a weight was lifted from my shoulders.

I felt good going up to the All-Ireland final because I went up to simply enjoy the day. Limerick were favourites going into the final but we had great support – we had huge crowds at training in the run up to a big game.

On the bus going to Croke Park, there were huge throngs of Galway supporters as we passed Barry's Hotel; the lads holding up their pints to greet us. It was only a few years later when I was a supporter watching as the Galway team arrived at Croker that I realised how badly I really wanted to be on that bus.

Whatever about the supporters, the big worry I always had was letting down the rest of the lads I had trained with. When you are the last line of defence, you don't want to be the cause of losing a game.

Before the 1980 final, Niall McInerney was picked to play full-back instead of in the corner. It was an unusual move, but it worked a treat and before the game I would say to him that if there was a ball dropping between himself and Joe McKenna, try and not let him pull on it. That meant I could stand my ground and read the flight of the ball.

We got into Croke Park for the start of the minor final and then left for the dressing-rooms after a few minutes. Cyril did most of the talking before the game and Joe Connolly, our captain, was a wonderful speaker and when he had something to say, you listened.

I very rarely had much to say; I was more preoccupied making sure I was in the corner in any dressing-room I togged out in.

Any time you start a big match, you want to get your hands on the ball early and right from the throw-in I caught a dropping ball under the crossbar from an Ollie O'Connor shot which gave me a huge boost.

Two minutes later we got out first goal when Bernie Forde kicked to the net and then only a few minutes after that, PJ got up from the ground after being hacked down and he buried a second. It was a dream start but it just showed the determination of the man.

If it were nowadays, the game would have been held up for five or 10 minutes. Straight away though Limerick got a goal when a ball came across between Conor and Eamonn Cregan, and I didn't even see it as Cregan flicked it past me, but after that we always seemed to be comfortable and the points kept going over for us.

I had one shot to save from Willie Fitzmaurice midway through that first-half and picked up a bit of a bang to the head in the goalmouth scramble that followed. By half-time we were ahead by five points. During the break we knew if we gave it everything in the second-half we could pull it off.

There wasn't any stage when I felt we wouldn't win, until late in the game when we got a bit jittery and the realisation of what we might be about to achieve hit home. Eamon Grimes came on as a sub for Limerick towards the end and hit a shot for goal that went narrowly wide.

I danced a jig in the goal after that because I knew we had it then.

People have often talked about the great game I had, but in truth I was far from happy with my display because I had let in three goals. I was particularly disappointed not to have saved the goal scored by McKenna but then again, there was one save that I recall from McKenna a few minutes before that which gave us a big lift during that second-half.

I went down low to save his shot.

The ball spun up over the in-rushing Eamonn Cregan.

And I ran by him to collect and clear.

When the final whistle went, you could not believe the relief we all felt. Eamonn Cregan was the first man in to congratulate me, no more than a lot of the Limerick lads.

Many lasting friendships were made that day.

Lord rest Leonard Enright, he was another of the Limerick lads we palled around with on the All Star trip to the USA that followed a few months later. Out on the pitch after the final whistle, it was bedlam, with back slapping and thousands of supporters in on top of us straight away.

As we were making our way across to the stand for the presentation, one lad tried to take one of my hurls but I wouldn't give it. I still have them at home, except for one that I signed and donated to a charity event in Abbeyknockmoy two years after the final.

When the cup was being presented Cyril was shouting at me to... 'GET DOWN... GET DOWN' because I was blocking the view of the RTE cameras, but it was my first time ever being up there so I had no idea about cameras or protocol. PJ came up beside me in the Hogan Stand and I thanked him for all he had done for me.

I told him I owed him three-quarters of my medal!

There was no lap of honour like there is now, so we were back in the dressing-room fairly soon after the presentation. Joe's memorable speech, the supporters calling for Iggy, and Joe McDonagh's unique rendition of *The West's Awake* all captured the emotion of the day.

We then went to the Clarence Hotel and from there to the RTE studios in time for *The Sunday Game* and the announcement of Man of the Match

When it came to a discussion about Man of the Match, I never for a minute thought I was in the reckoning. I was certain that Bernie Forde would get it because he had a great game, scoring 1-5 in an All-Ireland final. I was genuinely stunned when Mick Dunne presented me with the trophy. It wasn't engraved so I had to give it back to get my name on it and it was presented again to me a while later at a function in the Sacre Coeur Hotel in Galway.

Later, we went to the Grand Hotel in Malahide for the post match meal where it was absolutely thronged. If you left the dining-room, the chances were you would not get back in. My wife Marie went out to the bathroom and I saw her being shoved by the crowd against the glass doors as she tried to get back in.

I think it was Jim Carney from RTE that helped her, or she might have come through the glass. It was scary stuff.

It didn't take long for the celebrations to kick off the next day; after meeting the players from Limerick we headed home. We left Dublin between two and three o'clock hoping to be in Galway around six.

The celebrations began in Leixlip with people cheering us on, children waving flags – there was even a fire there. This reception was repeated in every town until we reached Kinnegad, where the gathering was so big we couldn't get off the bus.

We stopped outside the Dunner Arms, where Paddy Dunne brought sandwiches and champagne onto the bus for us. More crowds greeted us in Athlone and when Joe Connolly brought the MacCarthy Cup across the Shannon it was an exceptional moment for everyone. The crowds that turned out in Ballinasloe and Loughrea were unbelievable, as was the case in Craughwell and Oranmore.

We arrived in Galway city at two o'clock in the morning to huge crowds of people, finally sitting down to our meal in the Sacre Coeur Hotel at 4am.

All week long the scenes around Galway were crazy. Homecoming events were organised throughout the county that went on until Christmas. I went to all of them except one; they were great nights with huge crowds coming to celebrate with us.

A very special night was held in Ward's of Ballyfa, where we celebrated Sarsfields' county success as well as the All-Ireland; both cups were there and it was a memorable night. Another good night we had was in Tuam, where we arrived from Turloughmore on a Saturday evening to a marquee arranged by Frank Fahy of Western Pleasure. Frank had been involved with the revival of Galway hurling in 1974 and I always found him to be a great players' man.

We were absolutely mobbed in Tuam, so much so they had to open up the canvass at the back of the marquee to sneak us out. We ended up in the Bridge Bar until 5am. It was a famous night. Until the All Star trip to America in the middle of October, many such nights took place throughout the county.

Six of our lads had picked up All Stars a few weeks after the final, including my own club mate Jimmy Cooney, who had a great year with club and county.

Personally, I wasn't disappointed not to get an All Star as I wasn't expecting to and I was going to America anyway with the All-Ireland champions on the same trip. We went to New York, Chicago and Los Angeles and it was absolutely brilliant, a trip of a lifetime.

The way I look at missing out on an All Star is the same way I look back on getting Man of the Match. I didn't train to win individual awards, I trained to be part of a team that could go out and try and win a game.

We ended up losing the final in 1981 against Offaly in a game we were expected to win. I got a bad back injury in the drawn semi-final against Limerick that year, which is still part of my problem today.

That was to be my last championship game with Galway.

I went to a surgeon from Cork who advised me to pack it in and even though I tried to stay involved with Galway for the next two seasons, I wasn't right and eventually had to walk away. I was a financial rep on the road that time and did a lot of travelling.

Yet, from my first trial game in Tuam in 1974 until the All-Ireland final of '81, I only ever missed two training sessions. I came from Longford, Thurles, Castlebar and even Malin Head to go training because I loved it and always wanted to improve.

Marie and I have three children… Orla, Kenneth and Ailbhe, and there were plenty of evenings where I was gone to training or matches so their support was invaluable during all those years.

I never thought I would get involved in management, but Michael McGrath, Michael Kenny and Packie Cooney came to me about taking over the Sarsfields team in 1992 and after some consideration, I asked Michael Murray and Mike Mulkerrins to come in with me.

We got the job and I made clear to everyone that it was just for one year. We ended up in an All-Ireland final after winning the county championship and then heading down to play Buffers Alley in Wexford in the semi-final. Everyone thought we would be hammered but they were a special bunch of players whose like I haven't seen since.

On a bitterly cold Saturday we went down to Wexford to check out the pitch before that semi-final but were refused entry by one of the men in charge.

I gave him a tenner and he happened to 'disappear' for an hour as the lads togged out in the cold and rain to have a game for 20 minutes. The following day we beat Buffers Alley by 12 points and then went on to beat Kilmallock by seven in the final, even though we were underdogs again.

That summer, the players started fundraising for a holiday abroad and they raised enough to cover all of the flights and still have some pocket money. By the time we were heading off to The Canaries in January 1994, we were back in the following year's All-Ireland semi-final. We came back totally refreshed and you could see it lifted the whole panel and, sure enough, we went on to beat St Rynagh's and Toomevara to win back-to-back All-Ireland titles.

I look back with very fond memories on my time with Galway and the lasting friendships that were made. Indeed, a number of former county hurlers headed up by my good friend Vincent Mullins called around with a cameraman in tow to present me with a Báireoirí na Gaillimhe Hall of Fame award last year.

It was a lovely night; we relived many good memories and the grandchildren were on hand to see it. Orla's young lad Darragh, who was 11, sat in awe as Seamus Shinners started telling stories of Tipperary club championship games in the 1970s where one lad had his jaw broken with a hurl and another had his leg broken in a challenge.

The lads were all laughing and enjoying the stories when Darragh asked, 'Were there no red cards in those days grandad!'

It has now come full circle with my grandchildren continuing to play both hurling and football. Cormac, Darragh and Éanna Delaney play hurling and football for Ahascragh/Fohenagh and Caltra. Oisín, Éabha and Ciara Conneely play hurling and camogie for Sarsfields and the babies of the family, Donncha and Laoise Flaherty will play for Carnmore and Claregalway.

Practice, perseverance, and patience fulfil dreams.

ANTHONY CUNNINGHAM

GALWAY 0-10, DUBLIN 0-7
All-Ireland MHC Final
Croke Park
SEPTEMBER 4, 1983

It all started for Anthony Cunningham when he became the first Galway minor captain to lift the Irish Press Cup

★ **GALWAY:** J Commins; M Killeen, P Dervan, S Treacy; P Brehony, P Malone, G McInerney; D Jennings, JJ Broderick (0-1); T Monaghan, T Moloney (0-2), J Cooney (0-4); S Keane (0-3), **A Cunningham**, P Higgins. Subs: G Elwood for Higgins, M Shiel for Broderick, S Brody for Cooney.

★ **DUBLIN:** T O'Riordan; N O'Carroll, E Clancy, JP Byrne; D Byrne, J Murphy, S Cullen; P Williams (0-4), D Foley; M Hayes, B Collins, P Confrey; N Quinn (0-1), S Dalton (0-2), B Gavin. Subs: P Kearns for Foley, T Spellman for Hayes.

THE ACTION

GALWAY MINOR HURLERS made history at a windswept Croke Park by winning the county's first ever All-Ireland minor championship after a hard fought three-point victory over Dublin.

The gale force conditions ruined the game as a spectacle but that didn't bother Galway as Anthony Cunningham became the first minor captain from the west to lift the Irish Press Cup, having been one of the players to have lost the All-Ireland final in the previous two years. The Tribesmen played with the advantage of the elements in the first-half, but a lead of 0-7 to 0-3 never looked like it was going to be enough, especially when Dublin were only a point behind at 0-8 to 0-7 with 10 minutes to go.

Crucially though, the Galway defence really asserted their dominance at this juncture and the final two scores of the game were Joe Cooney frees for the winners. Tom Moloney and Sean Keane were the main scorers for Galway in that opening half with five points between them, while Dublin star Niall Quinn was being well marked by the excellent Sean Treacy at the other end and never exerted the influence which had been the hallmark of their historic Leinster championship campaign.

The Galway half-back line of Padraig Brehony, Pat Malone and Gerry McInerney were outstanding throughout and when the pressure came on in the second-half, it was the Galway rearguard that came up trumps.

★★★★★

"

GALWAY'S ALL-IRELAND senior win in 1980 was a huge event and not long after that famous success, the Liam MacCarthy Cup and the team came to Our Lady's College in Gort, where I went to school.

Past pupils on the team included Bernie Forde, Noel Lane and Pierce Piggott, as well as Sylvie Linnane, Steve Mahon and all from South Galway who went to school in the area. There was great excitement and pride on a day that was so inspiring; to see the cup return for the first time since 1923 and to get to greet our heroes whose photos adorned the walls of every secondary school at the time.

I was 15 that year and I remember there was also a lot of rivalry and banter in the school in Gort, particularly because three-quarters of the school were Galway and the rest were lads from just over the border in Clare.

Minor teams at that time were very much developed from college teams and I was in the same class as John Commins and Tom Helebert when we teamed up from First Year on. We had a good team that was successful in First and Third Year, and we were building nicely for senior; there was no doubt that hurling was the 'be all and end all' of school life.

We played Portumna quite a bit around that time and they would have provided Martin Kelly and the Brehonys, Tom Moloney, JJ Broderick and Noel Brody to Galway minor teams. Joe Cooney played with St Raphael's, Loughrea and he was a star player since I first saw him in First Year.

Vocational Schools hurling was very strong at the time also and I recall John Burke of St Thomas' winning several medals with both Gort VS and the county vocational school teams. John Fahy, who was Galway minor manager from the early 1980s, had great success as manager of those county vocational teams, winning eight All-Irelands in-a-row from 1980, and I remember viewing top class performances from those games.

The schools scene was healthy but the big downfall of our county teams was the lack of club games. For me, St Thomas's hurling club provided an excellent opportunity for developing my game – from a new pitch purchase to tireless voluntary work in supporting and training underage teams, but I now wonder why at underage level a lot of clubs were getting just one game at under-12, under-14 or under-16.

Knockout championship and no league was the 'order of the day' at that time and this surely would have contributed to Galway's lack of success. It slowed the development of younger players.

There were also plenty of hard luck stories involving Galway minor teams and 1981 was a perfect example of that. We had a brilliant team that included Tony Keady, Eanna Ryan, Pete Finnerty, John Burke, Tom Helebert and Joe Byrne.

I was on that team in the full-forward line but we lost out to Kilkenny in the final. The following year we beat Kilkenny in the All-Ireland semi-final and ended up being well beaten by Tipperary in the final, having missed many scoring chances.

Significantly, I think the big difference in 1983 was the fact that we got an extra game in that championship when the semi-final against Tipperary ended in a draw. John Fahy was the manager for those two years and Padraig Fahy from Carnmore and Galway hurling stardom was our coach.

Padraig was really inspiring in imparting tips and knowledge, and it was the first time that a lot of us got exposure to being trained by a former senior county hurler. There was also national and secondary school teacher involvement throughout the county – like Sean Devlin from Our Lady's College in Gort, and men like him served as brilliant tacticians and hurling craftsmen in guiding young players.

In 1983 it proved somewhat of a masterstroke to get Cyril Farrell involved as coach. He had stepped away as Galway senior manager the year before but to have an All-Ireland senior winning manager from just three years previously training a minor team was a huge boost. Cyril obviously saw a lot of good prospects in that team and he would have trained us five nights out of seven for several weeks in the lead up to the championship.

He brought a great deal of belief to the players and it was an honour for me when management decided to make me captain and trusted me to lead such a talented panel of emerging players. It was probably because I was hanging around the minor set up for so long! One of the first jobs I did was gather up John Commins, Sean Keane and a few of the south Galway lads and drive to Gerry McInerney's house in Douras, Kinvara to convince him to commit and come on board with the panel, because he had missed a few weeks of training through work and we knew he was extra special.

There was a strong backroom team behind John Fahy and Cyril in 1983, including three priests – Fr Tommy Tarpey from Ardrahan, Fr John Naughton from Ballinasloe and Fr McNamara in Killimordaly, as well as Tony McGrath from Oranmore, Jackie O'Shea from Athenry and Michael Fogarty from Woodford.

One night Jackie stood in goals for a few penalties and got knocked out with a sliotar. He smoked a pipe and even though he got such a belt from the ball, the pipe stayed in his mouth! Those backroom lads were tremendously supportive to us and the fact that so many players went on to win under-21 and senior titles after that with Galway shows that the development work, encouragement and backing was spot on.

Joe Cooney was the colossus for us that year.

You could see from an early age how good he was going to be and he was the man that made the forward line tick with his style and vision. The excellent Pat Malone at centre-back and John Commins in goal had excelled in previous years and they had the experience and knowhow throughout that 1983 campaign and proved their worth for many a day since.

The age old problem for Galway teams was going in cold to an All-Ireland semi-final against a team like Tipp or Kilkenny that had three games under their belts in Munster and Leinster. So when we managed to draw with Tipperary – 3-10 apiece in the 1983 semi-final – the extra game ended up being better than a month's training.

We led for most of that drawn game and were six points up with 10 minutes to go, when Tipp came right back at us and could have snatched it at the end. We got a big break when we drew that game and it gave us a chance to iron out a few things for the replay which was a dogged, hard hitting affair in front of a big crowd in Ennis; we were delighted to come through by two points, 1-7 to 0-8.

One thing I definitely remember from that second game was damaging ligaments in my shoulder that put me in real doubt for the final, but we lost our full-back Martin Kelly that day and to lose a player of that ability was a big blow. It was a real pity that Martin missed out on that final but in fairness, Martin Killeen came in at corner-back and had a brilliant game.

Martin Kelly was one of four Killimor lads on the panel alongside Noel Brody, Kevin Muldoon (Mull) and John Joe Broderick while the Tynagh lads,

Tom Moloney and Padraig Brehony had tremendous talent and they had success with both clubs as part of Féile under-14 winning teams. Unfortunately, Tom got a bad back injury a couple of years after that, but he would have made centre-forward on the Galway senior team, while John Joe Broderick, one of life's true hurling gentlemen, suffered a hand injury that forced him into a very premature retirement and he was a huge loss to the game.

Our opponents in the final were Dublin, who we knew were good because we had played them in a challenge match during the summer. It was no surprise that they came through Leinster because there was a lot of talk about them all year.

Niall Quinn, who went on to become a famous Arsenal and Irish soccer player, was their star man and he was the height then that he is now. Dublin hurling was really craving success and after a first Leinster title in nearly two decades, they were the focus of attention for that final.

We travelled up as ever on the Saturday to stay in the Ashling Hotel but unlike 1981, there was no Galway senior team with us that year.

There was the usual stuff with tickets and gear in the run up to the game but the big thing was getting our hurleys right; Paddy O'Dea from Ardrahan was our local man that we went to. The morning of the final was wild, wet and windy.

It was disappointing for sure, but the wind dictated that the game was always going to be low scoring and a game of two halves. Even today, with all the planning that goes into an All-Ireland final, there is nothing you can do when a gale force wind starts to blow. You think about the weather for a few minutes beforehand but then you just get on with it.

Cyril always said to play with the wind, if we won the toss, and it's a philosophy that I would be pushy about to this day. If you get a lead, even if it's only a point or two, you can get in at half-time and make a plan to defend it. It takes a very experienced team to play into the wind in the first-half and control the game.

Our lead at half-time was only four points. There was no major panic though because we knew it was a game we would have to grind out, regardless of the score. Our backs really came to the fore in the second-half.

I mentioned already about Martin Killeen from Beagh coming in for Martin Kelly in the full-back line. His father 'Staff' Killeen was a legend in south Galway and he had spent the first half of that final in the Canal End spurring Martin on, and then came around to the Hill 16 end to be behind him for the second-half.

He had bought two tickets for the game and was making sure his young fella could hear his father's instructions for the full 60 minutes!

Dublin came back to within a point at one stage but we just kept blocking and hooking and literally trying to hit one ball at a time. It was nearly impossible to hit the ball into the wind – Niall Quinn at one stage pulled on a ball and it went over the bar from around 90 yards out. That was the only score he got but he was certainly overshadowed on the day by the brilliant defending of Sean Treacy from Portumna and Pakie Dervan of Kiltormer.

Both men went on to serve their clubs and county for decades after and gave many similar defensive displays to the ones dished out to Quinn that day. I think the way we finished the final and dug out the win was largely down to the way we won our semi-final replay in similar fashion.

I still remember clearly going up to receive the cup from the Archbishop of Cashel, Thomas Morris who was GAA patron at the time. I didn't have any speech prepared and probably went on a bit, but then again I had a lot of people to thank. The Galway Association in Dublin organised a function that night for us and then on the Monday, the four teams that competed in the All-Ireland minor and senior finals came together for lunch in the Burlington Hotel.

Liam Fennelly from Kilkenny came in with the Liam MacCarthy, but it was a great feeling to be able to walk in with the Irish Press Cup this time, having looked on at Tipp and Kilkenny celebrating the previous two years.

The homecoming was really special on Monday night as we stopped in Ballinasloe and Loughrea, before we had a brief halt at the St Thomas' GAA pitch in Castledaly, a memory that was special to me and the many club patrons who had selflessly given their time to help develop our game over the years.

Then it was on to Gort, Clarinbridge and into Galway where we had a reception in the Sacre Coeur Hotel in Salthill. One of the most fulfilling memories about the aftermath of that win was getting around to all the national schools, which took several weeks. It was great to travel with Tom Monaghan, who went on to be a top class coach as well as a hurling giant, in bringing the cup to the Killimordaly schools or with Sean Keane when bringing it out to Beagh.

For me it was really special to go back to Peterswell National School.

Being captain, I went on a lot of the visits to clubs and schools and we were just hoping it would inspire another crop of young lads to go on and win the biggest prize in underage hurling. It was definitely a few days before I got back to college in UCG where I had just started out.

Hurling was the only thing we knew at the time and in a nutshell, it always comes back to your club, your schools and your county. You belong to the GAA and you always have a connection and a bond with your team-mates. That win was a huge springboard for me to go on and achieve further success as a player and subsequently, a manager. When you reach a certain age you always feel like you want to give something back and Sean Treacy and Pat Malone were just two of the lads who went on to contribute so much to the game after they finished playing.

Sean is still involved in the backroom team in Clare and you have to admire the work Pat has done with his club Oranmore Maree in developing the game in his own style. I think more lads came out of that minor team that got involved later on with other clubs and county teams and contributed more than most. Pat Higgins and Pakie Dervan went on to win All-Ireland senior club titles with their clubs, having being central to our run back in 1983.

As players, though, I was reading recently that Galway got more out of that successful minor team than most counties would have out of All-Ireland winning teams. The Tipperary minor team of 2006 produced eight All-Ireland senior winners but that Galway '83 team produced five, as well as several others who won an under-21 three years later.

Cyril Farrell went back in with the seniors for the 1985 season and he brought a lot of young players through from the successful minor and under-21 teams of 1983 and it all fell nicely into place when we won back-to-back senior All-Irelands in 1987 and '88. He was also the manager when a lot of us were involved with the under-21s in 1986 when we beat Wexford to win the All-Ireland.

We have had a few reunions as a team over the years and even met up with the Dublin lads at a charity fundraiser in the early 2000s led by Niall Quinn and Shane Dalton. We all togged out and played a game, and then it was more than fitting that we met up afterwards for a few drinks.

The Dublin full-forward from that team, Shane Dalton has kept in touch with me since then and the paths of a number of players from both teams have crossed over the years at different events. We had a get together for the 25th anniversary of the All-Ireland win in 2008 and only a couple of years ago we were honoured by the Galway Báireóirí in the Loughrea Hotel, along with the successful under-21 team from 1986.

Those nights are priceless because you never know the next time you will come together as a group, or who may not be around the next time we meet. I was marking a lad called Mick Foley in that under-21 All-Ireland final against Wexford in 1986. He was full-back and the father of current Wexford player Kevin Foley, but I only found out a few years ago that he had died in his early forties.

The Wexford goalie from that team, Paul Nolan contacted me to see did I still have Mick's jersey from after that final, as the family would have cherished his 1986 final appearance and jersey. I would not be great at collecting memorabilia and hadn't recalled if I ever had it, but went down to the home house to try and find it, which I eventually did – and I brought it with me to an under-21 game between Galway and Wexford one evening and presented it to his wife.

Those are the simple things we sometimes don't realise or recognise that can really matter so much after someone has had their time limited with us and I was only delighted to be asked to make it happen.

Thankfully, most of the players from those teams are still around and able to reminisce about bygone days with fond memories, and enjoy the eternal game today.

PETE FINNERTY

GALWAY 4-12, CORK 5-5
All-Ireland SHC Semi-Final
Croke Park
AUGUST, 1985

Pete Finnerty (left) made up one of the greatest half-back lines in hurling history when he teamed up with the late Tony Keady and Gerry McInerney

★ **GALWAY:** P Murphy; S Coen, C Hayes, S Linnane; **P Finnerty**, T Keady, T Kilkenny; M Connolly, S Mahon; PJ Molloy (0-5); B Lynskey (1-0), J Cooney (1-1); B Forde (1-3), N Lane (1-2), A Cunningham. Sub: M McGrath (0-1) for Cunningham, J Murphy for McGrath.

★ **CORK:** G Cunningham; D Mulcahy, J Crowley, J Blake; T Cashman, P Horgan, D McCurtain; J Fenton (3-2), P Hartnett; D Walsh (0-1), T Crowley (0-1), T O'Sullivan; T Mulcahy, K Kingston (1-0), K Hennessy (1-1). Subs: J Hartnett (for O'Sullivan), J Hodgins (for Blake), J Barry Murphy (for Kingston).

THE ACTION

IN ONE OF the most extraordinary upsets of all time in the All-Ireland Championship, 'no-hopers' Galway caused a sensation when they defeated reigning champions Cork by four points after an enthralling semi-final played in appalling conditions.

Just over 8,000 spectators turned out in Croke Park for a game that is perhaps best known for being the last ever commentary from the legendary Michael O'Hehir. Twelve months previously Galway hurling was described as being 'dead and buried' in the local media after the Tribesmen suffered a humiliating 14-point defeat at the hands of Offaly in the All-Ireland semi-final, but with Cyril Farrell back in charge, Galway looked a different animal as they took the game to Cork from the off.

An early goal from a penalty by John Fenton put the Rebels 1-2 to 0-3 ahead, but a Bernie Forde goal for Galway straight from the puck out – from a Noel Lane delivery – was a sign of things to come as the underdogs refused to buckle. Even a second Cork goal from Kieran Kingston didn't rattle Galway as they finished the first-half with two points from Michael 'Hopper' McGrath and one from PJ Molloy to lead 1-7 to 2-3 at the break.

A Kevin Hennessy goal for Cork was cancelled out by a similar effort from Joe Cooney early in the second-half, sparking a period of Galway dominance which included goals from Brendan Lynskey and Noel Lane as the Tribesmen score 3-3 without reply to move 10 points clear with 10 minutes to go.

★ ★ ★ ★ ★

66

WHEN YOU LOOK back at our performances since we won the All-Ireland in 1980, we gifted one to Offaly in the second-half of the final in '81, we lost by 10 points to Kilkenny and Cork in '82 and '83, and then in '84 we got absolutely annihilated by Offaly in the centenary year in Thurles.

In 1985 the Galway team was a mix of some of the established names who were still there, men like Noel Lane, PJ Molloy, Bernie Forde and Steve Mahon, and some of the younger crop that had come through from the successful 1983 minor and under-21 teams.

But a lot of the 1980 lads like PJ Qualter, Frank Burke, Joe Connolly and John Connolly had moved on at that stage; they had worked so hard to win the All-Ireland that they were nearly burned out, as they were going at it hard all the way up along since the league final win of 1975.

Then, after winning it, they were given the honour of representing Galway for another few years but there was no real investment in youth and it wasn't until the 1983 underage crop came along that we saw the *future* of Galway hurling.

In 1984 I was one of the under-21 players asked to join the senior set up but nobody really wanted to manage the Galway senior team. PJ Qualter was put in and I think Frank Burke and Josie Harte were involved as well, but the whole thing was very lacklustre.

At training there was no appetite for physicality, and in the games there was no bite. I thought it was very dead in comparison to the effort we had put in the previous year at under-21 when we would play the seniors in the run up to a big game and would be hopping off them.

That was never in it in 1984.

We went down to Thurles to play Offaly in the semi-final that year but I was injured after I burst a blood vessel in my leg, so I couldn't play. I had been training to try and make corner-back but as it turned out it was just as well I was hurt as Joe Dooley had the year of his life and scored 2-3 on the day from corner-forward.

I would probably have been marking him and might never have been heard of had I been running around after him that day!

There was a shake up after that and Cyril Farrell came back in. He brought in

Phelim Murphy and Bernie O'Connor with him and a lot of the 1984 team was let go. It was a bad time in Galway hurling but something had to be done.

One thing about Farrell, he has always believed in youth and was never afraid to wield the axe and try something different. In 1985 we trained with a different intensity and you could see he was trying to gel the likes of Lane and Hayes and Sylvie and Mahon, with the likes of Keady and myself and Joe and Anthony coming on to the panel.

Farrell was a great 'people person' and was brilliant at getting a young lad to train with two older lads; to learn a bit from them. So a lot of great work was done at training that a lot of the Galway hurling public didn't see.

When it came to picking the team for the 1985 semi-final, Phelim often commented that the question was asked at a hurling board meeting... 'Did ye pick that team from a hat?'

It was seen as a bit of a laugh to put myself at wing back and Keady at centre-back instead of centre-forward where he had played as a minor. Tony Kilkenny made his debut that day at 28 years of age, and Sylvie at corner-back was never that far back in his life.

If Galway hurling wanted a change, this was definitely it.

Farrell always sat us down in the middle of the field on the Tuesday before a game to announce the team and it would be in the press the following day.

I sat there and really did not expect to be playing.

There were still a number of established players like Seamus Coen, Conor Hayes and Ollie Kilkenny to fill the full-back line and Sylvie was there for half-back. Even though I was picked at wing back in training and had won an All-Ireland under-21 there, I wasn't given any real encouragement that I was doing well and so when the team was called out, I wasn't sure whether I had heard my name or not.

He did say my name... didn't he? I thought to myself, but it was only after the team was announced that the subs went away and the starting 15 remained for a chat. There was a lot of us looking at each other.

As if to say... *Jesus, he did say your name too!*

As we were coming off the field Sylvie said to me, 'You have the f***ing jersey now... you better hold on to it'.

What a bit of encouragement to get on your first championship start! I don't think he was too happy to be picked at corner-back.

What made it extra special for me as well was that it was the first game I was picked to play alongside Tony Keady and we played together side by side from that day until 1990. We built up a mighty friendship on and off the field, and it is still hard to believe he is no longer with us.

Nobody gave us a prayer of beating Cork in that 1985 semi-final.

In over a century of the GAA we had only beaten them twice, in the semi-finals in 1975 and '79. The fact that Offaly had hammered us in the 1984 semi-final and then Cork had hammered Offaly in the final made it even more implausible that we had any chance. I remember there would always have been a certain amount of people that time who would go down to Athenry to watch us training.

No matter how bad Galway hurling was going you would get people from a farming background from around Athenry and Mullagh and places like that who you would meet after training, and they were telling us to do our best and maybe we would keep them to within 10 or 12 points.

There was no vision of winning or going forward in the championship but a good few of us in the dressing-room had the advantage of being in a winning dressing-room two years previously and we had a different mindset to some of the people in the room. We had beaten Kilkenny at minor and under-21 and didn't fear the likes of them or Tipperary, and we had no baggage from being beaten by Cork.

So, looking back on it, we had that bit of bravery allied to the experience of lads like Noel Lane to let us know what we had to do, so it was probably a good mix.

Farrell always insisted that everyone travelled on Miko Donoghue's bus, no matter where you were coming from. Conor Hayes might have been in Cork at the time and there were a few lads in Dublin, but we all travelled on the bus together.

We always stayed in the Ashling Hotel in Dublin the night before an All-Ireland semi-final or final and we usually had a puck around in the Phoenix Park on the morning of the game. We didn't that morning though because of the rain, so we got the Garda escort down to Croke Park, parked where the hotel is now and walked in with whatever crowd was there.

When we arrived in Croke Park that day and we saw how wet and miserable it was, I said to Tony Kilkenny how I hated playing hurling in the rain.

I never forgot what Tony said to me.

'Anything that upsets favourites is to your advantage.'

Cork were the kind of team that always loved stylish, free flowing hurling. They had some fabulous hurlers like John Fenton, Tom Cashman, that powerhouse at centre-forward Jim Crowley, Ger Cunningham in goals, Buckley, McCurtin, Hennessy… they had household names and were All-Ireland champions, so in virtually everyone's eyes we were wasting our time.

In fairness to the Galway supporters, they made up most of the 8,000 strong crowd. The real diehard Galway supporter was there but I've met so many people since who told me they were at the game I reckon there must have been closer to 80,000 at it! The previous time I played in Croke Park was in the All-Ireland minor final in 1981 and after Kilkenny beat us, we looked around and there were 50,000 people looking back at us.

Three years later we ran out in our first senior All-Ireland semi-final and we expected a buzz and the crowd to lift us, but all we saw was a sparse scattering of Galway people in the Hogan Stand. It was nearly all Galway people in the stand; they were all huddled together because it was so miserable and wet.

Tactics played a big part in our preparation.

Defensively, we were told to go man-for-man with the Cork forwards. I got the job of following Tony O'Sullivan wherever he went.

At the time Tony was known as 'Baby Jesus', because he would score nine or 10 points every game but my job was to stop him. Farrell's message to me was simple… follow him to the sideline, follow him to the toilet… follow him everywhere.

It was intimidation more than anything else, but it worked and eventually Cork took him off. It was an unusual tactic at the time and what was even more unusual was Farrell never did it again. After that, if my man ever drifted over to the other wing, I stood my ground at right half-back.

The other tactic we employed up front was we carried every ball.

Lynskey and Cooney carried everything. In the second-half, Noel Lane carried the ball, passed it to PJ Molloy who gave it back to Lane and… back of the net! Looking back, we might have got away with a lot of steps that day as well! Lynskey was a powerhouse at centre-forward and that was his first big game for Galway.

I always say it, you can give credit to Cooney and Keady and Conor Hayes and a lot of household names that people know, but without Lynskey we wouldn't have won that game definitely and I don't think we would have won a lot of the games we won after that.

He was the target man, he was able to break up defences and centre-backs, and make room for players like Joe Cooney and Anthony Cunningham and lads like that.

Cork probably thought they were going to turn up and win by 10 or 15 points, without breaking sweat and be in another All-Ireland final in four weeks' time. They were thinking about not getting injured for the final but we came with a very different attitude.

We were new, we were hungry and we were hurt.

Galway hurling was down and we felt insulted. We had two options… fight for the jersey or throw in the towel. We decided to fight.

Cork saw this early on and knew they were in a battle and suddenly started wiring into it fairly hard as well. We matched everything they threw at us.

We got a couple of goals after John Fenton scored a penalty and we built up a good lead but typical Cork, they are never beaten, and came right back at us. It looked like the game was turning again and going away from us.

John Fenton got a ball and it broke, and he swung at it and missed it. Had he connected it would have been a goal and they probably would have gone on and won, but we went down the other end and Joe Cooney scored our last goal to give us some breathing room again. From there to the finish it was pure adrenalin and desire and hunger, and want that kept us going.

You could feel that in every player and in the atmosphere among the few Galway people that were there. I remember thinking we can't f***ing disappoint them now.

When the game was entering the final stages I remember the excitement of the Galway people lining up on the sideline, getting ready to come on to the pitch to congratulate us. After the final whistle we were carried off the field shoulder high. People celebrated like we had won an All-Ireland, probably because it was our first chance to shout in Croke Park since we won it in 1980.

It was the first time that I got to experience our own people coming onto the pitch and clapping us on the back after a senior championship game. You would be sore by the time you got to the dressing-room with lads trying to take the boots and hurl off you.

The late Miko Donoghue helped to carry Noel Lane off the pitch, and I often look back and think weren't they two men who served Galway well. For me, that win was the catalyst for all the success that came afterwards. It brought together the old and the new.

It could have been a beautiful sunny day and we could have beaten Cork by two points in a classic, but I don't think it would have been as important for Galway as beating them in a mudbath, in a wrestling game.

Tony Kilkenny sent a ball into Noel Lane that day and when Tony came on as a sub three years later in the final, he sent the exact same ball into Lane for the goal that sealed the All-Ireland against Tipperary. A lot of things started that day that were improved on until we got to win an All-Ireland.

I have a poster somewhere of the RTE Men of the Match from the 1985 semi-final with the names Pete Finnerty, Tony Keady and Tony Kilkenny on it.

Instead of the usual Man of the Match being selected, RTE decided that the Men of the Match were the Galway half-back line. It was most unusual at the time and I'm fairly sure it hasn't happened since!

It was also the last time that Michael O'Hehir commentated on a game; he came into our dressing-room before the match with all his stats on every player. It was an honour to meet such a legend and in many ways it took our minds off the battle that we were about to face but it was most unusual and in many ways unique.

One other aspect of that game I remember is how enjoyable the aftermath was. There were other days in Croke Park where we won semi-finals and finals, but there was more tension and pressure and nerves, and when the match was over it was more relief than anything. In '85 I think it was the fact that we went into it as no-hopers, with very little expected of us and suddenly we found ourselves playing above and beyond what other people thought was possible.

That day a good performance was nearly as much as could be expected from us, so there was a lot less pressure. I look back on it now and think had things gone wrong for us and had we lost and not performed, there was no way that half of us would ever be heard of again.

There would have been a lot of lads thrown on the scrap heap.

I would probably have gone back to corner-back, Keady might have had to go back to centre-forward, a lot more could have walked away but instead that day gave us all hope and lifted everyone in the county going forward.

99

EANNA RYAN

GALWAY 3-20, TIPPERARY 2-17
All-Ireland SHC Semi-Final
Croke Park
SEPTEMBER 4, 1988

Late goals from Eanna Ryan and Noel Lane saw Galway through in the thrilling All-Ireland semi-final win over Tipperary in 1988

★ **GALWAY:** J Commins; S Linnane, C Hayes, O Kilkenny; P Finnerty, T Keady, G McInerney; S McMahon (0-3), T Kilkenny; M McGrath (0-3), J Cooney (0-6), M Naughton (1-0); **E Ryan (1-4)**, B Lynskey (0-1), A Cunningham (0-3). Subs: P Malone for T Kilkenny, N Lane (1-0) for McGrath, PJ Molloy for Naughton.

★ **TIPPERARY:** K Hogan; J Heffernan, C O'Donovan, S Gibson; R Stakelum, J Kennedy, P Delaney (0-3); Colm Bonnar, J Hayes (0-1); M McGrath (0-2), D O'Connell (0-2), A Ryan (0-2); P Fox (2-1), B Ryan, N English (0-6). Subs: M Doyle for McGrath, M Edison for McGrath.

THE ACTION

GALWAY QUALIFIED FOR their third All-Ireland final in-a-row after seeing off newly crowned Munster kingpins Tipperary in a thrilling semi-final at Croke Park.

This was a high-scoring epic, which was ultimately decided by two late Galway goals, but Tipperary played their part and will look back with some regret at how they lost the game. Galway started in whirlwind fashion with a goal by Martin Naughton inside the opening minute and built up a commanding six-point lead until a Pat Fox penalty goal before half-time left Tipp training by 1-13 to 1-9 at the break.

Tipperary dominated the third quarter and a brilliant second goal from Fox saw them take the lead with 15 minutes to go. A Nicky English point stretched the Premier County's advantage, but Galway battled back and points from Steve Mahon and Joe Cooney levelled the game.

Then came the game's defining moment. Referee Gerry Kirwan surprisingly disallowed a Nicky English point, and in the next passage of play Eanna Ryan hand-passed to the net to give Galway a lead they would not relinquish. Minutes later, Ryan passed to Noel Lane for a third Galway goal and Tipp were left to ponder on what might have been.

★★★★★

"

HURLING WAS PART of our DNA in Attymon, Killimordaly when I grew up watching my brothers and sisters playing with the county, so there wasn't much choice but to play.

My Dad was very into hurling as well and any time we needed a hurl he would get one and put his own mark on it by spoke shaving it, doing the tape and the metal bands.

My good friend Tony Keady and I went to Attymon National School together and it was under-14 before I played my first game with our club Killimordaly. There was an under-14 county development squad at the time which a few of us were brought in to, but undoubtedly the biggest highlight from my time playing underage was when Killimordaly famously won the *Connacht Tribune* under-14 'Bikes' Tournament in Pearse Stadium in 1976.

We had already lost the county under-14 final to Mullagh, who had Pete Finnerty on their team, when we qualified to meet them again in the final of the *Tribune* tournament that had a first prize of 30 Raleigh Chopper Bikes.

The match was the curtain raiser to the 1976 senior county final between Killimordaly and Kiltormer, and there was huge excitement because there weren't too many young lads cycling around Killimordaly with new bikes at that time. It was a huge prize for a squad of under-14s to try and win, and thankfully we came out on top and we were all presented with our new bikes on the pitch, with a few lads taking them on a trial spin for good measure!

I still have the bike at home, inscribed with the words 'Connacht Tribune Tournament Winner'. The *Tribune* ran the same tournament the following year for the football clubs, so we entered a football team to try and win a second bike!

We won a few games but it ended up with Kilconly winning the bikes.

At under-16, there was a Mid-West inter-county tournament where we beat Clare in the final in Loughrea and that was my first real game playing on a Galway team, when I lined out at wing forward. I went on to play county minor after that and in 1981 we got to the All-Ireland final against Kilkenny after beating Clare in the semi-final. 'Hopper' McGrath, Anthony Cunningham and I scored a goal each in that final, but we were still beaten by five points by Kilkenny.

I moved up to under21 after that and we ended up winning the All-Ireland title in 1983 when we beat Tipperary in the final, with Michael Coleman and Tony Keady among the lads on that team. In the GAA's centenary year 1984, I got called up to the Galway senior panel, and was a sub for the All-Ireland semi-final against Offaly in Thurles.

We were 12 or 14 points down with about 10 minutes to go, when one of the selectors turned to the bench and asked one of the subs beside me to go on. When he refused, he turned to me and said, 'Ryan, you're going on!'

That was how I got to play my first game for Galway!

Worse still, as I was running on to the pitch, I met my idol Joe Connolly coming off. I hadn't a clue who I was coming on for, but when I saw it was Joe I thought to myself... *This doesn't feel right.* That was Joe's last game for Galway.

In 1985, I was dropped off the county panel, but the club was going well in the championship those years, so it wasn't long before I was in the shop window to get back. Killimordaly were in the county final in 1984, but lost out to Castlegar. We got to the final again in 1985 and lost to Turloughmore, but made the breakthrough in '86 when we beat Turloughmore by 0-17 to 2-7.

I was back in the county panel before then, even though I didn't play in either the All-Ireland semi-final win over Kilkenny or the final defeat to Cork, but after I got Man of the Match in the county final in 1986, I got my place on the team for the start of the National League in October and held on to it from there.

One league game in particular stood out, against Clare in Ennis in December, when I scored 3-1. We won the league the following May when we beat Clare again in the final, and that was a big boost because we hadn't won it since the famous 1975 team.

What was really driving Galway hurling at that time was the county championship, because you had a different winner every year throughout the 1980s and that meant there were two or three players from a lot of clubs that were being picked. There was a much bigger choice available to Cyril Farrell and his selectors Bernie O'Connor and Phelim Murphy. Killimordaly was well represented with the county as well, with Michael Haverty, Michael Earls, Tom Monaghan, Tony Keady and myself, while Eamon Burke went in for a couple of years at the end of the decade.

We went straight into an All-Ireland semi-final against Tipperary in 1987, and even though I was struggling with a groin injury ahead of what was my first championship start, I was deemed fit enough to play. Thankfully, it was the right decision as I ended up getting 1-4 from play and was named Man of the Match.

Tipp were just after winning Munster for the first time in 17 years and the hype around them ultimately was their downfall. The press went mad talking about the new era of Tipperary hurling and we had it in our minds that even though we had been in the last two All-Ireland finals, we weren't getting the same attention or respect at all.

The key to Galway's success in the mid-to-late 80s was the great bond that existed between the players. We had great craic together, but we were also well looked after by the management with hurls, gear and a few trips.

We even got to keep our jerseys at the end of the season! You always knew when the championship was coming up because the meals after training in Athenry Mart changed from bacon and cabbage… to steak, onions, mushrooms and chips!

We called Phelim our dietician.

Then, when it came to an All-Ireland final, a Club Milk bar was added to the menu. That was the diet of champions.

We always stayed in the Ashling Hotel before any of the big games in Dublin, but there were seven or eight of us who used to sneak off to a quiet pub the night before an All-Ireland semi-final or final and have two slow pints, play a game of pool or darts, and just relax and have a bit of fun.

I'm not too sure that Cyril Farrell knew anything about it, but if he did, he didn't say anything!

I was nervous but not too nervous before that Tipp game in 1987. The match started at 100 miles an hour and Nicky English scored a point after nine seconds, but a minute later our first score was a goal from Martin Naughton.

We went six points up, but then they got a penalty before half-time and got back to within four. We went further ahead and were dominating, but never really put them away and then they got a second goal and we were back level again. The big turning point of the game was when the ref disallowed an English point that would have put them ahead.

I think he thought that there was a late foul on John Commins, but I've watched it over and can't see where the foul was. Conor Hayes took the free, Brendan Lynskey won it, gave it to me and I ran in and hand-passed the ball into the net.

That was the bit of luck we needed and when Noel scored our third goal a few minutes later, we had it in the bag. Despite the nature of our win, we were still concerned about what had happened in the previous two All-Ireland finals and there was a bit of fear about how we let Tipp back into the game because if that happened against Kilkenny, we were dead.

The day of the final was atrocious, with lashing wind and rain, and I knew all day long it was going to be a day for the backs. The weather is a big factor when you are small and light, and you need a fast ball. That's exactly what we got in the semi-final, but the day of the final was the complete opposite.

Yet again, we got the bit of luck we needed in a big game when Liam Fennelly was going for a goal and hand-passed the ball against the chest of John Commins, and it was cleared. I got the ball, soloed up the field and it was finished into the net by Noel Lane.

That was a six-point swing and by the end we had won by six points!

I went to the U.S. for six weeks in January and February of 1988. I was working and playing hurling and there was no problem with being worried about breaking the rules because everyone was doing it.

I met more hurlers out there than you would see at a match in Athenry. What happened to Tony Keady just over a year later was wrong and absolutely terrible.

He was singled out by the GAA for doing the same thing that hundreds of lads were doing every year, and we were let down by the Connacht officials in so-called 'football counties' when it came to the vote to get his suspension overturned.

Tony was only 25 at the time and with the media spotlight of the whole country on him, that was serious pressure to be putting on a young amateur player.

Was it the cause of us losing the All-Ireland semi-final against Tipp in 1989? Well it didn't help, nor did the injury to Martin Naughton that kept him out of that game.

Then Sylvie and Hopper got sent off, while a few Tipp lads got away with far worse. It was pretty obvious that we were 'set up' that day. There was a lot of hassle about Tony's suspension and maybe Croke Park didn't like it.

We came back in 1990 and got back to the final after beating Offaly, but came unstuck against Cork. I've no doubt we were a better team than Cork, but we weren't a better team on the day of the final and have to accept that.

We scored 2-21, which would have won most All-Ireland finals, but Cork scored five goals and maybe they had the same attitude as we had in 1987 against Tipp, and that was to take us down a peg or two. We were absolutely gutted after that final and I wasn't to know that it was my last ever game for the county.

A few weeks later, Killimordaly were playing Turloughmore in the quarter-finals of the championship in Athenry, before Galway and Antrim were due to play in the National League. I got a blow to the head going up for a ball and ended up on the ground.

Doc McGloin came onto the pitch and said I needed to be carried off, but I said I would walk off. As I got up, my two legs went from under me and I fell back down.

I tried to get up a second time, but the same thing happened so I looked up at the Doc and asked, 'Is it bad?'

He nodded and said I needed to get to the hospital.

Luckily for me, there was an Order of Malta ambulance there for the Galway-Antrim game so I was rushed to hospital in Galway in 13 minutes. I went straight into A&E and then into Intensive Care. It was only later when the ambulance crew came in to see me that they told me there was no first gear or reverse in the ambulance, so when they got to the Regional Hospital in Galway, the staff had to come out and push the ambulance back to the Emergency entrance!

The stitches I got were fine but the big problem was the damage to the eardrum which affected my balance for the next few months. I had to learn to walk again, was four months off work and it took about a year and a half before my balance was back to being one hundred percent.

After the first two months I could cycle a bike so that gave me a chance to get out of the house for a while to clear the head. I got a huge amount of letters of support, and there were always phone calls and people calling to the house.

It got so manic that a good friend of mine, Paul Owens took me out to his holiday home in Roundstone so that I could get away from it all for a few days. While in hospital there was even a rumour that went round that I had died!

Apparently, I was rushed to Cork in the ambulance, then taken by helicopter to Beaumont in Dublin and had died. The proof of that is my late mother Maureen got two Mass Cards for the repose of the soul of Eanna Ryan!

Mam was very religious and she wasn't going to show them to me, but I told her we had to hold on to them… that they might come in handy some time!

The fact that my county career ended so abruptly was probably easier than having to make up my own mind a few years later. At 27 years of age I probably had four or five years left in me, but when I put things in perspective, hurling was the furthest thing from my mind.

I just wanted to get better.

I got married to Mary in 1992 and we have five children, Daniel, Shane, Eoin, Joshua and Evie, who has just started in Calasanctius College in Oranmore, where the four lads all went to school. They all play different sports and I encourage them to play whatever they want to because there are so many distractions for our youth, it's vital that they have something else to focus on.

They play hurling, camogie, football, soccer, golf and rugby, and it is great that they can meet with their friends, play their sport and socialise afterwards. Our home is in Clarinbridge and the reason Mary and I built a house there goes back to my work with Heineken when we sponsored the Clarinbridge Oyster Festival every year.

I got to know a lot of wonderful people in the village and it truly is a beautiful place to bring up a family. We had been living in Knocknacarra, but an opportunity arose in the mid 90s to buy a site in Clarinbridge and we have been very happy there since.

After my hurling accident, every time I went to an All-Ireland semi-final or final someone would come up to me and ask me about my head or my ear or what happened to me?

I came to the conclusion that if I went back for the club and stood out on the pitch again, then everyone would say, 'He's fine,' and there would be no more about it.

That is exactly what happened.

Plus, there was always that little thing in my head where I wondered if I could ever do it again on the field. So, in 2000, I went back training with Killimordaly with the added benefit of seeing my Mum on a more regular basis, as she was not well at that time.

Ahead of the start of the senior championship, we knew that if we won one of our group games, the chances were that would be enough to stay at senior level. That was the extent of our ambition at that stage, but we ended up beating Clarinbridge by a point in our last game in the group which qualified us for the quarter-finals.

That was a sweet one for me, because I was living in Clarinbridge and it meant I could walk into Paddy Burke's or Sherry's and not bear the brunt of any slagging! After that we beat Abbey by a point in the quarter-final and then drew with Sarsfields in the semi-final, but lost the replay and that was that for me.

I stayed away from hurling for a good few years after that, but when you have kids you invariably get involved so I was delighted to be over an exceptional group of players that won two minor championships in-a-row for Clarinbridge in 2015 and '16, and in more recent times I'm helping out at under-14 and under-16 level.

When I think back on the career I had, I packed some amount of serious hurling into the years 1983 to '90, from an All-Ireland under-21 final in '83, to county finals in 1984, '85 and '86, All-Ireland finals in 1987, '88 and '90, and an All Star in 1989.

I was nominated for an All Star five times in total and ended up getting one at No 10, where I seldom played. Much more importantly, I gained life-long friends and for a good portion of those years it was dream stuff, at a time when the economy was in dire straits and those victories were a big lift to the people in Killimordaly and Galway.

If I had the chance... I would do it all over again.

GERRY McINERNEY

GALWAY 1-12, KILKENNY 0-9
1987 All-Ireland SHC Final
Croke Park
SEPTEMBER 4, 1988

The flamboyant attacking style of Gerry McInerney breaking out of defence broke the hearts of opponents through the 1980s

★ **GALWAY:** J Commins; S Linnane, C Hayes, O Kilkenny; P Finnerty, T Keady (0-2), **G McInerney**; S Mahon (0-2), P Malone; M McGrath (0-1), J Cooney (0-5), M Naughton (0-1); E Ryan, B Lynskey, A Cunningham (0-1). Subs: N Lane (1-0) for Naughton, PJ Molloy for Cunningham, T Kilkenny for McGrath.

★ **KILKENNY:** K Fennelly; J Hennessy, P Prendergast, J Henderson; L Walsh, G Henderson, S Fennelly; G Fennelly (0-7), R Power; K Brennan, C Heffernan, L Ryan; P Walsh, L Fennelly, H Ryan (0-1). Subs: T Lennon (0-1) for Walsh, L McCarthy for Power.

THE ACTION

GALWAY CALLED ON all their reserves of resilience to claim the county's third All-Ireland title after a bruising encounter with Kilkenny which was in the melting pot right up until substitute Noel Lane scored the game's only goal seven minutes from time.

The greasy conditions meant that both defences were largely on top, and after a tight opening half it was Galway who held a narrow advantage, 0-5 to 0-4. All of Kilkenny's scores came from Ger Fennelly frees, while Galway's points came from two Joe Cooney frees, a '65' from Tony Keady and fine efforts from play by Martin Naughton and Michael McGrath. After the restart, Anthony Cunningham extended Galway's lead with a fine point, but Kilkenny dug in and slowly started to wrestle control of the game. By the 43rd minute, the Leinster champions had taken the lead, 0-8 to 0-7, but Galway answered back and landed the next three points to go back in front.

Galway wing back Gerry McInerney was exerting a huge influence on the game with his attacking style, while goalkeeper John Commins made a couple of astonishing saves from Liam Fennelly to keep his side in front. Lane's goal came at the most opportune time for Galway and extended their lead to 1-10 to 0-8.

There was no way back for Kilkenny, whose starting six forwards only managed one point against a brilliant Galway backline, and it was only fitting that full-back Conor Hayes was the one to follow in the footsteps of Joe Connolly seven years previously by leading his team up the steps of the Hogan Stand.

★ ★ ★ ★ ★

"

OUR HOME PLACE is in Dooras, about four miles from Kinvara on the shores of the Atlantic and I grew up with three brothers and four sisters in the house. Two of the lads, James and Paddy, were good hurlers and any chance we got after school or work, we always used to play out the back.

We had no interest in the television, it was all about being outside, whether farming seaweed and oysters or fishing. I remember at the time that sea urchins were being sold at five pounds a shoebox and there was a big market for them in France, so any chance we got, we would go out in the freezing water and spend hours collecting as many as we could.

The seaweed was quite lucrative as well and we used to bring it ashore and make small cocks of it, like you would with hay, and then fork it into the lorry that would drive along the shoreline. We were brought up knowing nothing else but manual labour, so we were naturally very fit.

We had a good under-14 team in Kinvara at the time and got to a county semi-final, and a lot of those lads were in Gort Vocational school with me. Gort had won the All-Ireland Vocational Schools title in 1978 before I went there, but a couple of years later I ended up making the county vocational schools team and winning three All-Irelands in-a-row, including one in Croke Park.

I was captain the final year when we beat Kilkenny in a replay in Cloughjordan. Niall McInerney, Barney Winston, John Fahy and Pat O'Toole were involved in looking after us – and the likes of Michael Bond and Cyril Farrell came to see all those matches and they were clearly looking for talent. The county minor management came looking for me in 1982 but I was so busy at home with the farming that I only went in a couple of weeks before the All-Ireland semi-final against Kilkenny.

I ended up making the team at wing back and got Man of the Match after we beat Kilkenny by a point. John Fahy, Bernard Callanan, Sean Kelly and Frank Burke from Killimordaly were involved that year, while Padraig Fahy was training us, but unfortunately we didn't play well in the final and Tipp beat us easily.

The following year Cyril Farrell took over training the minor team, with John Fahy, Fr Tarpey in Ardrahan and Tony McGrath from Oranmore Maree, and they had a good idea about the lads they wanted to bring in. I didn't miss too many training sessions that year and, as it turned out, I ended up being involved on teams managed by Cyril Farrell for nearly the rest of my career.

Trying to win a first ever All-Ireland makes the task that bit harder and in the minor final in 1983 we played a Dublin side that a lot of work and money had gone into, but we had a big, strong team and didn't mind the terrible conditions the final was played in and came out on top by three points.

The year after winning the minor All-Ireland, I went over to the United States for a few months and ended up staying with an aunt of mine in Boston. The hurling season was over at that stage, but a few of the lads involved in the GAA scene over there fixed me up with a job. There were a lot of Carnmore and Turloughmore lads over there at the time and they were awful sound to me.

I came back just before Christmas 1984 and at the time the dollar was worth the same as an Irish punt on the exchange rate, so the money I brought home was worth a fair bit. Cyril Farrell, Phelim Murphy and Bernie O'Connor had taken over the Galway senior team at that stage, so Cyril and Phelim came down to the house to chat about going into the Galway panel in early 1985.

I started working in Thermo King not long after that, but only lasted a few months as I was more interested in outdoor work. To be honest, I wasn't really that bothered about committing to the senior team that year and one evening Cyril had picked Pete Finnerty and Tony Keady and myself to play together in the half-back line against Offaly in a challenge, but I didn't turn up.

It must have annoyed Cyril because I didn't get a chance again for a while, but it didn't really bother me. I was 20 years of age and more interested in living life and chilling out!

I was still involved in the panel though when it came to the All-Ireland semi-final against Cork later in the summer and I was all ready to come on for my first senior championship appearance late in the game after Tony Kilkenny picked up a nasty head injury, but he got stitched up and I never got to come on.

After we lost the All-Ireland final to Offaly, a few of us were brought out to New York to play in the latter stages of their championship for Galway, and we ended up winning it out with the likes of Sylvie, Joe Cooney, Sean Treacy and myself on board.

In 1986 I took it a bit more seriously and put the head down a bit more to try and make the team. That was the year we beat Kilkenny in the semi-final with three in midfield and a two-man full-forward line, but lost the final to Cork when the same tactic didn't work for us.

We had the consolation of winning the under-21 final a week later against Wexford and then I hit off back to New York again. A few lads I knew from Galway got together to get a house in Yonkers and any lad that came over from Ireland often bunked in with us.

Around that time, Pete Finnerty came out to join us as well – the simple fact was there was very little work to be got in Ireland. In fairness to the Galway County Board, after we won the minor in 1983 they tried to fix up lads with jobs in places like Digital, but when you are used to the outdoor life growing up in Kinvara, a factory job just wasn't for me.

In New York there was no shortage of opportunities, but we had to work hard for it. It was always an early start but if you were a hard worker, you reaped the rewards. There was any amount of Irish bars over there as well, but we would always go to certain places to change our cheques every week and wait around for our money.

I had been going out with Ita for a year at this stage, so she came out to New York in 1986 as well and she stayed with her two brothers and a sister in Long Island and started up a hairdressing business. Myself and Pete stayed in New York until the summer of 1987, so we missed the National League that year and listened to the final on the radio in New York when Galway beat Clare by two points.

The Galway board paid for our flights back ahead of the All-Ireland semi-final against Tipperary and we were delighted to get over that one because it gave us a few extra weeks to get into the swing of training for the All-Ireland final against Kilkenny.

The famous white boots that I wore appeared in Croke Park for the first time in that semi-final win over Tipperary and I couldn't get over the reaction after we won that game. I got the boots in New York for a championship game in Gaelic Park earlier in the year because my old ones were busted – I saw this pair in the window of a sports shop that looked 'broken in' and ready to wear.

I wore the same boots to training in Galway for a couple of weeks before the

Tipp game and nobody passed any remarks, but after they were seen on the TV the whole thing blew up out of all proportion. I hadn't much time to be listening to the hype about the white boots, however, I just wanted to make sure I made my place for the final.

We never thought about any Kilkenny player's reputation before that game and in truth, we knew very little about any of them. Pete, Tony and myself were just establishing ourselves as a half-back line, so we were only concerned with operating together as a unit and calling 'my ball' when it came into our area... or telling each other who should go for it.

It helped that we got on great as friends because a big part of our success was our communication on the field with one another. The other big thing that helped us develop as a half-back line was the quality of forwards that we had to mark in training.

The simple fact was that we weren't going to come up against any better forwards in the country. We would end up marking a different lad every night, whether it was Joe Cooney or Hopper or whoever, and even though I would travel to training and matches with Noel Lane, he still wouldn't be afraid to hit me a belt before the ball would even come our way!

He knew he was preparing us for the kind of thing that Kilkenny would do and how right he was. There was no holding back in training and when I hear people talk about the famous Kilkenny training sessions in the last few years, I guarantee you Brian Cody took a leaf out of our book.

The A versus B games were very frustrating at times, because every lad knew which way you would turn to clear the ball and hook you every time. It was very enjoyable at the same time because coming up to a big game, we would have over a thousand people on a Sunday morning watching a training match in Athenry – that game would go a lot longer than 70 minutes!

There was real pressure on us in that 1987 final not to lose three in-a-row and we felt it. We said we would leave no stone unturned to win that game and with all the hard training that we had done, it didn't matter how physical Kilkenny got, we were well able for it. The game itself was played in wet and windy conditions, but I really enjoyed rolling up my sleeves and getting stuck in.

Our backs were well on top right throughout that game and they only scored four points in the first-half and none of them were from play. I got on a lot of ball in the second-half and it wasn't that I was under instruction to run with it, it was a style of hurling that suited both me and the conditions.

The game was really tight for long spells and in fairness to the Kilkenny backs, our lads up front were finding it awful hard to get a yard of space or even win a free. We had just got our noses back in front inside the last 10 minutes when Noel Lane came on and hit a shot that Kevin Fennelly half stopped, but the ball spun past him and over the line for a goal. In a tight match, that score was the difference and I could see the Kilkenny heads drop around me.

We ended up winning by six points and at 22 years of age I had my first All-Ireland senior medal to go with the minor and under-21 from the previous four years. Beating Kilkenny in the final in 1987 seemed to mean an awful lot more to the older generation in Galway than the players, or certainly the younger players, who had beaten Kilkenny at minor level and didn't see them as being different to any other team.

When we got back to the hotel after the game I got word about a Man of the Match presentation that night, so Conor Hayes and a few of the lads came with me when I picked up the trophy. There is probably a lot more made of it now than there was back then, but there was still a fair bit of interest in it as it was still a rare thing for a Galway man to get Man of the Match in an All-Ireland senior final.

Two weeks of celebrations followed the win for me, but then I headed off back to New York and it was a different world. There was hardly a mention of the win and it was a reality check as I went straight back to work.

I had no long term plan in mind at that stage, apart from continuing to work and enjoy life, but making New York a permanent home for myself and Ita was definitely an option. I came home for the All Stars banquet a few weeks later because I was nominated, but as it turned out I didn't get one on the night. After I returned to the U.S. I linked up with the Galway team later in the year when we played the All Stars team in Gaelic Park.

Ita and I were making good money in America, saving a bit and spending a bit too, and we decided to get married the following summer in July of 1988. Ita picked the date and I said no problem. I didn't even think about the hurling championship, but as it turned out the wedding was held less than two weeks before the All-Ireland semi-final against Offaly!

The reception was in Hayden's Hotel in Ballinasloe, and Farrell made sure there was training afterwards! Galway had already played London in an All-Ireland quarter-final but myself and Pete came home after that game and joined up with the panel just before the wedding. We ended up beating Offaly by seven points in that semi-final and were really relishing the final that year against Tipperary.

We were well battle hardened at that stage after losing two finals in-a-row, and then coming through a real dogfight against Kilkenny in 1987 released a lot of the pressure. Farrell was quite worried about the pace of the Tipp full-forward line before that final and he spoke to me on a number of occasions about stopping Nicky English getting the ball; and he got me thinking more about dropping back than bombing forward like I did in 1987.

I ended up in a bit of limbo because of that and Declan Ryan score 0-4 that day from wing forward, even though I managed to score a couple of points myself in response. Michael Coleman was flying for us that day at midfield; he proved a big addition to our team in 1988 after we lost a really important cog like Stevie Mahon to a knee injury. Winning in 1988 was sweet and it was only that evening that I heard about Tony going missing for the Man of the Match presentation that night. When he eventually came back to the hotel we had a great laugh about it!

The following May, the Galway lads came over again on the All Stars trip and while myself and Pete were working legitimately all the time in New York, Tony wanted to stay on to play with us. It was nearly all Galway lads playing for the Laois club against Tipp and Tony just couldn't resist having the All-Ireland winning half-back line back together again.

He wanted to stay for the craic as well, but the fact that we won that game in New York by a cricket score didn't go down well and it ended up causing all the hassle that led to his suspension. When Pete and myself came back from America for the All-Ireland semi-final against Tipp, we still thought that Tony would get off, but the damage was done at that stage because of the hype and distraction that it caused.

There was talk of us not turning up to play and we were all over the shop in the lead-in to that game. Things just weren't right and it ended up being the start of the break-up of that great team.

We got back to the final in 1990 against Cork and it was another one that got away. We just didn't put them away on the day, even though we were the better team for long stretches, but I honestly don't think we trained as hard as we could have and after hammering Cork in a challenge a couple of months earlier, maybe we took them a bit for granted. 1989 and '90 could have been brilliant, but things went a bit pear-shaped for us on a number of fronts and the golden era came to an end.

Our first child Colleen was born in New York in 1989 and after she was born, Ita and I came back to Galway and I got a job working with Tennants Lager as a sales rep. We were building a house in Oranmore and around the same time I opened a pub in Ballinasloe, so we had a lot going on in our lives.

We had another great chance of winning an All-Ireland in 1993, but threw it away late on against Kilkenny and it was after we lost to Clare in '95 that my time with Galway was coming to an end. At that stage we had two young boys in the family as well, Gearóid and Sean, so my attention switched to our club Oranmore Maree and it was great to see the club go from strength to strength in the past number of years, from underage right up to when we won the All-Ireland Intermediate Championship in 2019.

We were all very proud when Gearóid got on to the Galway senior panel in 2014 and even more excited when he became a big part of the starting team three years later. The whole county was on a high after beating Tipperary in the 2017 semi-final and when Tony Keady rang me the day after the game on the Monday, he was still hyper with the excitement.

I couldn't believe it when I heard the next day that he had taken ill that night and was gone from us. It was unbelievable.

Gearoid and Niall Burke would have been very close to Tony from their time in Calasanctius College; they were still young lads and must have found it very difficult to understand. Gearóid is a quiet lad anyway and tends to keep his emotions to himself, but I'm sure both he and Niall used Tony's passing as a big motivation going into that final against Waterford. Gearóid asked me about what is was like playing in an All-Ireland final and I told him that a small bit of nerves was a good thing, but that *this* was the place you wanted to be.

He was fit, well prepared and had nothing to fear.

'Just go out and hurl like you can,' I told him.

And he did. It was lovely to hear people talk about Gearóid playing so well at centre-back, just like Tony did when Galway had last won the All-Ireland in 1988. I get a great kick out of people still asking me about that half-back line I was a part of. It's great to be held in high regard wherever you go, because people will always remember us as Finnerty, Keady and McInerney.

Not long into my career with Tennants, I had to go up to Belfast with the former Meath footballer Robbie O'Malley on a training course. The first night we were there, I went for a quiet pint in a pub called 'The Fly', when a man came over and asked me in a heavy Armagh accent… 'Are you the man with the white boots?'

It is lovely to be recognised and appreciated.

I suppose we could have won more, but we had an awful lot of fun along the way and got away with a lot more than we probably should have. The county lads now are serious role models for the younger generation coming up behind them. They are watching to see what gear they wear and what food they eat, whereas when I was growing up we would regularly be told it was alright to have a couple of pints the night before a match!

I'm glad to have seen that aspect go out of the GAA and for me, the modern game is the best thing to ever have happened.

JOHN COMMINS

GALWAY 1-15, TIPPERARY 0-14
All-Ireland SHC Final
Croke Park
SEPTEMBER 4, 1988

A couple of astonishing saves from John Commins kept Galway in front at vital stages against Kilkenny in 1987

★ **GALWAY: J Commins**, S Linnane, C Hayes (0-1), O Kilkenny; P Finnerty, T Keady (0-2), G McInerney (0-2); M Coleman, P Malone (0-3); A Cunningham, J Cooney (0-1), M Naughton (0-2); M McGrath (0-2), B Lynskey (0-1), E Ryan (0-1). Subs: N Lane (1-0) for Cunningham, T Kilkenny for Naughton, G Burke for Lynskey.

★ **TIPPERARY:** K Hogan; P Delaney (0-1), C O'Donovan, J Heffernan; B Ryan, N Sheedy, J Kennedy; Colm Bonnar, J Hayes; D Ryan (0-4), D O'Connell (0-2), J Leahy; P Fox, N English (0-6), A Ryan (0-1). Sub: Cormac Bonnar for Hayes.

THE ACTION

GALWAY RETAINED THEIR All-Ireland title with a deserved four-point win over league champions Tipperary, but it was only in the first minute of stoppage time that they finally shook off the clutches of the Munster men, when 'Super Sub' Noel Lane got inside Conor O'Donovan to strike the match winning goal.

The intense rivalry between the two teams was obvious from the start, but Galway were on top early on and, backed by the wind, established a 0-9 to 0-3 lead coming up to the half hour mark. Nicky English and Declan Ryan kept Tipp in touch though and by half-time the deficit was back to a manageable four points, 0-10 to 0-6.

Slowly Tipp clawed their way back into the game during the second-half and a free from corner-back Paul Delaney had his side within a point at 0-11 to 0-10 after 10 minutes of the second period. Almost immediately Galway responded with a score by Michael McGrath, and that pattern continued for the remainder of an absorbing contest as every time Tipp got within a point, Galway went up the other end to score.

The issue was eventually settled when Lane latched on to a Tony Kilkenny through ball to hit a ground shot past Ken Hogan, sparking a pitch invasion from delirious Galway supporters who knew their side had retained the All-Ireland title for the first time.

★★★★★

66

MY CAREER AS a goalkeeper started in 1983 when I went into county minor trials. Up to that point I had played outfield for Gort and was centre-back for the club minor team that year, but in the county trial game that year I ended up marking Joe Cooney.

Cyril Farrell was minor manager in 1983 and he came to me after the session and asked me to try out for goalkeeper, because he already had the likes of Gerry McInerney, Pat Malone, Tom Monaghan and Padraig Brehony as backs who were a good bit better than me. My attitude was to give it a crack while I was in there, so Cyril played me in goal for a few challenge games and that's how I ended up being there for the year.

That same year the Gort senior goalie Tony Monaghan went to London for work, so I ended up training with the club senior team as well. I found the transition to being a goalie quite easy – only recently I was listening to a podcast where the discussion centred on modern day goalkeepers having to be accomplished outfield players as well. That was exactly how I saw it.

You have to be confident in your own ability and have really good hand-eye co-ordination, which I had from playing outfield. I adapted pretty quickly and while the level of goalkeeping coaching wasn't nearly as sophisticated as it is nowadays, I still learned a lot from the lads that worked with me that year.

Our first game with the Galway minors that year was the All-Ireland semi-final against Tipperary in Croke Park. We were cruising early on in that game until Tipp came right back at us in the second-half. We were still three points ahead when I made a serious error late on by coming out over the top of Sean Treacy to try and grab the ball, but misjudged it and the ball ended up in the net.

The game ended in a draw. I was thinking to myself that I didn't fancy going in goal again after nearly costing the lads an All-Ireland semi-final.

A couple of weeks later in the replay in Ennis, I had a steady enough game and we won by 1-7 to 0-8, so we could look forward to an All-Ireland final against Dublin. I will never forget the minor final either.

It was a terribly wet and windy day and I didn't actually touch the ball in open play for the entire match. The only time I touched the ball was for puck-outs, so I was as nervous in the last minute as I was in the first minute because I still hadn't got my hand on the ball.

Dublin were made out to be unbeatable after winning Leinster with Shane Dalton and Niall Quinn up front, but Farrell was working in Dublin at the time as a teacher so he knew most of them really well and had the match-ups done perfectly. Dublin never looked like getting a goal that day, but in the last play of the game a high ball dropped in our square and I thought to myself... *I'm not going up for that one!*

Out of nowhere Joe Cooney popped up to grab the ball above everyone else and the final whistle went. That was the first ever minor All-Ireland for Galway and it was great to be part of it, but the best bit was going up to the Cusack Stand with the Irish Press Cup to our parents, many of whom are no longer with us.

A lot of the mothers, in particular, were crying and it was such a good feeling. I don't think we even watched the senior match between Cork and Kilkenny!

Not long after winning the minor All-Ireland, I played in the county final with Gort against Castlegar. They were a right good team at the time, with six or seven Connollys involved and an All-Ireland club title in the bag only a couple of years before.

Gort had won the county title in 1981 so we had a good team as well and it proved a right battle, and another learning curve for me. At one stage I caught a ball at the edge of the small square and instead of running towards the sideline I put the head down and drove my way out the middle.

But as I threw the ball up to clear it, Joe Connolly flicked it into the empty net.

Despite that, we held out and won by three points but I said to myself afterwards... *That won't ever happen again.* The All-Ireland club championship was most unusual that season because it was played over a weekend in the middle of April 1984.

We played Midleton in the semi-final on the Saturday in Limerick and Shamrocks the following day in Birr. Midleton had a good few lads on the Cork panel and were a serious team who had beaten Sixmilebridge, and on the way to the match – with Kevin Fahy and Pearse Piggott – Kevin's car broke down outside Ivan's Corner Shop in Limerick, on the way in to the Gaelic Grounds.

As we were pushing Kevin's car to the pitch, the Midleton team bus went past us after they had done a half hour warm-up in Na Piarsaigh's ground and they were looking out the window at the three Gort lads doing a very different kind of warm-up!

They had a huge support and we had all our loyal, local people there and after a super game of hurling, we came out on top by four points. The following day, we struck off for Birr to take on Ballyhale, with the Fennellys, and despite dominating for long periods of the game, we just didn't put them away and the game ended in a draw.

We lost the replay to them a few weeks later in Thurles.

Looking back at my first 12 months as a goalie though, I had won an All-Ireland minor and a county senior and had played in an All-Ireland club final and replay, and it made me realise maybe it wasn't such a bad place to play.

That time in Gort we had Pearse Piggott, Sylvie Linnane, Josie Harte, Joe Regan and lads that I knew growing up that would help you along. We had a super full-back in the late John Nolan, who told me the first day ever I played that if I called… 'MY BALL'… he would make sure nobody came in on top of me.

The first game I played at senior for Gort was a challenge game against Pearses. At one stage I called for a ball and one of their hard men, Frank Finn came in to bury me, but I managed to side-step him. After I cleared the ball, I looked behind me and John Nolan was rolling around in the back of the net with Frank Finn telling him if he ever came in like that again he wouldn't be going out!

The message was there early on that I was going to be protected and that was still the case later in my career when I had the likes of Conor Hayes, Sylvie and Ollie Kilkenny in front of me.

In 1985 I was the Galway under-21 goalie and a sub on the senior team.

We lost to Tipperary in the All-Ireland under-21 semi-final in Tullamore, while the seniors lost out to Offaly in the All-Ireland final in a match we could easily have won. Cyril Farrell was under-21 manager again in 1986, as well as being over the seniors so I was really starting to get used to the training and the set up.

In those days the goalkeeping position was all about sending the puck-outs as far down the field as you could. There was no such thing as short puck-outs or focusing on distribution. Nowadays you hear people like Eamon O'Shea saying that if your goalkeeper has the ball in his hand on average 30 times in a game, why would you give the ball away?

That is 30 opportunities to set up your team for a score.

The really good lads, like Donal Óg Cusack, could puck it 40 or 50 yards to the right guy and set up an attack. That's the difference in goalkeeping coaching in modern times.

The one thing I would always say about Cyril Farrell is that he gave a lot of us the opportunity to become senior county hurlers. He knew he was merging the five or six lads from the 1980 team with the young lads coming through from '83 but the training matches were brilliant and if any of the younger lads started getting cocky or too big for their boots, they had their wings clipped and were brought back into line very quickly.

The goalies did the same training as the outfield players that time as well, so myself and Peter Murphy were every bit as quick as Martin Naughton or Eanna Ryan because we had to be. As a goalkeeper, you have to be the fastest man on the team over 10 yards and there were plenty of times where all those shuttle runs stood to me.

The 1986 senior final was huge for me as it was my first time to start an All-Ireland. Cork got a goal early on from a John Fenton free and my cage was rattled. They got four goals in total at crucial times that day and after that I got a goal from a 21-yard free, where I just hit it as hard as I could; we got a second from PJ Molloy, but fell short by four points at the end.

The following day we went to the funeral of Pat Hurney from Turloughmore, a young man who tragically drowned in Dublin on the All-Ireland final weekend and it was a desperately sad occasion.

On the Tuesday night we were back in training for the All-Ireland under-21 final against Wexford which was on the following Sunday in Thurles, so an awful lot was going on in a very short space of time for any young fella to try and take in.

Wexford were a really good team, but the five or six of us that had just experienced losing a senior final had vowed not to lose a second All-Ireland final in a week. The one thing I always remember about that under-21 final was that Cork won the football final beforehand against Offaly. Denis Walsh and a couple of the Cork dual players who were involved in the senior hurling final the Sunday before, clapped us on to the pitch coming out the tunnel and told us that this was going to be our day.

I thought it was a brilliant sporting gesture from those lads who should have been running around the pitch with the cup. And it did give us a lift.

We won that under-21 final by three points and we had a great evening coming home. It did take a bit of the pain away from the senior defeat.

In 1987 we won a high scoring All-Ireland semi-final against Tipperary, where the big turning point came late on when we were two points down. Tipp had what looked like a perfectly good point ruled out for a foul on me that I don't recall and then Eanna Ryan went down the field and got a goal that put us ahead.

The win put us back in the final and we vowed not to lose a third final in-a-row. The 1987 final against Kilkenny was a dour game, with a lot of hard hitting on a horrible day for hurling, but getting over the line proved the turning point for that bunch of lads. After the final whistle there was the usual pitch invasion and I had all my hurleys under my arm.

In all the excitement though I dropped the puck-out hurl that I got from a neighbour of mine, Jim Donoghue, and when I looked around to pick it up, it was gone. It was the only hurl I ever pucked out the ball with, so I met a few of the newspaper lads afterwards and asked them to see could they mention it in their report, and try and get it back.

A few days later I got a phone call to say a young lad in Renmore had found the hurl, so I called up to him and collected it and presented him with a hurl signed by all the lads. I went on to use that hurl in every match I played until I retired from the club in 1995, and I still have it in the house today.

It's 37 inches long and when I look at it now I ask myself, how in God's name did I ever puck a ball with it!

I didn't get an All Star in 1987 but ended up getting one for the following two years. To be honest, it was nice for my parents to see their son getting one but I'd give the two of them back for a third All-Ireland senior medal in 1989.

People talk about the professional training nowadays but at one stage we trained for 20 nights in-a-row! We were well looked after as well with steak and chips and onion rings after every training session in the canteen of Athenry Mart, not to mention the box of Mars bars which was also devoured.

Imagine eating that for 20 evenings in-a-row!

We were definitely putting on the pounds, like the American golfer Bryson De Chambeau! Those evenings after training though were great fun and that is where the lads really bonded. Lynskey and Sylvie were desperate for messing and they used to leave the spoon in the cup of tea and then come up behind lads and press it against their jaw.

Even the county chairman Tom Callanan was a victim at one stage, but at the back of it all great friendships were forged and there was great respect.

We played Offaly in the semi-final in 1988 and going into that game we felt we had a great chance to get back into yet another final. We got the scores we needed at the right time, won by seven points and were back in the final against our greatest rivals Tipperary.

There was no love lost between the two teams at this stage and even in league matches between us there was a lot of niggle. They were the new kids on the block after coming out of Munster for the first time in years in 1987, but we felt they never really showed us the respect we deserved.

The build up to that final was all about how good Tipp were and their supporters felt they had a divine right to beat Galway, as they had done in the past. The 1988 final was another tough, hard match and looking back at the game on YouTube recently, there was an awful lot of ground hurling.

Any time the ball came into our penalty area, the policy was to whip it away first time from the danger zone.

There were even two or three 'throw balls' where hurls were broken and the referee was happy to let things go. Declan Ryan and Gerry Mac had a ferocious battle… Sylvie followed Nicky English everywhere and even late on Noel came on and tried to pull on a ball but connected with Conor O'Donovan.

That was hurling back then.

It was no place for the faint hearted. It was a very tense match and with only a few minutes to go we were two points up when Pat Fox took a shot for goal through a crowd of players. The ball hit me more than I saved it, but even then I pulled on it when it hit the ground.

The second save I made was when Fox looped a ball over the top to Cormac Bonnar, and I left the goal to try and cut it out. We both pulled on it together and as the ball spun in the air I pulled and missed it, but pulled a second time and put it out for a '65'.

It was lucky I left the goal so quickly and went to ground or Bonnar would have scored a goal and the game might well have been lost. I never worried too much about keeping a clean sheet, so long as we won, but I got a great kick out of stopping Tipp getting a goal that day.

After Noel got the goal we had it in the bag and even with the last puck of the game, Nicky English put a penalty shot over the bar. I was happy to have played well, but I was also delighted that Tony Keady deservedly got Man of the Match that night.

Tony was a super confident player who had great belief in his own ability. The story has been told a thousand times how he was celebrating in The Hut in Phibsboro after the match when his name was called out for Man of the Match on *The Sunday Game* and Cyril Farrell had to accept it.

When he eventually made it back to The Burlington Hotel, Tony told Ger Canning that he had already been given the award at half-time!

He was a brilliant character and we were devastated to lose him a couple of years ago.

Even though we had a serious rivalry with Tipperary, to a man Babs Keating and all the Tipp players travelled to Tony's removal which showed great respect to Tony and his family.

I got my All Star in 1988 and the one thing I loved about those nights was meeting the lads from other counties. I got very friendly with a good few of the Antrim boys like Niall Patterson, Sambo McNaughton, and Danny and James McNaughton. They were really good hurlers who would prove it in 1989 when they beat Offaly in the semi-final. A few of us went up to the final in '89 when they played Tipp and shouted for them from Hill 16.

We were due to play Antrim at a pitch opening in Mountbellew around that time and only 12 of them made it because a couple of car loads had been stopped by the British forces at the border and turned back.

I ended up playing in goal for Antrim because we made two teams by mixing up all the players from both sides.

You wouldn't see that happening nowadays.

Losing the 1989 semi-final against Tipp was hard because of the circumstances, but losing the '90 final to Cork was even tougher.

We were seven points up at one stage but Cork had a knack for scoring goals against us and the five goals that went past me ended my career in goal. The final score was 5-15 to 2-21 and I was one of the casualties of that scoreline.

I was a sub in 1991 and dropped completely off the panel in '92 when a new management came in. I was 26 years old.

I was asked back into the panel after the second league game in 1992 when Richie Burke broke his leg, but I was just after getting married to Christina, had moved into a house in Ennis and started a new job with Heineken so I decided I would leave it.

We have three kids. Paddy was on the Galway minor panel in 2019 and just finished his Leaving Cert, Therese is 20 and studying Child, Youth and Family Policy Practice in NUIG and Jack, who is 24, is in Australia for the last year and a half.

I got great support from my mother and father all throughout my career. My Dad Johnny played for Clarinbridge before moving to Gort and he is still going strong and going to matches at 85 years young!

I enjoyed every minute of my time playing with those lads and it was an honour to have played for Galway, but the way I always look at it is, you only ever have the loan of that jersey and in 50 years' time some other young lad will have that No. 1 on his back.

I ended up playing with Gort until 1995 when I had to pack it in due to injury and no more than Galway, it was an honour to play with so many great Gort hurlers down through the years. I'm still helping out the Gort minors and as long as I have a breath in me, I will always be involved.

MICHAEL COLEMAN

GALWAY 2-16, TIPPERARY 4-8
NHL Final
Croke Park
APRIL 30, 1989

Michael Coleman had to bide his time before playing an electrifying role for Galway through the late 1980s

★ **GALWAY:** J Commins; S Linnane, C Hayes, O Kilkenny; P Finnerty, T Keady, S Treacy; **M Coleman (0-1)**, P Malone; M McGrath (0-1), B Lynskey, M Naughton (0-2); G Burke (1-2), J Cooney (1-7), E Ryan (0-3). Subs: N Lane for Lynskey, P Higgins for Finnerty, T Kilkenny for Malone.

★ **TIPPERARY:** K Hogan; B Ryan, C O'Donovan, P Delaney; R Stakelum, N Sheehy, Conall Bonnar; Colm Bonnar, D Carr (0-1); D Ryan, J Hayes, J Leahy; M Cleary (1-3), Cormac Bonnar (1-0), P McGrath (2-3). Subs: J Cormack (0-1) for O'Donovan, D O'Connell for J Hayes.

THE ACTION

ALL-IRELAND CHAMPIONS Galway added the league title to their growing list of honours after a titanic tussle with Tipperary in Croke Park which maintained the Westerners winning run against the Premier County.

The biggest rivalry in hurling attracted a crowd of over 35,000 to HQ but it was Tipperary supporters who heavily outnumbered Galway as Babs Keating's side looked to avenge their All-Ireland final defeat the previous September. An early Joe Cooney goal gave Galway a tonic start, but Tipp captain Pat McGrath responded with a goal direct from a 40-metre free which went straight to the net in the 10th minute. A second Galway goal from the lively Gerry Burke was also answered by Tipperary corner-forward Michael Cleary – at the end of the first quarter the sides were level at 2-2 apiece.

A Joe Cooney free put Galway in front, but Tipp got a huge boost with a goal from Cormac Bonnar as a tremendous contest really came to life. Michael Coleman pointed from play and this seemed to inspire a purple patch from Galway as they took a lead of 2-8 to 3-3 into the half-time interval. That lead was stretched out to four points with 10 minutes to go as Galway kept the scoreboard ticking over thanks to fine scores from the full-forward trio of Burke, Cooney and Ryan.

Trailing 2-15 to 3-8, Tipperary were thrown a lifeline with eight minutes to go when referee John Denton awarded a penalty for a foul by Sylvie Linnane. Pat McGrath converted to set up a tense finale, but it was Galway who kept their composure and a late Joe Cooney '65' ended the scoring as Galway ran out winners to claim a fifth National League title.

★★★★★

66

I FIRST GOT involved with the Galway senior hurling panel back in 1984 under the management of PJ Qualter. My first outing in a senior Galway jersey was against Clare for the opening of Crusheen pitch, and I got a rude awakening at wing forward marking Ger Loughnane.

I got the call up again in January 1986 under Cyril Farrell, and that followed through to '87 when I eventually made the team for the last three games of the league, including the semi-final win over Waterford and the final against Clare in Thurles. I don't think I had a particularly good game myself at midfield that day but we won by two points – and took our first league title since 1975.

Two weeks later, I got a letter saying the panel was picked for the 1987 championship and I wasn't part of it. I wasn't sure what way to look at it.

You spend all your life trying to break into the Galway senior panel and after almost two years of being involved I thought for sure I would be at least part of the panel for the championship. From my own perspective, I just had to accept that maybe there were better lads out there, but I did feel a bit let down at the time and thought the only way to get back was keep hurling away.

I still came away from the All-Ireland final that year delighted that Galway had won but disappointed not to have been at least a sub. That All-Ireland win gave me a lot of belief that I could get back into the panel – and the only way for me to do that was impress in the club championship.

I didn't hear from anyone in the Galway set up until the Monday after my club Abbeyknockmoy played Ardrahan in the quarter-finals of the senior championship in July 1988, around the same time my father passed away – he was an avid supporter of club and county. I was brought back into the county panel ahead of the All-Ireland championship and made the team for the quarter-final against London.

I thought I'd make the semi-final team to play Offaly but didn't, and was disappointed not to even get a run. I knuckled down again for the couple of weeks in the run up to the final and in training one famous night about 10 days before the 1988 All-Ireland final the subs played the first 15.

Cyril Farrell had asked us not to hold back and give the team a good run for their money. We gave them a good run alright, because at the end of the 70 minute game with no-holds-barred we won by three points – and had five of the first team nursing injuries. As it turned out, the subs were the only team to beat Galway that year.

A few days later I got the nod to start the All-Ireland final at midfield, which was a place I wasn't normally accustomed to as I was usually at centre-back, but Cyril Farrell told me I was going to playing at No 8. There were a few injuries going into that game and I know Steve Mahon was having problems with his knee but it was a big chance for me.

It proved to be big news in the national newspapers. I thought a few journalists might have known me from a couple of years previously, yet it seemed like nobody knew who I was.

The day after the team was announced one paper ran the headline... *COLEMAN IN, LANE OUT.* Noel was very disappointed to have been left out but he made up for it without a shadow of a doubt because without his performance and late goal I don't think we would have won it. Looking back on it, the whole build up to the final was a blur and a bit crazy at times.

The biggest problem I had was staying away from the media because there were a lot of people looking for me. I just stayed at home out of the way because I had a point to prove that I was selected on merit and on behalf of the club. There is no doubt the only reason I got a look in was because of Abbey's great run in the 1988 club championship.

Not alone did we storm through the Galway championship to get to the final, but every one of the players we had in Abbey dug deep and I suppose that was where I got the bit of recognition to get back onto the county team. We had won the intermediate championship in 1985, just about stayed senior in '86, but then in '87 we lost to Sarsfields by two points in a quarter-final that we really should have won by 10 points given all the chances that we missed.

We were naive but we knew we were building and when 1988 came along we just got some momentum going. We only had around 17 or 18 players, including a very young Tomás Mannion, but we had great comradeship for three or four years and had a reputation for a never-say-die attitude built into us which meant whatever team we played, we would not back down.

There were a good few nerves before that final in 1988 against Tipp.

Even in the puck around beforehand it was difficult to see the posts with the huge crowd that was there. It took me a little while to settle down but there was one incident at the end of the first-half which I think came back to haunt me when I was noted by referee Gerry Kirwan for a late shoulder.

I got away with it and in the second-half I got into my usual routine and powered ahead no problem. Winning that final was a new and tremendous experience for me. Most of the lads were there the year before, but for me it was a bit overwhelming and there were times when I was overawed by it all. The celebrations went on for about a month but the club championship was still going so I had to keep focused on that.

That time there was huge interest in the Galway club championship. It was seriously competitive and nearly every year through the 80s there was a new team winning it. The amount of people going to club games way surpassed anything in today's terms. We won most of our games by the skin of our teeth and in the semi-final we edged out Gort by 0-5 to 0-4 on a very wet day.

Even the final went to a replay, and I know Athenry probably look back on it as a missed opportunity but they were the ones who snatched the draw against us the first day. The second day, we knew we would be well able to compete with them again and came away with another famous win by the narrowest of margins.

The National Hurling League had started by the time we had won the Galway county championship. Galway started with wins over Offaly and Waterford and next up was a home game against Kilkenny in Pearse Stadium in the middle of November, just two weeks before Abbeyknockmoy were down to play Four Roads from Roscommon in the Connacht Club final.

There were huge crowds following Galway at this stage so when Cyril asked me would I tog out and play I considered it an honour and didn't hesitate. We were expected to beat Four Roads anyway so there was no real issue with me lining out.

One remarkable memory I have of that Kilkenny game was how late I was getting to the stadium. It was a dreary, wet day and around 15,000 had showed up and trying to get through the traffic was impossible.

Looking back, I often wish I didn't tog out at all given what transpired during the game. As I ran into the dressing-room, the team was ready to run out onto the field but they waited for me. Five minutes into the second-half, I was sent off for the first time in my life, along with the late Lester Ryan by the man who had refereed the All-Ireland final, Gerry Kirwan. To this day, I have no idea why we were sent off – maybe we were the unlucky victims of what was a tempestuous affair, but the sending off had huge consequences for me and for Abbeyknockmoy as it meant I was suspended for the Connacht club final, due to an automatic two week suspension.

Coming off the field I was so frustrated I flung the hurley at Cyril Farrell as he came towards me. Abbey lost that Connacht final to Four Roads and I suppose I have to take a certain amount of responsibility for that. It was a day when the late John Blade collapsed on the field and it didn't help that I was watching on from the sideline unable to play.

At the time the All-Ireland club championship was wide open so it was a sickening defeat. I remember Lester coming up to me in New York the following year on the All Star trip and asking me why the two of us were put off? All I could say to him was I didn't know, but that I had paid a huge price whereas it probably mattered little to him.

Maybe the referee had remembered something from the All-Ireland final, or we were just in the wrong place at the wrong time, I don't know. There certainly wasn't any niggle between myself and Lester because we were actually good friends on the hurling circuit.

Galway won all their league games that season, before and after Christmas, but I wasn't involved again until the semi-final because I got glandular fever in February and it put me out of action for two months. Dr McGloin was looking after me at the time and he said there was no earthly way I could play until I was over it.

It was a very trying time. I lost two stone in weight and didn't eat for weeks but eventually got stronger and by the time the league semi-final against Dublin came around, I was back in training.

Farrell asked me to come on for 10 minutes at the end of that game as Galway were winning well, but it was all geared to being ready for the final against our great rivals Tipperary at the end of April. The Galway-Tipp rivalry was huge at the time and in the build up to the final, there was something in the papers every second day.

We knew everything about each other and both counties were hurling mad. We had beaten them in the All-Ireland semi-final of 1987 and the final of '88, so there was no doubt we had a little edge at the time. But the reason I look back on that 1989 league final with such fond memories is that I was back on the Galway team; management wanted me to be there and from two years previously where I was taken off with 10 minutes to go in a league final, here I was getting Man of the Match.

I suppose it was the day I came of age in the county jersey.

The one thing about the Galway dressing-room in that period is that every time you went in, the place was full. There was no such thing as lads being missing for any reason because every player was fighting for his place on the team.

Trying to break on to the team was nearly impossible.

You were nearly waiting for a lad to get injured. Look at Noel Lane, a goal poacher supreme, who came on early in the second-half of that league final when Brendan Lynskey got concussed. That's the key to a successful team. You need someone to come on who is equally as good as the man who is going off.

A good few of us had gone to Pete and Claire Finnerty's wedding on the Friday in Ballinasloe but we were minding ourselves ahead of the game on Sunday. When you get into a winning culture, you just went out to win at all costs and we had a real habit of winning built up from the 1987 league final right through to '89. We had that swagger and were not really overawed by Tipperary but that day there was a huge Tipp support in Croke Park and they outnumbered Galway at least two to one.

The game itself was pretty hard hitting but we always seemed to have the upper hand. Even when the goals were flying in, we just kept going and pulled ahead when we had to. In the second-half we always seemed to have a gap of four points, unlike the All-Ireland final when there wasn't a puck of the ball between us.

Tipp got a late penalty but we went straight up the field and got a point, and when you look at the scoring, whatever about the goals, eight points was a poor return from a seasoned Tipperary forward line. It was another very satisfying win for the Galway players and supporters and the team could now look forward to a trip to New York the following week along with the All Stars, where we could make up for the lack of real celebrations at Pete's wedding!

We had an excellent eight-day trip to New York and Florida, which came after a long campaign in the 1988 championship with club and county and then the National League. Nowadays most teams go away in early January but that time it was always at the end of the league and before the championship started.

We played the All Stars twice and the fact that we were in New York meant there were a lot of Galway people there and nearly all the players had relations over there because emigration was so high during the 80s. The lack of work at home was a major issue in 1989 so it was no big deal when four of us decided to stay on after the All Star trip to play hurling with the local Laois team, which was ran by a man from my own parish, Monty Maloney.

The team headed back on the Tuesday, but myself and the late Tony Keady, Aidan Staunton and Michael Helebert stayed on and were going to meet up again on Sunday for a game against, of all teams, Tipperary. However, on the Thursday, I got a phone call from home to say Abbey were fixed to start the defence of the championship against Mullagh and I was expected to be back for it.

I flew back on the Friday and it is a game which still lives with me to this day because after about 20 minutes in Athenry, our full-forward Johnny Blade collapsed and died. It was heartbreaking for everyone, but especially his family. It was a very sorrowful period in our parish.

Three weeks later it came through that Tony had played in that game in New York, along with Aidan and Michael, and that Croke Park had an issue with it. Little did we know it would blow up into the 'Keady Affair' and become one of the biggest controversies in GAA history. I think by the end of the year, the records will show that a large number of players were banned for similar reasons, including lads from Kerry, Limerick, Cork... from all over the country. I would have been one of those statistics had I stayed on and played that day.

Okay, everyone knew that it could have been illegal but it was the 'done thing' due most to the economic circumstances of the day. Tony's suspension took us away from what we were programmed to do and our goal of winning three in-a-row. It got more and more media coverage as every week passed and it proved a major distraction as we knew we had a big game to play against Tipperary, again in the All-Ireland semi-final.

Normally the whole thing should have been dealt with by the CCCC, as we know them today, but it went to a vote of all the counties, and Tony lost and was unable to play. The loss of Martin Naughton to a cruciate knee injury the week before that semi-final was another huge loss, but perhaps the most crucial part of the build up was the huge cheer we heard in Croke Park before we ran out – which was the Antrim team being given a guard of honour by Offaly after beating them in the first semi-final.

Now we knew that we were going out to play a game of elevated importance which, with no disrespect to Antrim, was probably going to be the final.

All of a sudden the whole temperature of that fixture went through the roof. We had chances but we didn't play particularly well. Yes, there were mistakes made by the referee but maybe Tipp were that bit sharper.

Whatever way you look at it, it just wasn't meant to be that day

MICHEÁL DONOGHUE

GALWAY 1-13, WATERFORD 2-4
All-Ireland MHC Final
Croke Park
SEPTEMBER 6, 1992

Micheál Donoghue was a leader for Galway as a young man and also as a triumphant manager in 2017

★ **GALWAY:** L Donoghue; T Healy, M Spellman, C Moore; N Shaughnessy, C O'Donovan (0-2), **M Donoghue**; F Forde (0-3), S Walsh; M Lynskey (0-1), D Coen (0-2); P Kelly (0-3); S Corcoran (1-2), C O'Doherty, D Walsh. Subs: J Murray for Lynskey, J Kerans for O'Doherty.

★ **WATERFORD:** P Haran; T Morrissey, P O'Donnell, J O'Connor; A Kirwan, G Harris, T Feeney; T Kiely, F O'Shea; JP Fitzpatrick, D McGrath, JJ Ronayne (0-1); R Ryan (0-1), P Foley (2-0), P Flynn (0-2). Sub: B McCarthy for Kiely.

THE ACTION

GALWAY WON ONLY their second ever All-Ireland minor hurling title in fine style, after coming back from the concession of two early goals to earn a fully deserved six-point win over Waterford. The Munster champions were looking to win their first minor crown in 44 years and with under-21 star Paul Flynn up front, they looked good value for their favourites tag after two goals from full-forward Paul Foley established a 2-2 to 0-2 lead, with the wind, after 19 minutes.

But with Tom Healy marshalling Flynn superbly and the half-back line of Shaughnessy, O'Donovan and Donoghue in inspired form, Galway steadied the ship and finished the first-half strongly with points from Dara Coen and Michael Lynskey, leaving them 2-3 to 0-5 in arrears at the break.

With the elements at their backs for the second-half, Galway scored two quick-fire points from Frannie Forde and Sean Corcoran to cut the deficit to two – and even though Raymond Ryan pointed for Waterford after 37 minutes, it would prove to be the loser's last score. Points from Dara Coen, Peter Kelly and Conor O'Donovan had the sides level with 14 minutes to go and the game was effectively ended as a contest two minutes later when Corcoran finished to the net for Galway. From there to the finish it was one-way traffic and despite 12 second-half wides, further points from Forde, Kelly and O'Donovan sealed a very impressive win for Mattie Murphy's young side.

★★★★★

66

MY FATHER MIKO was well known for driving Galway teams over the years, so it was a real treat growing up and watching the teams in the 1980s leaving our house on their way to winning All-Irelands in Croke Park.

Clarinbridge were in the Community Games national final in 1988, which was played on the morning of the All-Ireland final, so we missed out on seeing Galway beat Tipperary to win the two in-a-row. I remember on the Monday evening naively thinking that because dad was driving the bus, we would be able to get up close to the team when they arrived back into Eyre Square with the Liam MacCarthy Cup, but not realising the thousands of people that had turned out!

Dad wasn't just driving teams around though, he had a huge involvement in hurling and was a selector on various Galway minor and intermediate set-ups over the years and we often went to see the Galway seniors train in Athenry, so we had huge exposure to it when we were young because of the interest he had in it.

My two older brothers Joe and John are twins and the other two lads in the house, myself and Liam, are also twins. We went to Killeeneen National School at the same time as the likes of Darragh Coen, Mark and Alan Kerins, Paul Kennedy, Aidan Quinn, and Liam Madden, and several others were all within a year of each other.

Michael Browne, the principal, was a massive influence on all of us, while Monty Kerins and Stephen Coen got involved also and they stayed with us throughout all our underage careers as we won the All-Ireland Community Games, and under-12, under-16, minor and under-21 championships.

When it came to secondary school, Liam went to Athenry Vocational and I went to Pres Athenry. I think mam learned a lesson or two from John and Joe both going to the Pres and breaking her heart, so Liam and I were always likely to be split up! The vocational school had an unbelievable team at the time with the likes of Liam, Declan Walsh and Franny Forde and they were winning All-Irelands on a regular basis, whereas I only ever played in an All-Ireland senior B final with the Pres which we lost to Scariff.

At 17, I made the Galway minor panel in 1991.

That side was managed by John Fahy, with PJ Molloy, Tony Dervan and dad all involved. In 1991 I was a sub on the Galway minor team and I had a few friendly arguments with dad about not being on the team because he was a selector, but we still had a good team that lost to Tipperary by five points in the All-Ireland semi-final.

In 1992, I was dealing with a back injury but made the Galway team at corner-back for the All-Ireland semi-final against Kilkenny. We had a new manager in Mattie Murphy, who was very stern but very fair. He was extremely driven and focused and he instilled that into an exceptional group of players.

In that semi-final, Colm O'Doherty from Ardrahan got a goal late on that earned us a draw and we came on in spades for the replay in Limerick, which we won well. I was wing back the second day against Kilkenny and winning that semi-final meant Galway were back in the final for the first time since we won the title for the first time in 1983.

Our opponents in the final were Waterford and there was huge hype surrounding their star forward Paul Flynn, who was also on their under-21 team that had qualified for the All-Ireland final. There were five Clarinbridge lads on the Galway panel and one of them, Kevin Donoghue, who set up the equalising goal in the drawn semi-final, had his appendix out and missed the final.

An All-Ireland final is a massive occasion for any young fella, but Mattie had us really grounded and even though we had beaten the defending champions Kilkenny, all the talk around the country was about Waterford so it was an ideal way to go into that game.

The big novelty, of course, was staying in Dublin the night before the final and seeing how different lads react to not being in their own beds, but it made little difference to us. Mattie Murphy's record in preparing teams for a big day was second to none, but we also had a very mature bunch of hurlers, with some incredible leaders.

Only a few years ago we had a 25th anniversary reunion and, as each lad walked in the door, I could see how well they had done in sport and in life. One of those leaders was Tom Healy. In fairness to the Galway management, there were no special tactics devised to stop Paul Flynn with a sweeper system or anything like that; we all had complete faith in Tom's ability to do a man-marking job on him.

As it turned out, Tom did a brilliant job on him that day. I started wing back for the 1992 final beside our captain Conor O'Donovan and Nigel Shaughnessy. Conor was marking a young centre-forward with a distinct yellow helmet called Derek McGrath. It's totally mad how things work out in life and who would have known that 25 years later Derek and I would be standing on the sideline in Croke Park managing our counties in an All-Ireland senior final.

I have got to know him pretty well in recent years and we are occasionally in contact. The day of that minor final was quite windy and we were playing into the elements in the first-half. Waterford got a goal early on when Flynn mis-hit a shot which went straight to Paul Foley standing all alone at the edge of the square.

We got a couple of points to steady the ship but they got a second goal on the rebound from a save that Liam made, and suddenly we were two goals behind. We never panicked though, largely because there was massive composure in the team – we had it back to 2-3 to 0-5 by half-time.

If ever a performance reflected the old adage that you don't panic after conceding an early goal, then this was it. Right from the start of the second-half, we set about dominating Waterford and they would only score one point in the last half an hour. Franny Forde had a great game at midfield all through and, after he scored one of our early points, Conor O'Donovan, who was immense at centre-back, scored the leveller.

When Sean Corcoran flicked home our goal to put us in front, it felt like we were in total control from there to the finish. The final whistle was sweet music to the ears of all Galway people and we got a huge reaction to the win with massive crowds coming out on the Monday night in Ballinasloe, Gort, Clarinbridge and eventually Galway city.

It was also the first of the six All-Irelands that Mattie Murphy would win as a minor manager over the following 20 years and when he took the Galway senior job in 1996, he showed a lot of faith in the lads that were on that minor panel.

A good few of us went straight into the under-21 set-up the following season and we ended up beating Kilkenny in the 1993 All-Ireland final replay. We were managed by John Cody, with Cyril Farrell involved, while Liam Burke from Kilconieron was our captain. I was also involved with the senior panel under Jarlath Cloonan after the under-21 championship was over and played in the early rounds of the National League before Christmas. I was only 19, but all the young lads that went in, like Franny and Shaughs, were flying it. Wequalified for the league semi-final, but I broke my collar bone in an under-21 club semi-final that would keep me out of action for a few months.

I was back later in the year, 1994, when Clarinbridge won the intermediate championship in Galway. Even though I played in the semi-final, the back injury was really starting to flare up and I missed the final against Tommy Larkins. That was when I went for the first of my three back operations and after taking several months out, I came back to play senior hurling with club and county in 1995.

I played in 1996, the year we lost to Wexford in the All-Ireland semi-final. The following year I was on the bench as we lost to Kilkenny by two points in the All-Ireland quarter-final and then in 1998 back operation number two came along (and we lost to Waterford by 10 points). Mattie was back as Galway manager in 1999 and 2000 but I didn't feature in the championship defeats to Clare and Kilkenny those two years and was struggling physically with my back. I finished up with Galway in 2000.

In 2001 John McIntyre came in to train Clarinbridge under manager Billy McGrath and he brought huge energy and experience to the club. He made me captain and it was like giving me a new lease of life.

I was 26 years-old and after we won all our group games, we were building huge momentum. I missed the last group game after I got married to Siobhan in June. I played well at centre-back for the club for the rest of the championship and we went on to beat Athenry in the final and win our very first senior title.

In May of 2004 I had my third and final back operation, just after Cian, our eldest, was born. At that stage I had the total realisation that I had to get my back sorted for any kind of quality of life. It was nothing to do with hurling.

I spoke to Dr Ian O'Connor and we talked it out and he said that it was in my best interests to finish playing. At the time I was working with Vincent Mullins in Tom Hogan Motors and almost straight away after ending my playing career, he asked me in as a selector with the Galway under-21s for the 2005 championship.

I learned so much from him and the rest of the management group, including Mattie Kenny and Mike Ryan, about group dynamics and what constituted a good set up. I stayed involved with the under-21s for four years, from 2005 to '08 and we ended up winning two All-Ireland titles. I came out of that period with a lot of knowledge to take back to the club.

I became manager of the Clarinbridge senior hurling team in 2009, working with a bunch of players who were so successful at underage but had won only one county senior title. At that time I put together a very strong backroom team. Even though we exited the championship to Mullagh in our first year in charge, the following year we changed things up a little bit and after getting out of the group on score difference, we suddenly had a focus and a pathway to success that gave us the incentive we needed.

The other big advantage we had was that we had nobody in with the county panel, so every night we went training we had a full complement at our disposal. We got on a roll and ended up in the county final against Loughrea.

The first game ended in a draw. We learned an awful lot from the game and for the replay we changed our game tactically, and we won our second county title by three points – that sent us into an All-Ireland semi-final against De la Salle from Waterford and their star man John Mullane.

Of all the matches I have been involved with as a player and as a manager, this was one that took on a life of its own. When the game was level at normal time, we asked our lads in the very short space of time to draw on all their experiences from the county final against Loughrea in terms of the replay and our learnings, and to put them into our performance for extra-time. I still look back at the last 90 seconds of added time in extra-time of that game and can see that our lads, despite trailing by two points, kept doing everything that we had worked on in the training ground.

Everybody was going forward with intent. Paul Coen turned and went for goal, Alan Kerins did likewise and Eanna Murphy got the winning touch. I still get great satisfaction from that. That group deserved their success and an All-Ireland club title followed a few weeks later in Croke Park.

I look back now and think how lucky I was that Vincent Mullins asked me to be a Galway under-21 selector. After winning the All-Ireland title with Clarinbridge on St Patrick's Day 2011, the following year I went for the Galway senior job but knew very early in the process that I wasn't going to get it.

Shortly after that, another county came knocking on my door and I also got chatting to Eamon O'Shea, who had just taken over Tipperary. Eamon asked me to get involved in his backroom team and I knew that this might be the opportunity I needed to learn more and enhance my CV. Maybe managing Clarinbridge to an All-Ireland title just wasn't enough to become a top county manager.

I went straight into a top class set-up with great people and a top class team. I stayed two years with Eamon and the second year, Dave Morris came down with me and we learned so much that would stand to us if the opportunity to manage a county team arose for us.

That opportunity arrived in late 2015.

In 2016 we lost Joe Canning and Adrian Tuohy at half-time in the All-Ireland semi-final against Tipp. We were just unlucky to lose by a point, but we were getting a massive buy-in from the players so we knew we were on the right track for 2017.

To date I have worked with great people without whose knowledge, support and friendship I would not have had any success. I have learned so much from them and other managers within the GAA and outside from other codes.

Being a county manager is a pressure cooker, 24/7 job and your life is consumed by it. Don't get me wrong, I loved it but I also have a home life and a work life.

It's all about getting the balance completely right.

When I left the Galway job after the 2019 championship, it took me a long time to get back to being 'normal' again. Maybe Covid has helped me with recharging the batteries and my own three lads are involved now with Clarinbridge under-12s, under-14s, under-16s and minors so I'm getting the bug back again.

Do I envisage doing it again?

Maybe. Will I look at an offer if I am approached?

Possibly.

But right now, I'm just building back up to get to that point.

99

PADRAIG KELLY

SARSFIELDS 1-17, KILMALLOCK (Limerick) 2-7
All-Ireland Club SHC Final
Croke Park
MARCH 17, 1993

*Padraig Kelly shone for Galway, but winning the All-Ireland club title in 1993 with Sarsfields
(inset) is the game that makes him proudest of all*

★ **SARSFIELDS:** T Kenny; Pakie Cooney, B Cooney, M Cooney; **Padraig Kelly (O-2)**, D Keane, W Earls; N Morrissey, J Cooney (O-1); M McGrath (O-4), J McGrath, A Donoghue (O-5); Peter Kelly (O-3), M Kenny, Peter Cooney (O-2).

★ **KILMALLOCK:** G Hanly (1-O OG); S Burchill, JJ O'Riordan, S O'Grady; D Barry, D Clarke (O-2), D O'Riordan; M Houlihan (O-3), B Barrett; P Barrett (1-O), M Nelligan, P Kelly (1-1); P Tobin (O-1), B Hanley, D Hanley. Sub: T Nelligan for M Nelligan.

THE ACTION

GALWAY CHAMPIONS SARSFIELDS ensured the Tommy Moore Cup stayed west of the Shannon for another year at least, after a thoroughly comprehensive victory over Limerick and Munster champions Kilmallock.

Following Kiltormer's success in 1992, Mike Conneely's side were in determined mood to match that achievement and had one hand on the trophy at half-time, leading by 0-11 to 1-1. Backed by the breeze, Sarsfields opened up with the game's first three points from Peter Cooney and Michael McGrath (two), before Pat Barrett struck a goal from a ground shot to the net to level the scores. Sarsfields never flinched and after Aidan Donoghue (two) and Peter Kelly had re-established the lead, the Galwaymen finished the half in blistering fashion with five points in quick succession.

A brief comeback at the start of the second-half, which yielded 1-1, brought Kilmallock back to within four points, but Sarsfields were in no mood to be denied and an unfortunate own goal five minutes from time ended the game as a contest. Wing back Padraig Kelly, who landed a point from a sideline cut in the first-half and another from play late on, was Man of the Match but he had plenty of help, as Sarsfields put in one of the truly great all-round team performances in the history of the club championship.

★★★★★

"

I WAS AT the county final in 1980 when Sarsfields won the title for the first time ever. I was 12 at the time and wasn't the tallest, so all I remember is being on the opposite side to the stand in Duggan Park and only catching a glimpse every now and again through the crowd of what was happening.

After we had won, all of a sudden we had heroes of our own and it probably lit the spark to go on and try and do something similar myself. Twelve is a very impressionable age and at that time you are looking for heroes in different sports. Eamon Coghlan was very prominent at the time so when you went out running, you were him.

It depended on what was on the television, but when Galway won the All-Ireland hurling final a week after Sarsfields' county final win, the whole county went mad. I wasn't very musical growing up, but I remember the word going round that the local band in New Inn were going to lead the Galway team with the cup into New Inn village, so I picked up a tin whistle and joined the band just to be at the front!

I was only pretending to be playing but it didn't matter, because I got to be beside the cup. I remember Galway goalie Mike Conneely, a local lad, saying to me that one day I would bring it home and even though that didn't happen, it set the ambition.

At underage I used to play centre-back, but then one day when I was 15 I went down to see our under-21 team training and a man called Tommy Shea asked me why I wasn't out training with them. In my eyes that under-21 team were all big men, but I headed off on the bike one evening to Bullaun and started training with them.

They always put the 'small lad' in corner-forward, and that year (1984) the under-21s got to the county final where we played a Turloughmore team that included Martin Naughton. At one stage in the first-half one of our lads got injured – I was brought on at corner-forward and ended up getting a goal as we won our first under-21 title.

I was picked to play in the forwards for the county vocational school team the two years after that and won two All-Irelands with Galway playing corner-forward and taking the frees. Those finals were always played before the National League final so there was a good crowd in by the time the second-half was on and we ended up completing six in-a-row and seven in-a-row.

I went to the America for four summers in the late 1980s and early 90s when I was in Thomond College and also played in the forwards over there before I ended up corner-forward on the Sarsfields senior team that won the county final in 1989. I scored a goal that day against Athenry after a pass from Michael Mulkerrins and like most young lads, I liked the feeling of scoring.

It was only when 'Big Mike' Conneely took over the team in 1992 that I went back to play in the half-back line again.

I loved the practical subjects in school, and I was good at them.

Our deputy principal in St Killian's New Inn, John Fahey also looked after career guidance and one day he brought in a newspaper advertisement for a woodwork teacher and he left it in front of me. He told me I should look at it seriously as a career, so the seeds were sown.

From around second year in St Killian's, I worked in the evenings and weekends in our local shop in New Inn called Finnerty's. A few years later, when I was 20, I was filling petrol for a local man home from the U.S. when he got chatting to me and ended up inviting me out to America for the summer to play hurling.

For a lad from a farming background this was a dream offer and once I got the okay from home to travel, I was off. I played with the Harry Boland's club in Chicago and worked hard, saved some money and it helped to put me through college in Limerick. I knew I wouldn't be missing anything in Galway because the club hurling scene was put on hold from June until the end of August when the county team was training.

I really loved those years in the U.S. and made a lot of friends back there.

After my fourth summer in America, in 1991, I returned home to a part-time teaching job in Ballaghaderreen and then took a chance by applying for a part-time position in my old school, St Killians. I got the job and started officially in January 1992.

That same month, the Sarsfields AGM was held and Mike Conneely was in line to take over as senior team manager. The players always had the height of respect for Mike because of his personality, reputation and achievements and I knew people would look up to Mike for all those reasons. The day of the AGM proved a strange one for me.

Not far from our home place, Cappataggle Cross was a notorious accident black spot at the time and my brother Brendan and I were coming back from visiting relations in the area. I knew the crossroads very well and as I pulled across thinking the road was clear, a car came from nowhere and ploughed into the passenger side.

Brendan took the brunt of the impact as the car was pushed along the road sideways until finally coming to a stop after what seemed like an age.

We were brought to hospital by ambulance, but thankfully we both survived, although Brendan's injuries took some time to heal. It was definitely a traumatic experience for all our family. I'm the oldest of six, four lads – myself, John, Brendan and Peter, and then came the two girls Angela and Claire. Both our parents were from the locality and would have known each other from a young age.

Early in 1992, Mike Conneely and his management team of Mike Murray and Mike Mulkerrins called a players' meeting in the national school in New Inn. The three Mikes were all part of the breakthrough 1980 Sarsfields team and they set out their stall for the year ahead.

One of the changes was putting me back into the defence and before long we started playing lots of challenge games and tournament games, and regularly had 15-a-side training matches on our own pitch. We ended up building up a great habit of winning those games and Big Mike seemed to be ahead of his time in setting us scoring targets for different periods of the game – something that is second nature to teams now because of all the stats that are available.

We always focused on our own game and hitting the targets set for us by the three Mikes, and before long we had advanced to a county semi-final showdown with reigning All-Ireland club champions Kiltormer. They were legends at that stage with household names like the Kilkennys, Conor Hayes and Damien Curley, and the game between us in Duggan Park was a real milestone in our club history, as we won by 0-11 to 0-7.

In our first year with the new management set-up we were in a county final against Carnmore and the excitement really started to build in the parish. We had a serious team at that stage. Everyone looked up to our county stars, Joe Cooney and 'Hopper' McGrath and what they had achieved with Galway, but we had a great team ethic and while the two lads were great leaders, they also knew how to bring other lads into the play.

We also had a tremendous mental strength and dug out results in a lot of matches that we might not have in previous years. The first county final against a great Carnmore team was a perfect example as Peter Cooney, Lord rest him, scored seven points, including one at the very end to draw a match that we really should have won comfortably.

It was probably the most important score in Sarsfields' hurling history, because our journey would have stopped before it even began, only for Peter. We won the replay by nine points and could celebrate being county champions again.

We enjoyed Christmas and we had our club social at the end of 1992 but it was a joy to be going back training for an All-Ireland semi-final, regardless of how bad the weather was.

We also had a point to prove after coming up just short in the All-Ireland club semi-final in 1990 against Ballyhale Shamrocks, which has its own story, and we knew if we prepared properly we had a right good chance of matching any team from anywhere.

In those days there weren't many top class pitches either and even training for an All-Ireland semi-final was difficult because we were relying on the generosity of other Galway clubs to allow us to use their facilities. We were up against Buffers Alley that year and they had home advantage, so the game was fixed for Wexford Park.

We travelled down the night before, but the hotel we stayed in was obviously closed for the winter and only opened up to accommodate us. It was freezing there and lads got up in the middle of the night to put on their tracksuits.

A big crowd travelled down from Galway as well and the day of the match was bitterly cold with an Arctic wind blowing. What struck me as we looked out from the dressing-room was the number of people from other clubs who had made the journey. That gave us a big lift.

We ended up winning the game by 12 points, thanks mainly to the four goals we scored and could now look forward to a clash with Limerick's Kilmallock on St Patrick's Day.

The three Mikes kept us very grounded for the All-Ireland final.

The excitement in the parish reached levels never seen before and everybody was heading to Croke Park that day. We stayed in The Burlington Hotel the night before the final, which was new to all of us bar the county lads, and it was hard not to get carried away.

All of the supporters were at the hotel for breakfast on the morning of the game. Fr Michael Burns said Mass for the team and we headed off on a double-decker bus to Croke Park. We had a Garda escort as well and this was also a novelty, until we came to a bridge that the bus couldn't go under so we had to swing around and take a different route, passing the people getting ready for the St Patrick's Day parade along the way.

We watched the first-half of the club football final between O'Donovan Rossa of Cork and Éire Óg from Carlow, before heading back to the dressing-room at the corner of the Hogan Stand. They turned out to be a big let-down, with pillars in the middle of the room and everyone squashed together, but it didn't matter, because I was about to fulfil a lifetime ambition by running out onto the field in Croke Park.

I thought I would be playing in Croke Park in 1986 when I made the Galway minor team for the All-Ireland semi-final against Offaly. Unfortunately the game was moved to Thurles after Croke Park was dug up by fans at a Simple Minds concert, and we ended up losing to an Offaly team that included Michael Duignan and Johnny Pilkington that went on to win their first minor title.

After that, even when Galway were winning All-Irelands in 1987 and '88, I never ran out on to the pitch afterwards to celebrate as a supporter, because I was determined only to go on to the pitch as a player. It was more of a feeling of relief than anything when I ran out with the lads before the Kilmallock game – my first impression was how hard the ground was, much more solid than any other pitch we had played on.

The waiting was finally over, this is what we wanted all our lives. Now was our time.

The calmness in our team was notable.

We had confidence in our game plan, everything was very measured and calm and this was, again, down to the management. It was a game I really enjoyed, even though we got a few body-blows throughout, because it felt like we were playing the free-flowing hurling we knew we were capable of.

There was great satisfaction in what seemed to be a great team performance. Lots of lads were getting on the scoreboard; overall we ended up getting 12 points from play, and even at half-time we felt in command when leading by 0-11 to 1-1. I scored a sideline cut in the first-half and although I would have spent hours and hours practising the skill – because it's something I always enjoyed – the wind definitely helped to drag it over the bar.

No final is ever won easily though and our minds went back to the drawn county final against Carnmore when we were leading comfortably, only to have to snatch a late point at the death to earn a draw. When Kilmallock scored a second goal just after half-time to get back within four points it didn't knock us off our rhythm and our discipline was so good – we hardly gave their free-taker Paddy Kelly any scorable chances.

We got our goal late on which gave us great breathing space and I added my second point straight after in unusual circumstances. The best advice I would always give any young player is never turn your back to the ball. Just after Joe's free ended up being spilled into his own net by the Kilmallock goalie, the corner-back was so frustrated he pucked the ball out quickly and it ended up coming straight towards me.

Most other players including my marker were running out with their backs turned to the goal and did not realise that the ball had been pucked out, but I was jogging in reverse and saw it coming. I was expecting the referee to blow the whistle for the puckout to be retaken but he let play continue.

It felt like time stood still as I grabbed it. I went past my man (who was running towards me) and drove it over the bar. It was all over after that.

Almost straight away, after the full-time whistle, there was absolute euphoria, but within seconds a steward was grabbing me to bring me over to the stand. He said I was getting the Man of the Match award. The cup was presented to Pakie Cooney first and then I got my trophy.

We went back to The Burlington for dinner, then hit for home. The first stop was Ballinasloe and there was a brilliant reception for us there, organised by Councillor Michael Mullins. Then it was on to Kilconnell for another quick stop, before arriving in Ballyfa for a great night of celebration. St Patrick's Day 1993 was a Wednesday, so I was back at work on the Friday.

I never drank, so the only thing that might have affected me was tiredness, but I never minded going back to work after winning!

My performances with Sarsfields in 1993 led to Jarlath Cloonan bringing me into the Galway senior panel that year. The first game I played with Galway was the Sunday after winning the club final, when we played Cork in a challenge.

We had a couple of group games in the county championship a couple of months after that, but when June arrived the county team started serious training and it was a level above anything I had ever done. I wasn't really expecting to start the All-Ireland semi-final that year against Tipperary and got the shock of my life when I was named at No, 7. I would be marking Michael Cleary, a top class player who was running amok in Munster that year, while Tom Helebert was on the other wing, with Gerry McInerney in the centre.

We ended up putting in a good performance and beat Tipp by two points, which wasn't expected, and suddenly we were back in an All-Ireland final against Kilkenny. The club final with Sarsfields in Croke Park a few months earlier had given me great confidence, albeit this time round would be a few levels up. There is a huge amount of nervousness involved in a first All-Ireland final and mental preparation is hugely important. A lot of players freeze on a big day because they are more conscious of not making mistakes than going out to play in a positive way.

The 1993 final was bitterly disappointing to lose.

It was a nip and tuck game that was there for us to win, but we fell on the wrong side of a couple of plays late on and Kilkenny had the experience to see it through. That night we were back at The Burlington Hotel having our meal when a couple of RTE lads started setting up lights beside our table. I took no notice until the announcement was made that I was named Man of the Match, despite being on the losing team.

When you are playing in an All-Ireland final, you have no idea who is analysing the game on TV, but I heard afterwards that Jimmy Barry Murphy had picked me as Man of the Match. Jimmy was also one of my heroes and one of those players that you had to admire for his stickwork and ability, regardless of what county you came from, but he was under pressure to come up with an alternative Man of the Match from the winning team, which would have made life a lot simpler for RTE.

I asked him years later when I saw him going into an All-Ireland final in Croke Park if the rumours were true that he was under pressure to change his decision, and he verified the story. I thanked him for standing by his principles that he felt I was entitled to it and wasn't swayed by the powers-that-be.

It said a lot about Jimmy Barry Murphy as a person to me.

I also managed to pick up an All Star award a few weeks later. Also, 1993 was the year I met my wife Catherina; we were married five years later and we now have four healthy children, Pádraig, Réitseal, Caoimhe and Saoirse.

Whatever about the *Game of my Life*, 1993 was certainly the Year of my Life!

KEVIN BRODERICK

GALWAY 2-15, KILKENNY 1-13
All Ireland SHC Semi-Final
Croke Park
AUGUST 19, 2001

Kevin Broderick was part of a 14-man Galway team that shocked the whole country by toppling an 'invincible' Kilkenny in 2001

★ **GALWAY:** M Crimmins; G Kennedy, M Healy, O Canning; D Hardiman, L Hodgins, C Moore; D Tierney, R Murray (0-1); A Kerins, M Kerins (0-1), **K Broderick (0-2)**; J Rabbitte (0-1), E Cloonan (2-9), F Healy. Subs: B Higgins (0-1) for F Healy.

★ **KILKENNY:** J McGarry; M Kavanagh, N Hickey, JJ Delaney; P Larkin, E Kennedy, P Barry; A Comerford, B McEvoy; J Hoyne, J Power (0-2), S Grehan; C Carter (0-1), DJ Carey (1-1), H Shefflin (0-9).

THE ACTION

FOURTEEN-MAN GALWAY caused a major upset by toppling the seemingly 'invincible' Kilkenny in a thoroughly entertaining All-Ireland semi-final in Croke Park. Tough underfoot conditions meant it was not a day for the purists and Galway's no-nonsense approach was outlined before the throw-in when 19 year-old Richie Murray thundered into his opponent to spark an early dust up.

Galway got a huge boost early on when a Eugene Cloonan free from 55 yards out dipped into the net in the fourth minute, and after Joe Rabbitte had added a point, it was the 11th minute before a Henry Shefflin free opened Kilkenny's account. Three more Shefflin frees had Kilkenny within two points of Galway after 27 minutes (1-4 to 0-5), but a minute later Galway were dealt a cruel blow when corner-back Gregory Kennedy was unluckily sent off on a second yellow card after a collision with DJ Carey.

The extra man proved to be of little advantage to Kilkenny though as Galway won a penalty minutes later and Cloonan's effort was touched over the bar for a 1-6 to 0-6 half-time lead. There was still three points in it midway through the second-half when that man Cloonan booted the ball to the net from close range to put Galway in the driving seat, and a famous Galway win was rounded off in the most glorious style imaginable two minutes from time when wing forward Kevin Broderick took off on a mazy 45-yard run, flicking the ball over an onrushing opponent, before volleying over the bar for one of the greatest points ever scored in Croke Park.

★★★★★

66

WHEN I STARTED out hurling with the club at under-12 level, I played in goals and it was the same story at under-14 when I was part of a Galway squad that lost the final of the annual Tony Forrestal Tournament in Waterford.

By the time I got to under-16, I was first choice goalkeeper for Galway and was on the team that won the 1993 Nenagh Co-Op Tournament in Tipperary. A good few of that team went on to play senior for Galway, like Alan Kerins and Fergal Healy, while future Galway minor manager Jeff Lynskey and Sylvie Linnane's son Shane were also on that team.

The year before, Galway won the 1992 All-Ireland minor title for only the second time ever with Liam Donoghue in goals and the sub goalie that year, Pat Scully was young enough for minor in 1993. A lot of the 1992 team were underage again the following year, so there were great hopes of Galway doing the two in-a-row.

Unfortunately for Pat, he picked up a bad knee injury that meant he was out for the year, so I was shocked when they called me in to the panel as a 16 year-old. I played in the All-Ireland semi-final against Tipperary in Thurles and we were miles better than them – I only got one or two touches of the ball.

At the other end, they had Brendan Cummins, who made around 10 top class saves that prevented us from giving them an even bigger beating. So it was on to the final against Kilkenny. That was my first taste of playing in Croke Park and because it was Galway against Kilkenny in the senior final as well, there was a bigger crowd than usual in for the minor game.

We were probably favourites going into that final but we had no complaints as Kilkenny beat us; they were better on the day. I let in a soft goal as well from David Buggy and it was an awful experience at the time. That year, Mattie Murphy was in charge of the minors and in training one evening he played me outfield to make up the numbers. I scored a goal and a few points that night and it was only after we lost the minor final that Mattie said to me he was sorry he hadn't played me outfield!

The following year I was wing forward for Galway and we went on to beat Kilkenny in the semi-final and then Cork in the final. That Cork team included Donal Óg Cusack, Joe Deane, Sean Óg Ó'hAilpín and Diarmuid O'Sullivan, and they were all still around for my final year as a minor in 1995 when they beat us in the semi-final and went on to hammer Kilkenny in the final.

Still, when I look back on my time playing underage for Galway, I got my All-Ireland minor medal and it's one of only three I have, so it's one I treasure.

The second All-Ireland medal I won was in 1995 with St Raphael's College, Loughrea when we won the All-Ireland Colleges Senior A Hurling final against Midleton CBS. Those same Cork lads – Cusack, Deane and O'Sullivan – were on the Midleton team and it proved to be the one and only time a Galway college has won the title to date.

When I left St Raphael's I went to Athlone RTC for two years to study mechanical engineering and after we won the Ryan Cup in my first year, we were promoted to the Fitzgibbon Cup the following year when I played my one and only match in the competition as we lost away to Waterford.

At the end of my second year a job offer in the bank came up, so that was where my career ended up going. At the end of 1995 though, I was called into the Galway under-21 squad that included the likes of Frannie Forde, Micheál Donoghue, Conor O'Donovan, Peter Kelly and Nigel Shaughnessy, all part of the minor winning team of 1992. I played in the drawn under-21 semi-final against Kilkenny and also in the replay, which we lost, but only a few weeks later I was picked to play for the Galway seniors in the opening round of the National League against Cork in Athenry.

What made that day extra special was my club mate and local legend, Mattie Kenny was playing as well. He had been called up by senior manager Mattie Murphy because he was playing so well in the Galway club championship, even though he wasn't exactly a young lad!

We beat them that day and I got on the score sheet with a point, but it also meant I had played minor, under-21 and senior for Galway in the same year.

By May of 1996 we had qualified for the league final and when it came to picking my favourite match for *Game of my Life* that game against Tipperary was right up there. Galway hadn't won any silverware for seven years, which was a long time given the success the county was used to in the 1980s.

The game was on in Limerick and for a 19 year-old to get to play alongside my idols – Joe Cooney, Michael Coleman and Gerry McInerney – made it an extra special day for me. I will never forget another Galway legend, Eanna Ryan wishing me good luck on the way into the match and thinking to myself... *He knows who I am!*

We only scored 0-2 in the first-half and were behind for most of the game until I got a goal with around 15 minutes to go that levelled it up. It was a ball that should have been cleared, but it fell nicely for me and I pulled on it first time and it flew into the net. I will never forget the Galway roar that day after I got that goal in what was a packed Gaelic Grounds.

Tipp went four points up again after that, but Joe Cooney got a brilliant goal with five minutes to go and we won the game late on with points from Frannie Forde, Liam Burke and Joe Rabbitte, 2-10 to 2-8. The championship that summer was a big disappointment though as we lost to Wexford by three points in the semi-final. There was actually a Connacht hurling final those years from 1994 to '99 – we beat Roscommon that year before going on to play New York in the quarter-final in Athenry in what was a real novelty match.

Our first 'real' game however was a disaster and we were very flat that day against Wexford. It all seemed a lifetime away from the league final win three months earlier.

Later in the year, I was part of the under-21 panel under manager Cyril Farrell as we came up against Cork yet again. On a wet day in Ennis, we beat them by four points to set up a meeting with Wexford in the final, just one week after they had won the senior All-Ireland for the first time in 28 years.

They had senior stars Rory McCarthy and Garry Laffan on their team, and Thurles was packed, mainly with Wexford supporters, but we beat them by 10 points to win with a bit to spare. I still had two more years playing under-21 but in 1997 I got my first bad injury when I tore a hamstring against Derry in the semi-final and even though I wasn't right, I started the final against Cork but didn't last long and they beat us by seven points.

We lost to Cork again in the final the following year after I had scored 1-6 against Kilkenny in the semi-final. By 1997 I was well established in the senior panel; Cyril Farrell was back in charge and that was the first year that the GAA brought in the 'back door' system in hurling. We ended up playing Kilkenny in an All-Ireland quarter-final after they had beaten Dublin in a Leinster semi-final and then lost the provincial final to Wexford.

I was thinking about some of the best games I was involved in with Galway and those years in the mid-90s were a boom time for hurling with new teams coming to the fore. Our quarter-final with Kilkenny was voted the match of the year in 1997, but from our perspective it was very disappointing because it was a game we lost 4-15 to 3-16, having been nine points up at half-time. It was right up there with one of my best performances for Galway as I scored 1-4, but DJ Carey was unreal for Kilkenny and he scored 2-8 to win the game for them.

I got the first of my two All Star awards later that year and even though there were no All Star trips in the 1990s – they brought them back in the early 2000s – I eventually got to go on two of them. Galway had a lot of hard luck stories during the 90s, matches that could and should have been won but for lady luck deserting us, but 1998 was not one of them. We were well and truly beaten up by Waterford in a quarter-final by 10 points and that meant another change of manager, with Mattie Murphy coming back for 1999.

You talk about other great games that I was involved in – the drawn All-Ireland quarter-final with Clare in 1999 is still talked about as an all-time classic. We were nine points up midway through the second-half after Ollie Fahy got his second goal, then Clare got three goals in eight minutes to go a point up with 10 minutes to go.

We went back in front by two points late on, before Seanie McMahon levelled the game with two late frees. Even then it looked like we had a free to win it when Ollie Canning was fouled, only for Pat Horan to blow the final whistle after just five seconds of injury time.

I felt so sorry for Ollie after that game because he started his Galway senior career in the forwards and he rattled the crossbar with a shot three minutes from the end that would have sealed the game for us had it gone in. Everyone played really well for us that day against a really good Clare team, but they hung in there and got out of jail.

When we lost the replay it was devastating, as Galway's desperate losing streak in championship matches continued for the sixth year in-a-row. The one big regret I have in my career is playing in that replay because I had to get an injection in my knee after I picked up a knock in the drawn match, and I just wasn't right.

I can still remember how upbeat everyone was in the dressing-room at training on the Tuesday night after the drawn game because it was the best Galway performance in a big game in years but, as I looked around, half the lads were bruised and battered. We did hardly any training that week as all we could do was try and recover for the following weekend. It didn't work out and we were beaten by seven points.

The year 2000 was a big personal disappointment because, after playing all the league matches up to the final, I got injured and couldn't play against Tipperary in the decider. Ollie Canning got two goals that day, while Rory Gantley and Ollie Fahy were brilliant as well in the forwards. David Tierney got my place and he had a really good game, so I didn't get my place back for the championship.

We beat Tipperary again in the championship quarter-final, our first win in seven years, and I got a point after coming on as a sub with a little over 10 minutes to go. We went on to play Kilkenny in the semi-final and it was one year I definitely think the All-Ireland was there for the taking.

I think we just didn't believe we could beat them.

I came on again late in the game and Joe Cooney set me up for a goal chance which hit the post, but the match was virtually over at that stage and we lost by eight points. Kilkenny went on to beat Offaly well in the final.

2001 saw yet another change of management in Galway. In fairness to Mattie Murphy, he won two league titles in his time and probably got longer than a lot of managers did in two different spells. Noel Lane came in and he brought John Connolly with him and Mike McNamara from Clare, probably to toughen us up!

The first time we met the new management in Craughwell we all expected a cup of tea and a biscuit and a sit down discussion about where we could improve, and our plans for the year ahead. No such luck.

On a dirty, dark night, Mike Mac dogged us from the start.

He didn't even say anything on the first night, he just got us doing warm up laps that were worse than any training session. I remember Mark Kerins getting sick because he only had his dinner a couple of hours beforehand.

It was pure 'old school'; constant laps of the pitch in pairs where the back two had to sprint to the front on the whistle. In fairness to Mike, he got us in serious shape. We didn't do anything spectacular in the league and lost to Tipperary in the semi-final at the end of April but it was obvious we were being trained to peak later on in the summer.

The worst thing about the championship structure from a Galway perspective is we trained for weeks and weeks after that without knowing who we might be playing in an All-Ireland quarter-final. We had a poor year with the club as well that summer and we were gone out of the Galway championship by the group stages, so I was finished with Abbey Duniry for the year before the All-Ireland quarter-final in July.

The training remained intense and we did several nights running up and down the hill in Kilnadeema, as Mike Mac looked to copy his winning formula with Clare in the 1990s. Because I had lost my place the year before, my attitude was to train harder than I ever did in my life and earn my place. I could feel myself coming into form as we prepared for a quarter-final meeting with Derry.

I scored 2-3 that day and got Man of the Match as we won easily, but any chance I had of going into the All-Ireland semi-final against Kilkenny under the radar went out the window when I got a big write up in the *Independent* after playing well in a challenge game a week later... telling everyone... *Kevin Broderick was back in form*... and... *food for thought*... for Brian Cody and the Kilkenny management.

Training was going really well and despite being heavy outsiders against Kilkenny, we were really confident about our chances. The team had really taken shape, with Eugene Cloonan at the peak of his powers, yet outside of our own group there was little belief in Galway that we could turn things around just 12 months after losing to Kilkenny at the same stage.

Our supporters had endured some bad days in the previous eight years and I'd say a lot of people who had come to support us in the 2000 semi-final said no way could they suffer another hiding at the hands of Kilkenny. The few supporters that did go knew that there was something different in the air that day.

Before the ball was thrown in, Richie Murray hit a serious shoulder on Brian McEvoy, who was an All Star the year before. Richie was only 19 at the time and it put down a marker straight away. Kilkenny knew they were in a game.

The first score of the game was a goal from a free by Eugene Cloonan that dipped in under the bar. It was a great boost for us because we had trained so much for this one game and we so desperately wanted to perform.

The other big lift we got in that first-half was when we blocked a DJ Carey 21-yard free when he went for goal – that kept us ahead at half-time. The other big incident involving DJ saw Greg Kennedy being sent off just before half-time for a second yellow card. When you looked at it first all you saw was Greg's elbow making contact with DJ's head, but DJ had slipped into the tackle and Greg was very unlucky.

It only added to our achievement that day that we could beat them playing with 14 men for the entire second-half. We promised ourselves that we would fight like dogs to the very end and Greg's sending off only intensified that determination. It certainly didn't feel like we were a man down for large portions of that second-half. Eugene kicked a great goal midway through the half to put us six points up, but at that stage I had started to get on a lot of ball because I was playing much deeper in our half of the field. I scored two points in that second-half; for the first one I played a one-two with Mark Kerins and put it over the bar for a seven point lead.

Kilkenny responded with a point, before I took off on the solo run that ended with me flicking the ball over the head of Eamon Kennedy and then volleying it over the bar. It was just pure instinct. It wasn't that I set out to go on a run like I did, but my mind went back to a similar score I got in an under-16 C final in Ballinasloe!

The reality is we were a man down and you just had to carry the ball until a better option became available. There was a feeling after that score that it was going to be our day. DJ got a goal late on for Kilkenny but it was only a consolation score and we were back in an All-Ireland final for the first time since 1993.

The feeling of satisfaction afterwards was unbelievable and the celebrations even included Mike Mac fulfilling a promise that he would drink a pint out of his shoe!

There are always regrets when a county player fails to win a senior All-Ireland medal in their career and 2001 was my best chance. We played fairly well against Tipperary but not well enough to win. There was plenty of talk about refereeing decisions that didn't go our way, including a goal I got that was disallowed, but at least I can look back with satisfaction that it was my best display in a Galway jersey as I ended that final with 0-5.

Joe Rabbitte got a lot of punishment that day as well without getting any frees but you just have to live with it.

I picked up my second All Star that year and finally got to go on the trip to Argentina the following January. Even though Eugene couldn't travel, my club mate Liam Hodgins and Ollie Canning were there, along with Joe Rabbitte and Cathal Moore. It was a brilliant experience.

Later that year we lost by a point in heart-breaking fashion to Clare in the All-Ireland quarter-final and they weren't far away from beating Kilkenny in the final, but the Galway County Board still decided to get rid of Noel, John and Mike Mac after just two years. Conor Hayes came in and stayed in charge until 2006, and then Ger Loughnane took over. My last match for Galway was when I came on against Kilkenny in the 2007 quarter-final.

Nowadays, I'm living beside our home house in Duniry with Niamh and our three kids, Emma, Grace and baby Tommy. The two girls play camogie with our local club Davitts, where I am manager of the under-8s, although they haven't shown any inclination just yet to put the ball on the hurl and take off on a solo run!

GER FARRAGHER

GALWAY 5-18, KILKENNY 4-18
All Ireland SHC Semi-Final
Croke Park
AUGUST 21, 2005

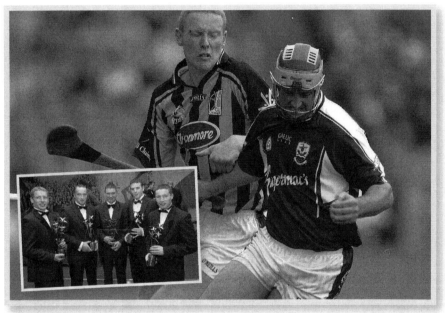

His performances in 2005 ensured Ger Farragher was one of five Galway All Stars by the end of the year

★ **GALWAY:** L Donoghue; S Kavanagh, O Canning, D Joyce; D Hardiman, T Óg Regan, D Collins; F Healy (0-1), D Tierney (0-2); R Murray (0-2), D Forde (0-2), A Kerins; **G Farragher (2-9)**, N Healy (3-0), D Hayes (0-1). Sub: K Broderick (0-1) for N Healy.

★ **KILKENNY:** J McGarry; M Kavanagh, J Tennyson, J Ryall; R Mulally, P Barry, JJ Delaney; T Walsh (0-1), D Lyng; M Comerford (0-1), H Shefflin (1-9), J Hoyne (1-0); E Brennan (2-4), DJ Carey, E Larkin (0-1). Subs: R Power (0-2) for Hoyne, B Hogan for Barry, E McCormack for Lyng, J Tyrrell for Larkin.

THE ACTION

GALWAY QUALIFED FOR an All-Ireland final meeting with Cork after a sensational win over Kilkenny in a nine-goal thriller at Croke Park. It was an extraordinary achievement for Conor Hayes' side, given they lost to the same opposition by 19 points a year previously, but there was no doubting the merit of this Galway win.

In a good old fashioned 'shoot-out' Galway had heroes in star forwards Ger Farragher, who bagged 2-9, and full-forward Niall Healy, whose second-half hat-trick will live long in the memory. An early scoring burst of 1-2 by Eddie Brennan must have had Galway fans fearing the worst, but Farragher's free-taking eventually edged his side 0-9 to 1-5 ahead and then the Castlegar maestro proceeded to score two goals in a minute to put real daylight between the sides.

The first was set up by rampaging midfielder David Tierney and the second was a rebound from a Damien Hayes shot that was well saved by James McGarry in the Kilkenny goal. Leading by 2-10 to 1-5, Galway looked in control, but they got a sharp reminder of Kilkenny's danger up front when Henry Shefflin and John Hoyne both pounced on defensive blunders to hit the net just before half-time and reduce the deficit to 2-11 to 3-5 at the break. The Cats kept up their pursuit of Galway's lead and were level by the 43rd minute, but then Niall Healy rebounded to the net from a Richie Murray shot to re-establish a three point cushion for Galway.

With excitement levels at fever pitch and Kilkenny soon back to within a point, Healy bagged goal number two after he latched on to a throw-in ball that was pulled in his direction – his hat-trick was completed with 13 minutes to go when the Craughwell star kicked to the net after receiving a pass from Alan Kerins.

★★★★★

"

I WAS ONLY eight years-old when Mam passed away suddenly from a brain haemorrhage. She was only 35, and Dad was left to rear five kids from two years-old to 10 at home in Ballybrit Crescent beside the racecourse.

I was the second oldest and I remember him bringing me to under-8 and under-10 hurling training, but when we were young we played whatever sport was on the telly at the time because we had a large green area outside the house and there was always a gang of lads around.

In Briarhill National School we had Sean O'Flynn, who was also involved in Castlegar GAA club, so from a young age we had a big interest in hurling. The Connollys were always to the fore in the club and Gerry, in particular, was involved in coaching a lot of the teams I was on growing up.

I got onto the Galway under-14 and under-16 squads under Jim Bishop and Damien Coleman, but the peculiar thing was I ended up playing county minor in 1999 before I played under-16! John Hardiman was over the minors that year and, to be honest, he was probably one of the best managers I ever had. He was well ahead of his time and when I look back, it is every young lad's dream to play county minor in Croke Park on All-Ireland final day – and I got to do it three times.

I put a lot of that down to John Hardiman. Even at training, he used to involve every player in drills and in games; he was always encouraging lads, never put anyone down and just seemed to get the best out of everyone.

Before the second final in 2000, he put on a video in the hotel which had clips of the best bits of play from every player on the team put to music. From the Citywest Hotel into Croke Park nobody said a word on the bus because we didn't have to. He had us in the right frame of mind.

In the 1999 minor championship, I came on as a sub in both the quarter-final win over Clare and the semi-final win over Kilkenny, but I started at midfield for the final against Tipperary. I got two points that day as we won 0-13 to 0-10, but one of my points was from a sideline ball. I used to practice them a lot when I was young with a neighbour of ours, Gary Long and we would spend ages taking sideline cuts over and back between two sets of cones.

My first ever run out at Croke Park was in the quarter-final win over Clare, which was the curtain-raiser to a cracking senior game between the same two counties that ended in a draw. Croke Park was being re-developed at the time so we were in the old dressing-rooms between the Canal End and the Hogan Stand and they were tiny and old fashioned, nothing like they are now.

That 1999 team produced a lot of great hurlers for Galway like Fergal Moore, Richie Murray, Brian Mahoney, Damien Hayes and our captain John Culkin, while Tipperary had Eoin Kelly, Donal Shelly and Dermot Gleeson.

The following year we beat Limerick and Offaly to get back into the final, this time against Cork. They had Setanta O'hAilpín and Tomás O'Leary on their team, but two goals from David Greene helped us to a 2-19 to 4-10 win and we became the first Galway minor team to win back-to-back titles.

That gave us a shot at the three in-a-row in 2001 and it was even bigger because the senior team were in the final as well. When you are playing minor you think you are the be-all and end-all, but I met a reporter in the run-up to that final and he didn't even know we were playing! The entire focus being on the seniors suited us down to the ground, but in fairness to the Galway supporters, they came in early to see the minor final.

For the third year in-a-row, I managed to score a sideline cut and ended up with a personal tally of 1-6, but Cork centre-back John Gardiner beat us on his own that day and it was probably a match we left behind. I played under-21 with Galway for four years from 2000 to '03 but that happened to coincide with a great Limerick team who won three All-Irelands on the trot.

They beat us in two finals and a semi-final, and I remember their fans went nuts when they hammered us to make it three in-a-row down in Thurles. We lost the 2003 final to Kilkenny after overcoming Tipp in a cracking semi-final that went to extra-time, so the under-21 grade ended up being a bit of a lull for Galway hurling during those couple of years that followed losing the senior final in 2001.

In 2002, Noel Lane was in his second year as senior manager with Galway and both myself and Damien Joyce made our championship debuts when we came on against Down in the first round of the qualifiers in Belfast.

After hammering an out of sorts Cork in round two, we had qualified for an All-Ireland quarter-final against Clare in what was my first 'big' game as a

GAME OF MY LIFE

sub for Galway. I came on with 10 minutes to go and late in the game, when we were a point down; Damien Hayes won a ball and passed it out to me to score the equaliser.

I was certain it was enough to earn us a draw, but Clare went up the field and Colin Lynch scored the winner with the last puck of the game, and we were out. It was an absolute sickener.

Conor Hayes took over then but I didn't really get much game time in his first two years in charge and felt I wasn't making much headway so I pulled away and concentrated on playing with the club. In 2005, Conor invited me in because I was going well with Castlegar, so he gave me a start in the opening round of the league against Dublin.

I did well and scored 0-4, but in the next outing in Nowlan Park against Kilkenny I scored 0-15, even though we lost by four points. We didn't make the final that year but I ended up top scorer in the league and by that stage I was the main free taker as well. When you are playing well it's very hard for a manager to drop you, so it progressed from there to the first round of the championship against Laois.

One of the best hurlers I ever played with, Eugene Cloonan, was out with a back injury for a lot of 2005 after Athenry had lost the club final in March to James Stephens. Eugene was very under-rated for Galway in my opinion, especially when you see what he could do for Athenry when he won many big games on his own. But with Eugene unavailable, I was given the task of taking the frees and in the qualifiers group stage I racked up 1-31 in three games against Laois, Antrim and Limerick, before we prepared for an All-Ireland quarter-final against Tipperary.

The game against Tipp was one of the rare occasions where we came back from the dead to win a game late on. I remember we were six points down with about 10 minutes to go when a ball came to me in the corner and as my man came to push me over the line, I just pulled on the ball and it went straight to Damien Hayes, who threw his man out of the way and hit the roof of the net.

It was the turning point as we outscored Tipp 1-6 to 0-1 from there to the finish and ended up winning by 2-20 to 2-18. The win kind of came out of nowhere to be truthful though, because in the run up to that match we were well beaten by Offaly in Killimor in a challenge match – that match ended up being a turning point for our season.

Conor Hayes went absolutely cracked so Liam Donoghue, who was captain in 2005, kept the players back for a meeting and there were a lot of home truths spoken in the dressing-room after that Offaly game with lads telling each other straight out what they thought of each other. I was only 22 and a pretty quiet individual, so I kept the head down as best as I could! It was a heated meeting but it was no harm that things came to a head.

The players decided to take responsibility from that moment and it ended up being the spark we needed to turn things around. We were also blessed to have great leaders like Ollie Canning and Liam Hodgins to help steer lads in the right direction. After the comeback win against Tipperary, we quickly came back down to earth when we realised what was between us and a place in the All-Ireland final. Kilkenny had beaten Galway by 19 points the year before in Thurles and they were expected to put us to the sword and have a crack at winning back their title from Cork, who had beaten them in the 2004 final.

They had all the big names – Henry Shefflin, DJ Carey, Martin Comerford, Eoin Larkin, Eddie Brennan, Peter Barry, Tommy Walsh, Michael Kavanagh, James McGarry. They had them all over the place. We were building momentum after the Tipp game though and regardless of the pre-match odds, we believed in ourselves and that was the main thing.

It started lashing rain on the morning of the game and I remember Sean Silke saying to me that my frees would be very important because it was certain to be a low scoring, tight game. How wrong would that prediction be?!

The game started at 90 miles an hour and the second ball that came to me, I went down and some people thought I was injured. I just couldn't get my breath.

It was up and down the field without any break and without doubt was the fastest game I was ever involved in. Eddie Brennan was on fire early on and he scored 1-2 in the first 10 minutes, before Shane Kavanagh went over on him and won the first three balls that came between them. We settled down after that and both David Tierney and Fergal Healy were having massive games at midfield.

We were level by the 20th minute after I knocked over a couple of frees. The Kilkenny crowd weren't happy with referee Seamus Roche all day and while a few frees we got might have been 'borderline', he certainly didn't go out to 'do' Kilkenny. The game had settled down at that stage, but the end of the first-half was just crazy stuff.

David Tierney made a great run in from the left but looked to have carried it too far when my man went across to him; he flicked it over to me and I had the simple task of finishing it past McGarry to the net. Then a minute later the exact same thing happened again, only this time Damien Hayes came in from the same side and took a shot, which was saved but fell nicely for me to pull on the ground and into the net.

I couldn't believe it... 22 years of age in an All-Ireland semi-final against Kilkenny and already I had scored 2-7.

Tierney landed a great point straight away and we were 2-10 to 1-5 up. It was dream stuff. All we had to do was play out the last minute of the first-half and we would have been in the driving seat at half-time. Then Kilkenny do what they do best and, in the blink of an eye, they got two goals of their own through Shefflin and John Hoyne and, somehow, we were only three points up at half-time.

Still though, we would have taken that position before the game and when we got in at half-time, we talked about lads at the back playing in their positions rather than following their men, and keeping the work rate up all over the field to put them under pressure. I came a bit further out the field in the second-half and a lot more ball seemed to go in to Niall Healy at full-forward.

Niall will be the first to admit he wasn't having the best of days, but he ended up scoring a hat-trick that will be talked about forever and the thing about it was all three goals were so different – one of them he kicked in, one he pulled on, and the other he took on his man and buried it in the corner.

Before that though, Kilkenny had got back level and the pace of the game in the second-half never let up. I thought to myself at one stage... *Here we go again!* Another big game that we would let through our fingers, but Niall's three goals changed everything and put us back in the driving seat big time.

One of the goals came from a Kilkenny lad 'mouthing' at the referee after they had got a free out. David Forde pulled on the throw ball into Niall, and he finished brilliantly. Leading by 11 points with just over 10 minutes to go, surely they couldn't come back again?

But of course, they did.

One thing we did have that year was fitness.

Gerry Dempsey was training us and we were as fit as we could possibly have been, but Kilkenny were a brilliant team and when Eddie Brennan got his second goal, we were hanging on a bit. Then Kevin Broderick came on for Niall, who had cramp, and he scored a crucial point late on to ease the pressure and put us four ahead.

The final whistle was pure elation. We were just overjoyed at beating one of the greatest teams to ever play the game. For the lads that had to endure the 19-point humiliation the year before, this was redemption.

Some lads might have said that revenge wasn't the motivating factor, but of course it was. If you get a beating like Galway got, you want to set the record straight the next day. There was also the immediate realisation that we had qualified for the All-Ireland final for the first time since 2001.

Most of the 2005 lads were not around in '01 so it was a new experience for a whole bunch of young lads who always dreamed of playing in a final and now would get their chance. The only pity about the whole thing was that the Kilkenny game wasn't the final. There we were after beating a brilliant Tipp team and a brilliant Kilkenny team, and we still had to go and beat Cork to try and win an All-Ireland.

Still, that was in the future. The management enjoyed the win over Kilkenny every bit as much as the players, as can be seen by the photo of Conor Hayes and Pearse Piggott that appeared in the papers!

The final against Cork was a big disappointment but they were a serious team and worthy winners. I ended up as the championship's top scorer and picked up a coveted All Star award later that year. I'm not really into individual awards and all that, but I was delighted for my late father that I got the All Star and the trophy sits proudly on his mantelpiece at home.

The late Gerry Connolly was at the Kilkenny match as well and I was delighted for him because he and my father brought me up from underage all the way up along to senior, so it was great to see his work being rewarded. It was also great to be on an All Star team with the other Galway lads selected, but to see your name on a list of fifteen hurlers that includes some of the greatest hurlers to ever play the game, you'd take that any day of the week.

The All Star function was in the Citywest Hotel and it was a brilliant night, followed later again by a brilliant trip to Singapore, while the Galway team holiday was to China, so some of us did a serious amount of travelling around Asia that year! The China trip after Christmas was more like a school tour. It was mighty craic but we had hardly any time for letting the hair down because nearly every day we were taking a different flight to various parts of the country.

We got back into action for the 2006 season but ended up losing to Kilkenny by five points in a quarter-final in Thurles and that was the end of Conor Hayes.

Ger Loughnane came in, and he had no time for me at all and I didn't get a look in in his first year or 2008 – I only came on as a sub a couple of times as we lost to Cork in the qualifiers. It was only when John McIntyre came in, in 2009, that I got a chance to really show what I could do. I asked him to play me at midfield, which was my proper position, and not corner-forward where I just happened to play in 2005 under Conor Hayes.

Without a shadow of a doubt, the best hurling I played was in 2009, '10 and '11 under John Mc. I was nominated for an All Star in 2010, the same year I was Player of the League, and in two of the last three matches I ended up playing for Galway in 2011, I got a crystal hurl for the game against Clare, and Man of the Match against Cork.

What I could never have predicted was our defeat to Waterford in the quarter-finals that year would be my last game for Galway. What was sickening then was Anthony Cunningham took over as manager and felt I was surplus to requirements.

At 28 years of age I felt I was playing better than I ever was, but the new manager thought differently. I thought I had another three years in me at least, but in fairness to Anthony he got rid of a few lads and ended up getting to two All-Ireland finals in the four years he was there.

I kept going with Castlegar but we never really progressed beyond the group stages so there was no chance of me getting back in the Galway set up based on club form. I'm 20 years playing with Castlegar and in all that time, we got to one semi-final, in 2007. This year (2020) we were nine points up on St Thomas' and got caught with a goal at the death and we were hard done by against Sarsfields in another match we should have won – but we are a long time saying we are in hard luck.

At least we have a lot of good young lads coming through, so please God we will have a better run of luck soon. No matter what game you play in, you need a bit of luck. Sometimes it's all about timing.

I happened to be in the right place at the right time in 2005 in a game that I'm still reminded of on a regular basis. For nine goals to be scored in an All-Ireland semi-final and for Galway to come out the right side of a result against the great Kilkenny team was the stuff of dreams. That match is right up there alongside the 2017 semi-final win against Tipp when Joe landed that unbelievable winning point.

The way it all finished for me left a sour taste, but I loved every minute I had with every Galway team I played on from underage to senior.

DAVID COLLINS

GALWAY 1-15, KILKENNY 1-14
All-Ireland Under-21 HC Final
Gaelic Grounds, Limerick
SEPTEMBER 14, 2005

The one-point All-Ireland under-21 win over Kilkenny in 2005 was a crowning day for David Collins in maroon

★ **GALWAY:** A Ryan; P Flynn, A Gaynor, K Briscoe; G Mahon, B Cullinane, A Garvey; B Lucas (0-1), **D Collins (0-1)**; J Gantley, A Callinan (1-1), E Ryan; K Burke (0-2), N Healy (0-1), K Wade (0-8). Subs: F Coone for E Ryan, C Dervan (0-1) for Gantley, D Kelly for Cullinane.

★ **KILKENNY:** D Fogarty; S Maher, J Tennyson, D Cody; J Dalton, PJ Delaney, C Hoyne; M Rice, M Fennelly (0-1); J Fitzpatrick (0-2), A Murphy, E Larkin (1-9); E Reid (0-1), R Power, W O'Dwyer (0-1). Sub: D McCormack for Murphy.

THE ACTION

KILKENNY'S BID FOR three All-Ireland under-21 titles in-a-row ended in dramatic fashion at the Gaelic Grounds as Galway rattled home four points in the closing minutes to snatch an unlikely victory and a first under-21 crown since 1996.

A week after losing the senior final to Cork, the Tribesmen looked set for further disappointment when they trailed a star-studded Kilkenny outfit by 1-14 to 1-11 with only five minutes to go, but a long range free from David Collins sparked an incredible comeback which culminated in Kerrill Wade firing over a last gasp winner.

Kilkenny roared out of the blocks with an early Eoin Larkin goal, but Aongus Callanan found the net for Galway at the end of the first quarter and by half-time, Vincent Mullins' side had forged ahead by 1-7 to 1-6. A Wade '65' doubled Galway's lead after the restart, but Kilkenny then hit a purple patch and, inspired by the unstoppable Larkin, had forged ahead by 1-13 to 1-9 with 13 minutes left. The Cats kept Galway at arm's length until Collins, one of four seniors on the team, landed a long range free in the 56th minute. That point turned the game on its head as Galway went for broke, and points from substitute Cathal Dervan and two injury time strikes from Wade, the first from a contentious free, saw Galway complete the minor-under-21 double for only the second time ever.

★★★★★

66

THE ONLY MAJOR All-Ireland I have is the under-21 medal I won in 2005. Beating Kilkenny at any stage is sweet, but coming on the back of losing the senior final to Cork a week before and to win it the way we did, was incredible.

It was a chance at redemption and after the devastation of losing to Cork in Croke Park, we were back training with Vincent Mullins on the Tuesday night. I recall saying to the lads that night that we had one more week to put in... just focus and go for it.

Plus, the few of us that were involved in the senior team had the experience a month before of winning an epic senior All-Ireland semi-final against Kilkenny by 5-18 to 4-18. That was the game where Niall Healy saluted the crowd in Hill 16 after scoring his hat-trick and I'm sure he was thinking... *What the hell is after happening here?*

Himself and Farragher were class that day and, thinking back, to beat Kilkenny twice in the space of a few weeks in a senior All-Ireland semi-final and then an under-21 All-Ireland final was unbelievable. Going back to the senior win, I will never forget catching the very last ball and as I was running out, the final whistle went and for some unknown reason, I kicked the ball away.

I often ask myself why I didn't keep the ball because it was one of my best sporting memories ever! I got Young Hurler of the Year the same year and that award is sitting on my mother's mantelpiece and is the pride and joy of that whole era that I played in, but 2005, for me, was incredible and was really the year that I cemented myself as a senior hurler.

I never really made it at county minor level and it was only in my final year as a minor that I made it on to the under-21 team. Still, as a young fellow growing up, making the senior team was the goal and at the time, I saw under-21s as a real stepping-stone because it was a lot more physical than minor. I was playing Third level Fresher and Fitzgibbon Cup hurling with GMIT at the time and marking the likes of John Tennyson and Henry Shefflin, who were playing with Waterford IT. I developed massively once I went in to GMIT.

We played a good few times in the Ragg in Tipperary against the likes of WIT and UCC and we were getting hit way harder than we were ever hit before, so it was a real learning curve. It was a massive turning point in my career and

I think the hits that went in at Third Level and under-21 that time were a lot harder than nowadays – you got away with a lot more pulling and dragging and the refereeing was far more lenient.

I will never forget marking Henry Shefflin in a colleges game in my first year in GMIT and we were losing by six or seven points down in Waterford. He ended up commenting on what I was doing right and wrong during the match, telling me about my positioning, balls that I should and shouldn't have gone for and I thought to myself... *Here is a Kilkenny man educating me on how to play hurling!*

I was only 17 and, to this day, I have massive respect for Shefflin for the way he coached a young lad starting out. To think then that a few years later we would be tearing strips out of each other in a senior game in Croke Park. I often say hurling is an amazing sport where you make a lot of friends and also get a chance to play against lads that you regard as icons growing up.

I was very raw as an underage hurler and I was a sub on nearly all the Galway underage teams, from the Tony Forrestal under-14 team under Josie Harte right up to minor. I got a No. 24 jersey at under-14 and I remember thinking... *I never want to wear a jersey like this again!* As it turned out, I think it was one of the final jerseys I got at the end of my senior career, so it's funny how things started and finished.

Thankfully, the middle of it was 2005 to '07 and they were three years that I would describe as epic. When I look back on the way Galway teams were prepared in my time, things went to a new level in 2007 when Ger Loughnane came in. Anthony Cunningham took it even further as regards weights programmes and conditioning, but we had to move with the times because Kilkenny had already got a head start on everyone – by the time they had their run of four in-a-row from 2006 to '09 they were really at their top level of physicality.

When you hit Larkin, Power or Fennelly you knew all about it. I remember running out with a ball against Kilkenny in one of those years and Jackie Tyrell hit me in the chest, right into the sternum. I couldn't show weakness and go down, so I just turned away and coughed up blood.

He hit me so hard, he made me realise we were not physically prepared for the battle at all. By the time it came to 2012, I believe we were at the level that we needed to be at to compete with the likes of Kilkenny. That year we won the Leinster final for the first time when we beat Kilkenny by 10 points and we knew we would probably end up playing them again in the All-Ireland final.

We were eight points up in that final coming up to half-time when I got penalised for over-carrying and before we knew it they had rattled over three frees and cut the gap to five. I always remember things like that even more than games we won, especially as they came back to draw the game and beat us well in the replay.

When Micheál Donogue took over in 2016, I had told him I would give it one more year and see could I contribute something. My training ethic was always to go flat out all the time and that probably worked against me in the end because I never gave myself the time to recover from any injuries I suffered.

Andy Smith was the same way and we were great buddies on and off the pitch, but I knew my time with the seniors was coming to an end in 2016. I only told Micheál that I was done; it felt like more of a relief than anything else.

I had 13 years done at that stage, so then you roll on to 2017 and Galway go and win the All-Ireland! Do I regret not winning an All-Ireland with Galway?

Of course I do, it was always my dream and what drove me, but it won't define me and the fact that Liam Mellows went and won a first Galway senior championship in 2017 after 47 years shows to me that my decision was justified. I remember the call being made to bring Louis Mulqueen to Liam Mellows, and the first question he asked me was whether I was packing in county hurling?

When I said yes, he agreed and brought us to a new level of 'professionalism'. Knowing that standard would be there, it was easy for me to row in behind him and bring everyone along with us. That is exactly what happened.

We were lucky as well to have players like Aonghus Callanan and Tadhg Haran, but you can see what Louis sought to achieve. County players have been training with their clubs all the time and the standard has improved dramatically as a result. The executive of the club bought into what Louis was bringing as well and believed in what he was doing, so it all added up to a famous county final win over Gort.

Mellows is a fantastic club, with great people behind it and volunteers for all age levels. Mellows is one big family I always say to people that ask and I'm hugely proud to be a member of it.

My first involvement with the Gaelic Players Association came as a 21 year-old in 2005; the GPA was only formally recognised as the players' representative body by the GAA at its annual Congress in 2010 I remember. I was always very passionate about players getting a lot more than they were back then.

Nowadays it's a different story because players get their expenses, gear and whatever they are entitled to, but in 2005 when I went in as a representative from Galway, that wasn't the case. I spent a year as the Galway rep and then served as GPA secretary and I was president for two years, which was a massive honour.

It kept my finger on the pulse of what was going on in other counties. I was one of the youngest members of the GPA reps at the time in 2005, but I always had that belief in myself and felt that I had some chance of making a difference once I was in a position, rather than mouthing off from the outside.

Looking back now, I was confident in 2005, but my involvement in the GPA made me grow up a lot over the next couple of years and in 2007 when Ger Loughnane came in, I was captain of Galway and it was a dream come true! My style of hurling in those years was very aggressive, maybe I had a point to prove from not making all those underage teams. It stood to me in the end.

College was also a means to play hurling, as was my job with HP and that is not the way it should be. Your career is so important because if you get injured in a game or suffer a serious injury then you are gone, and what are you left with? That happened to me in 2007 when I got injured and missed the next 18 months because of it.

I was told I wouldn't get back playing and that really opened my eyes when it came to talking to other players after that because I could ask them one simple question, 'If it all ended tomorrow with hurling… what is your back-up plan?'

That is really what the GPA do. They work with players to transition from GAA to real life. I worked in Hewlett Packard for 13 years and that job allowed me to play hurling; it is only in the last three years that I have focused on my career. If I had my time over I would definitely have given more time to my career, but essentially it is a player's choice. I know other counties have sorted lads out with jobs as teachers and in banks over the years, but I think players now have the opportunity to arm themselves with a lot more information with the career development courses that the GPA provide.

It is a service that is very under-used, but the opportunities are there for players to learn now and that simply wasn't there back in the day.

My first involvement with the Galway seniors was in 2004 under Conor Hayes when we got to the league final against Waterford. Dan Shanahan scored 1-3 on me and I was taken off but instead of going into the dug-out, I walked up and down the sideline with a water bottle, trying to encourage the lads.

We won the game by five points, but that was my mentality at the time. If I can't do it on the field, I might be able to do something off it. We had some legends in those days, between Eugene, Ollie, and Kevin Broderick. The craic we had under Conor Hayes was unreal, with Pearse Piggott and Gerry Dempsey with him.

I remember the three years I had training with them better than the times I had 10 years later. At one stage we went over to Lough Lomond in Scotland at the end of 2005 and just played golf, drank, bonded as a group and did a small bit of training one of the days. When we lost the All-Ireland senior final to Cork, we 'celebrated' for a few hours I think.

When we won the under-21, we celebrated for a fortnight!

It was unbelievable and there is no way you would get away with it now! The other thing about 2005 was we went straight into an All-Ireland under-21 semi-final against Cork. We won that game by six points, but the challenge in the final was going to be far stiffer as we had to try and stop Kilkenny from winning three in-a-row.

There were battles all over the pitch in that under-21 final right from the start. It wasn't mean or nasty stuff, just hard hitting man-to-man stuff.

They fleeced us and we fleeced them.

I remember myself and Richie Power nearly taking the heads off one another at one stage and it was just 'play on'! I loved games against Kilkenny because there was no filth, just real hard hurling. There was a great Galway crowd at the game as well and that helped us immensely.

Kilkenny got off to a flyer when Eoin Larkin scored a goal after two minutes. I was midfield that day, so I wasn't marking him but he broke my heart on more than one occasion in the years that followed. Aongus got a goal for us about 10 minutes later and the game turned into a shoot-out between the free-takers after that as Larkin and Kerrill Wade went point for point. Brendan Lucas and Niall Healy scored two raspers of points and by half-time we were one ahead.

The second-half was an all-out war and it seemed like there were fights breaking out all over the place, but the referee John Sexton didn't see half of it! It was a typical Kilkenny game because when I looked up at the clock there was only five minutes left and I thought to myself… *Where has the time gone?* We trailed by three points.

Then we won a free in our own half-back line and why I stood over it to take it, I will never know. I remember distinctly trying to drop the ball into the square because we were three points down, but I hit it so hard it went over the bar. Next thing Cathal Dervan, who had come on as a sub, scored an unbelievable point to bring it back to one, and then Wade got a dubious free out of nothing to level it in the first minute of injury time.

There was war over that free.

Then came Wade's winning point and it was an absolute cracker. From nowhere, we were All-Ireland champions and the feeling was pure elation. I asked my dad recently if he remembered anything about the closing minutes of that game and he said all he remembered was the final whistle and seeing Brian Cody walking out of the Gaelic Grounds with a 'bould head on him!'

It's hard to credit that nearly all of those Kilkenny lads ended up with seven or eight All-Ireland medals, while it took us another seven years to get back to an All-Ireland senior final. A lot of those Galway lads never really pushed on, which is unfortunate. We hadn't a star-studded team, but a lot of lads were real work horses and played above themselves that day. We had plenty of quality too and Kerrill Wade went on to make the senior team two years later under Loughnane when we played Clare.

That was the day he got the nickname 'The Assassin' because for some reason when Ger was calling out the team, he named the full-forward line… 'Hayesey at 13… Eugene at 14 and at 15… is the Assassin'. We hadn't a clue who he was on about!

We really celebrated that under-21 win and spent a good few nights in the 'Earl Inn' in Killimordaly and the 'Hole in the Wall' in Galway. They are very fond memories of a brilliant time in my hurling career.

People often ask me is county hurling gone too serious now and I say that if we can get the changes that are being spoken about now into practice, whereby the focus in any year is equally split half and half between club and county, then it will be for the better. The average amount of time spent training by a county player is 31 hours a week.

You would be on a salary of €35,000 starting out as a developer for that. Something has to give from both a family and work perspective, otherwise the game is going to go semi-professional and I don't ever want to see that. I just don't believe in it and it's one of the main reasons I got involved in the GPA.

Communities are built on GAA clubs and I would be a strong advocate for players not being paid to play. Will the split season help county players? I believe it will, because it will make them realise that the club is so important to them and we can run off the club competitions in a much shorter time frame than in the recent past.

OLLIE CANNING

PORTUMNA 2-17, JAMES STEPHENS 0-11
All-Ireland Club SHC Semi-Final
Semple Stadium, Thurles
FEBRUARY 12, 2006

Portumna becoming the greatest club in Ireland brought equal joy to Ollie Canning as his glorious county career

★ **PORTUMNA:** I Canning; M. Gill, E McEntee, **O Canning**; G Heagney, M Ryan, A O'Donnell; L Smith, E Lynch; D Canning (0-1), K Hayes, A Smith (0-4); D Hayes (1-4), N Hayes (0-1), J Canning (1-7). Subs: P Smith for K Hayes, P Treacy for L Smith, E Lynch for N Hayes, T Quinn for Ryan.

★ **JAMES STEPHENS:** F Cantwell; D. Cody, M Phelan, D Grogan; J Tyrrell, P Larkin, P Barry; B McEvoy (0-3), P O'Brien; J Murray, E Larkin (0-5), G Whelan; E McCormack (0-2), R Hayes, D McCormack (0-1). Subs: M Ruth for Murray, S Egan for Whelan.

THE ACTION

PORTUMNA DETHRONED CHAMPIONS James Stephens with a ruthless and comprehensive performance that was every bit as dominant as the final scoreline suggests and leaves the Galway side on the verge of a first All-Ireland title.

Seldom has a Kilkenny team been so outplayed in an All-Ireland semi-final and for Portumna, this victory may well signal the arrival of a new superpower in club hurling. The Galway side tore into the game from the off and with 17 year-old Joe Canning, Damien Hayes and Andy Smith all adding points to their tally, they led by two points after 22 minutes when Davy Canning set up Hayes for the game's opening goal.

James Stephens had an opportunity to cancel out that goal just before the break, but Ivan Canning made a brilliant save from Gary Whelan that helped Portumna to a 1-9 to 0-6 half-time lead. When Joe Canning pointed from a sideline cut to extend the lead after the break the signs were ominous for James Stephens – and the goal that killed the game off entirely arrived 12 minutes into the second-half when Ollie Canning, who was supreme in defence, started a move that involved Aidan O'Donnell, Leo Smith and both Damien and Niall Hayes. The ball was eventually transferred to Joe Canning, who blasted home to put Portumna out of sight at 2-11 to 0-8.

The final quarter saw Portumna cement their lead and frustration eventually got the better of James Stephens as they had both Philip Larkin and Shane Egan sent off on double yellow cards. By the end, Portumna were thinking of an All-Ireland club final against Newtownshandrum long before the final whistle brought the curtain down on an emphatic 12-point win.

★★★★★

"

I'M THE FIFTH of seven children in the Canning house and we all went to Gortanumera National School. Dad coached the hurling team there, as did my brothers Frank and Davy in later years.

It was only a small, two-teacher school, so we played seven-a-side competitions and we won a couple of titles during my time there. All the Hayes' went to school there, as did Connacht Rugby star John Muldoon so there were a few sporting families in the area.

Portumna wouldn't have been steeped in hurling history by any stretch of the imagination and there was a time in the early 1970s when there wasn't even an adult team in the parish. A number of players had to go to neighbouring clubs to stay hurling.

Dad and a few more played with Killimor and others played with Tommy Larkins and Tynagh. We were like a lot of rural clubs at that time, suffering from emigration – in 1966 Portumna had six county minors on the Galway panel and they all had to emigrate to England and the U.S. for work.

As a club, we are as east of the county as you can go, right on the edge of the Shannon. I can remember on the odd occasion while hurling for Portumna being told to… 'Go back to Tipperary', which underlined the general feeling of how far east we were.

Growing up, the great Castlegar team of the 1980s would have been spoken about, but then Kiltormer came along in the early 90s. Their All-Ireland club success was a big thing in our house because our mum Josephine is one of the Lynch's from Kiltormer and she had brothers playing at the time.

When Kiltormer were playing in the 80s and early 90s we spent many a Sunday supporting them. That kept us going until we made our own breakthrough to senior hurling. The key years in Portumna hurling history that spring to mind for me are 1982, when we won the county junior title, 1992 when we won the intermediate title and then 2003, when we won our first senior title.

Every decade we were making steady progress back then, with club facilities improving all the time. You could see the hurling landscape was changing for the better and the question was whether we could sustain that over a period of time.

Portumna's early years at senior level were dominated by the great Sarsfields and Athenry teams. The Galway championship was, and still is, notoriously difficult to win. I was a sub on the intermediate team in 1992, but broke into the team the following year so, like a lot of recent Portumna players, I was very lucky to be playing in an era where all we knew was senior hurling.

We never had to play in a junior or intermediate championship after 1992 because of the work the previous generation of players and management had put in, and we were acutely aware of that. I know it was mentioned in the dressing-room on a few occasions before and after we won our first county title in 2003.

We did get to a county final in 1995, but Sarsfields were going really well at the time and they beat us by five points. We always felt we would get back to another final, but with the nature of the Galway championship and the quality of teams competing, it took us eight years to get there. A number of lads who played in 1995 had moved on at that stage, but we were very lucky to have county championship winning minor teams in 1998 and '99 – that provided seven or eight players to the senior set up within three or four years.

Those young lads coming through our underage structure including the Smith's, Lynch's, Hayes', my brother Ivan, Aidan O'Donnell and others, probably sustained us for the next 10-to-12 years. A lot of clubs lose players around the 18-20 age mark, but we were lucky in Portumna that they all continued to hurl and progress.

I was a minor with Galway for three years.

In 1992 I was a sub when we won the All-Ireland, in '93 some people said we had the best team of the three years but we lost the final to Kilkenny, and we won it again in '94 against Cork. The following year I was training with the Galway under-21s and seniors.

By the time it came to 2003, when our own crop of minors had come through to the Portumna senior team, I was excited about the energy and enthusiasm they were bringing to the team even though I had been hurling for 10 seasons with the club at that stage. We got back into a county final in 2003 and this time we were successful, winning our first ever senior title against Loughrea.

It was just reward and a dream come true for some of the older lads who were still playing from the 1995 team. That Portumna team contested seven county finals in-a-row from 2003 to '09, winning on five occasions which was a great return in a very competitive championship.

After winning the county final in 2003 we had serious celebrations because it was all new to the people of Portumna. We were back in training the first week of January for an All-Ireland club semi-final against Dunloy in Clones. They were a very good team, who had put it up to Birr in the final the year before, but even though we gave it a good shot they beat us by three points on the day.

It was definitely a learning experience for us and maybe the loss was easier to take after the excitement of a first Galway county title had been secured. Dunloy were too strong for us on the day so we can have no complaints. The All-Ireland club series was totally new to us and real learning experience at the time.

A simple aspect of club training during the winter was trying to find pitches to train on. Our facilities back then were nowhere near as good as they are now, so we travelled for miles to find floodlit pitches for training in the evenings. Many clubs really facilitated and helped us at that time, and we appreciated that.

Later that year, in 2004, we lost the county final to Athenry, who were still going strong. The late Mike Monaghan had been manager for the minor successes in 1998 and '99 and had coached many of the minor players to progress onto our senior team. Mike managed us to the 2003 county senior final win and subsequently handed the reins over to Jimmy Heverin in 2005, with Sean Treacy in a coaching role.

We were blessed for years in Portumna that we had managers and coaches within our own club that looked after teams voluntarily. We never really had to go looking for 'outside' managers that would have been a cost to the club. Following on from Jimmy, we had Johnny Kelly and my brother Frank in charge of successful All-Ireland winning teams in the years that followed.

All those lads had played senior hurling for Portumna and were there for the right reasons. In Jimmy Heverin's first season in charge we won the 2005 county final in a high scoring encounter with Loughrea, so we were back again at the point of preparing for an All-Ireland club semi-final.

Having lost the All-Ireland semi-final in February 2004 and the county final nine months later, there were question marks over whether we could sustain the level of performance needed to be real contenders once we had gotten out of

Galway. Our opponents in the 2006 semi-final were the defending All Ireland club champions, James Stephens from Kilkenny and in our pre-match analysis of our opponents, we were aware of their half-back line of Jackie Tyrrell, Philly Larkin and Peter Barry, not to mention the threat of Eoin Larkin and Brian McEvoy – and Donncha Cody in the full-back line was on the Kilkenny panel at the time as well.

We knew it was going to be a big task to try to stop them and at the time I don't recall any great expectation from outside our squad that we would cause an upset. The fact that the game was in Thurles was a help to us.

We looked at it in similar terms to the dimensions of Pearse Stadium and the fact that we were a young team meant we really relished the wide open pitch and just wanted to get out there and hurl. We felt as well that we had the players up front that could do the damage if the game was open.

What was really pleasing about how the game turned out for me was the link-up play within the whole team and while there were games where we scored more goals, to me it was a complete performance that I always knew was in Portumna. I've played against plenty of Kilkenny teams in the past and even though you feel you are doing well and on top, the next thing you look up at the scoreboard and they are two points up and you are saying to yourself… *How the hell did that happen?*

It was a bit like that after 20 minutes against James Stephens.

We felt we were doing a lot of the hurling, but just weren't putting any daylight between the two teams, but then the first goal arrived.

The two goals we got that day were massive scores, but the first goal was the product of great build-up play. Eoin Lynch played a cross-field ball to Davy, who could have shot himself, but he fed it back inside to Damien who roofed it to the net like he did so often in his career. It was a goal that was built on composure and I felt this now was a new, fresh Portumna team, who demonstrated it again in the second-half when Damien linked up with his brother Niall, who passed it to Joe and he finished it to the net.

There was no hint of luck about them, just really well created goal opportunities that were dispatched ruthlessly.

The value of goals in big championship games cannot be overstated. After we got the first goal that day, you could sense that James Stephens knew they needed a lift before half-time to balance the books and get back in the game. Their No.

12 Gary Whelan let rip with a rasper of a shot, but Ivan brought off a terrific save in goal that was probably one of the defining moments of the game.

It meant we went in at half-time six points up, but more importantly it took away the opportunity for James Stephens to say that they were only three down after hardly doing any of the hurling. Of course every moment is important in a game, but some moments are more important than others and that save was definitely one.

My own role that day was at corner-back, having moved back from centre-back where I played in 2003 when we won our first county final. I was No. 4 with the county for most of that period and I ended up playing the majority of the remainder of my career in the same position.

We weren't overly focusing on anyone on the James Stephens' forward line for me or others to pick up, it was more a case of picking up whoever came into your space on the pitch. When Philly Larkin got sent off late on, I ended up as a sweeper for the last 10 minutes. They needed a few goals at that late stage, and we were probably home and hosed with a few minutes to go.

You try your best in those last few minutes to stay focused and not let your mind wander, but we were far enough in front it was hard not to start thinking about qualifying for an All-Ireland final which was really satisfying. Everybody takes different things from that game, but for me it was the coming of age of that Portumna team when we proved that we could compete at this level.

For me also, I felt that every line on the field performed so well for Portumna that day and I think that game gave us the confidence to go on and do what we did over the next 10 years.

The All-Ireland club final that followed on St Patrick's Day was a bitterly cold day against Newtownshandrum, a side that had been All-Ireland champions two years previously.

You always look for something to motivate you in the run up to a big game and we found it in the newspapers the week of the match.

We had played them in a challenge game in Cork a few months earlier and there was little expectation that we would be meeting in the All-Ireland final. The challenge game was very physical, and their manager made reference to it in the build-up to the final by suggesting we couldn't cope when the going got tough.

That was all we needed to get us going and focus our minds firmly on the final.

We went out and won our first All-Ireland club final by 2-8 to 1-6.

That victory kicked off a glorious period in the club's history and out of the six county championships we won, we ended up winning four All-Ireland titles, which is a fantastic return considering the teams that we came up against. I was just blessed to be around when that group of players came along, because so many lads in the past never had the opportunity to go to Croke Park and pull on the Portumna jersey.

When I look back at our time, we probably won as much as we could have won. Maybe there were some matches that could have gone either way, but these things tend to balance out over a person's career. It's comforting to know that we gave it our all when we had the opportunity.

It was a fantastic period in our club's history and will be in the record books forever.

I often get asked the question, 'Have you any regrets?' with regards to my county career, especially after Joe and the Galway lads won the All-Ireland in 2017. I'm a fairly practical person in life and in sport, so I have no problem saying that if we were good enough to win it when I was playing, we would have done so.

We did come up against some great teams, like the Cork side that had their time and Kilkenny, who were at their height when I was playing. I don't think we will ever see a team like that Kilkenny team again. There are lots of reasons why you don't win, but were we really good enough?

Probably not.

I was so delighted to see Galway win the All-Ireland in 2017 because it brought a massive sense of pride, huge satisfaction and enjoyment and a sigh of relief after 29 years of waiting. I looked at those lads winning the All-Ireland and felt they were the same as myself and many other hurlers down through the years in Galway, giving it everything and putting social lives and family lives on hold.

Hurling was their number one priority for the years leading up to that victory and when they won, it was a great achievement for themselves, their families, their clubs and for the whole county. As a side note, it also stopped a few of the 'naysayers' and people who knock Galway players and Galway hurling from mouthing off, at least for a few months.

Ideally, I feel if you could win an All-Ireland title every four or five years it would be great for the county and keep everyone going. I was there for my time and it didn't work out for me, so I move on and pass the jersey to the next man, and that's just the way it is.

For me, I have no regrets at all.

99

ALAN KERINS

CLARINBRIDGE 3-22, DE LA SALLE 1-27 (AET)
All-Ireland Club SHC Semi-Final
Semple Stadium, Thurles
FEBRUARY 20, 2011

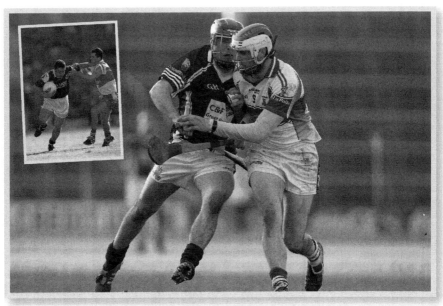

Winning for Clarinbridge in an epic in 2011 lives with Alan Kerins' dual career with Galway as a shining memory

★ **CLARINBRIDGE:** L Donoghue; C Forde, B Burke, P Callanan; J Cannon, D Forde (0-1), M Donoghue; B Daly (0-1), E Murphy (1-0); S Burke (0-1), M Kerins (2-5), S Forde (0-1); E Forde (0-5), **A Kerins (0-6)**, P Coen (0-2). Sub: A Armstrong for S Forde.

★ **DE LA SALLE:** A. S Brenner; D Russell, I Flynn, M Doherty; B Phelan (0-3), K Moran (0-1), S Daniels; C Watt, D Twomey (0-2); P Nevin (0-1), D Greene, J Mullane (0-11); J Keane (0-2), E Barrett, J Dillon (0-3). Subs: E Madigan (1-3) for Watt, L Hayes (0-1) for Twomey, Twomey for Dillon.

THE ACTION

IN ONE OF the most exhilarating club championship games of all time, Galway champions Clarinbridge were the team left standing after a last-gasp goal by Eanna Murphy at the end of extra-time proved the knock-out blow for a shell shocked De la Salle.

The Waterford and Munster champions looked certainties to make it through to their second All-Ireland club final in three years when they led by three points coming up to the end of normal time – and by two deep into stoppage time at the end of extra-time – but on each occasion Clarinbridge rescued their hopes with crucial goals.

Fine points from brothers Mark and Alan Kerins, and David and Eoin Forde, had given Clarinbridge a 0-11 to 0-8 lead at half-time in normal time, but the Galway men needed a late goal from a Mark Kerins' free to level the match at 1-18 to 0-21. Even then there was time for Alan Kerins to point what looked like the winner, but Bryan Phelan salvaged extra-time for De la Salle with the last act of a breathless encounter.

With the floodlights on for extra-time, Clarinbridge struck first with Mark Kerins' second goal of the game but that was cancelled out by sub Eoghan Madigan, who rebounded to the net after John Mullane was denied by Liam Donoghue. The sides were still level four minutes from the end of extra-time when Mullane and Lee Hayes pointed to put De la Salle two up, but in one final twist, Alan Kerins' shot at goal deflected in the air and Eanna Murphy wrote his name into Clarinbridge folklore with a goal to break the Waterford side's hearts.

★★★★★

66

GROWING UP IN Clarinbridge in the 1980s and early 90s, we knew nothing else except hurling. My dad Monty was captain of the Ardrahan team that won the Galway senior championship in 1978 after they beat Ballinderreen after extra-time in a replay.

Coincidentally, the only other time a Galway senior championship was won by a team after extra-time in a replay was in 2010 when Clarinbridge defeated Loughrea.

He won three championships in all and we grew up listening to stories about the great Ardrahan team of the 1970s. Monty built the house in Clarinbridge then after he got married to Anne Broderick from Kilbeacanty. We went to National School in Killeeneen, where we were blessed to have Michael Browne as a teacher and mentor.

He went on to become a selector with Clare and won county titles with Crusheen and Tulla, but he set up a real nursery in Killeeneen and coached us brilliantly, especially from six to eight years of age, which modern research shows is the time to engrain the skills of a technically difficult game to learn.

When Galway won the 1992 All-Ireland minor title, there were five Clarinbridge lads involved and four of them came from Killeeneen National School. A lot of the club team that ended up winning an All-Ireland title nearly two decades later also came from that school. We had the Spellmans, Coens, Donoghues, Kennedys and many others, and we won everything from schools titles, under-12s, under-14s, two under-16s, minor, under-21, intermediate and eventually senior with that generation of players. In the space of 17 years we went from being intermediate to All-Ireland senior champions, thanks to the production line of Killeeneen and the subsequent work of Stephen Coen and dad.

After winning the intermediate in 1994, we got to the Galway senior championship semi-final in 1996 against Athenry, but lost after extra-time in a replay. They went on to win the All-Ireland and the following year we lost in the final to Sarsfields.

We never performed that day and faded away for the following three years until John McIntyre came in and injected a new energy into the club. We got on a roll in 2001 and ended up winning our first title by a point against Athenry in

Duggan Park.

It was a huge mental barrier to break and, as it turned out, came at the end of a crazy time in my life where I had just played in both All-Ireland football and hurling finals with Galway in the space of a few weeks.

My football career started in first year in St Mary's College under Liam Sammon but never progressed past that because I was concentrating on hurling with the Galway under-14s. I actually played a lot more soccer than Gaelic football when I was younger and represented the Galway Town team in the Oscar Traynor Cup for two years in the late 1990s.

I was even invited in by Galway United for a trial but I was studying in Dublin at the time and didn't fancy the journey down, so I didn't bother.

That is something I really regret because it would have been nice to say I played at least one season with them. After a year in the University of Limerick, I was offered physiotherapy and transferred to Trinity College. The hurling team was quite poor there, so in the winter of 1999 I started football training with the three Cavan lads I was living with to keep fit.

I really started to enjoy the football, so they put me in corner-back as a man marker and at one stage I marked Derek Savage in a 'Colours' game and did well on him. In the summer of 2000, I made enquiries to a few football clubs in Galway about how to go about joining because there was no team in Clarinbridge.

Salthill-Knocknacarra were the only ones to come back and I ended up playing a few intermediate league games for them after we had lost the All-Ireland hurling semi-final to Kilkenny in 2000. At the end of the year I was made captain of the Sigerson team in Trinity and we got to a quarter-final in early 2001, which was a big achievement for us, but the competition was postponed because of the outbreak of Foot and Mouth disease and played off over a number of weekends.

John O'Mahony must have been made aware of me playing at this stage because after Galway lost to Mayo in the National League final at the end of April, there was three weeks to the opening round of the Connacht championship against Leitrim and I got a call from Salthill to say I had better play in the senior football league game against Annaghdown on the following Friday night.

I hadn't intended playing because Clarinbridge were down to play Turloughmore on the Bank Holiday Monday in the first round of the senior hurling championship, but I was told that O'Mahony wanted to have a look at me. Needless to say, John McIntyre wasn't too impressed when I told him, but I ended up kicking 0-4 from centre-forward for Salthill in that game and afterwards the football board chairman Pat Egan came to the dressing-rooms and said the Galway footballers were playing Westmeath in a challenge on Sunday in Athlone and John O'Mahony wanted me there.

As if playing on Friday was bad enough, now I had to tell McIntyre I was playing football on Sunday as well! I will never forget walking into the dressing-room in Athlone. I was mortified.

These lads were All-Ireland champions in 1998 and had lost the final the year before, and I'm sure they were saying to themselves... *Where the hell does this lad think he is going with his gear bag?* I played wing forward and kicked a couple of points against Westmeath and after the game O'Mahony asked me to stay down and train Tuesday and Thursday night, and play another trial game on Saturday.

He said he would let me know where I stood then.

That was fine, except I was doing my final exams for physiotherapy in Trinity the day after the Leitrim championship game which was now two weeks away.

The Tuesday after the trial game I was named in the Galway team to play Leitrim and there was war. Michael and John Donnellan pulled out of the panel as a result and I felt really bad because even though it was John O'Mahony's call, in my eyes I was responsible for one of the greatest players of all time not being part of the Galway football team.

I never felt as nervous in my life before a match than that day in Tuam. In my head everyone was there to see this hurler trying to play football, but thankfully I did okay and kicked two points as we won easily. That match started at two o'clock, then I had to head to Athenry to play a senior hurling match against Liam Mellows at 6pm – and I got the 5am train on Monday morning to Dublin to sit my final exams.

Talk about a crazy couple of weeks!

In 1994 I was goalie on the All-Ireland winning minor team, two years later I was outfield when we won the under-21 final against Wexford, and the following year I was involved with the Galway senior hurling panel for the first time.

We lost that year in the All-Ireland quarter-final to Kilkenny and lost to Waterford, Clare and Kilkenny again over the next three years before we made the breakthrough by getting to the final in 2001 against Tipperary.

After the Leitrim game for the footballers, the Donnellans had returned to the football panel but we lost to Roscommon in Tuam and then we ended up going on a tour of Ireland in the back door qualifiers, which ultimately led us to the All-Ireland final against Meath. It was hard to believe that just 11 months after joining a football club for the first time, here I was getting ready for an All-Ireland football final with Galway!

There was a lot of pressure from the hurling side as well to concentrate on their championship preparations, and rightly so, but John O'Mahony was very accommodating with me and knew I didn't have to do the physical training because I never missed a training session with the hurlers. We were robbed in the 2001 hurling final and I felt sorry for Noel Lane, who was a very professional manager and put great systems in place, but didn't get the luck he deserved. Two weeks later I ended up winning an All-Ireland senior football medal as we beat Meath by nine points.

Our first cut at winning an All-Ireland club title with Clarinbridge came in early 2002 when we beat Ballygunner from Waterford in a cracking semi-final, but with Croke Park being redeveloped, the final against Birr was in Thurles.

I had pneumonia going into that game and we never really got going as Birr beat us 2-10 to 1-5. It was probably a combination of us not performing and Birr being a serious team. For the next nine years we slipped off the pace in Galway, as Athenry and then Portumna took over.

We just weren't demanding high enough standards of ourselves and it wasn't until Micheál Donoghue took over in 2009 that things began to change again for the better. In between, I finished up playing football with Galway in 2004 and won an All-Ireland club football medal with Salthill-Knocknacarra in 2006 when we beat St Gall's in the final, but I can't remember a thing about that game because I suffered concussion after about 20 minutes and was taken off at half-time.

We had a great management team in Salthill, with Eoin O'Donnellan and Mark Butler, and we went on a great run after winning the Galway championship as we beat Crossmolina, St Brigid's and Kilmacud Crokes en route to the final.

Michael Donnellan had transferred to Salthill the year before as well, so he made a huge difference.

2005 was also the year that I first went as a volunteer physiotherapist to Zambia, having spoken to Fr Dan Joe Mahony in Blanchardstown, who I knew through college. People often ask me why did I first go to Africa?

I go back to the time I was watching *Live Aid* in 1984 and as I saw the emaciated children from Ethiopia on the news, it left a lasting impression on me. Around that time as well my dad backed himself to win the Captain's Prize in Gort in 1984 and he donated every penny of his substantial winnings to *Live Aid*.

That's why I always say never underestimate the power of your positive or negative reactions on children, because it might be 30 years later that it triggers an action, as in my case. That message was reinforced in National School when Michael Browne would take us carol singing for Goal at Christmas, and Ronan Scully would come into the school and talk to us about the work that the charity was doing in Africa.

My first experience in Zambia was seeing queues of people outside Sister Cathy's door looking for food, and it proved a life changing experience. The poverty over there was unbelievable and I couldn't help thinking that just because they were unlucky to have been born into those circumstances, the best they could hope for in life was to just survive.

If anything, my first trip to Africa made me try to enjoy my hurling even more when I returned as I had a different perspective.

Sister Cathy told me she needed €5,000 to sink a well in order to provide water, so I organised a couple of fundraisers and the money started to roll in. It was the height of the Celtic Tiger and I remember Joe Connolly, Frank Fahy, Noel Grealish and a large group of people doing a skydive up in Edenderry for one of the fundraisers.

Then by pure chance, the photographer Damien Eagers, who had been on the same trip to Zambia, sent me some stunning photographs he had taken of me putting up some blocks and holding some of the sick children. We made a brochure which had a huge impact and before we knew it, five grand became €100,000. I was awarded a Rehab People of the Year Award in Dublin and a Galway Person of the Year Award, and after that the credibility and awareness of our work went through the roof.

TV3 commissioned a documentary then which followed me from the end of the 2005 championship until I went back to Zambia in 2006 and it aired in December of that year. DHKN helped me manage the funds coming in and we set up a board of directors, and I ended up leaving physiotherapy at the end of the year to focus on the charity work full-time because I simply couldn't keep everything going, as well as hurling and football.

After Micheál Donoghue took over as Clarinbridge manager in 2009 we really upped our game. Noel Burke and Tom Helebert were with him and the whole set up was top class.

We were building up a head of steam again, when we lost out to Mullagh in the quarter-finals. The following year, we made a really slow start to the championship as we lost to Portumna and Kinvara in the group stages, but we hammered Killimordaly, and in the very last game we drew with Beagh and qualified for the preliminary quarter-finals on score difference because three teams got out of the group.

Whatever happened over the summer, things clicked into place.

We beat Tommy Larkins in the preliminary quarter-finals and that was when their manager Cyril Farrell came into the dressing-room afterwards to congratulate us and told us we would win the All-Ireland. All the lads started laughing.

We thought he was daft, but he obviously saw something that day and how right he would prove to be six months later. We beat St Thomas' and Tynagh-Abbey-Duniry to get to the county final and then showed great resilience to come from four points down with a couple of minutes to go to force extra-time with Loughrea in a replay – and then beat them in extra-time.

Early in the New Year we were getting ready for the All-Ireland club semi-final against De la Salle when my brother Mark had to go into hospital with a virus. He was there for the week leading up to the game and was a major doubt.

The Novena was on around the same time so I remember saying one or two prayers that he would be alright! Mark was our free-taker, our playmaker and a real leader, so he would have been a huge loss. Thankfully, he recovered sufficiently to be able to play and his performance against De La Salle was unbelievable.

We were fairly confident going into that game but started slowly and they went four points ahead early on. We settled into the game and scored the next six points, before they came back at us to level. That was the start of the topsy-turvy nature of the game.

We led 0-11 to 0-8 at half-time and I really started to come into the game after the break, scoring 0-4 from play and really enjoying being brought out to midfield. We went four points up early in the second-half but then they came back and scored six points in-a-row, before Mark fired over a couple of frees to level the game again with around eight minutes to go. The pace of the game was unreal throughout and there was no let-up. De la Salle came again and Mullane was really driving them on, so with time almost up they led 0-20 to 0-17. In the last minute, Eoin Forde was pulled down outside the '21' and I knew Mark would have to score a goal or we were gone. In fairness to him, he roofed it into the net and straight from the puck-out, I won the break and put it over for what I thought was the winning point.

The next thing I knew, they had a free from way out the field which Brian Phelan drove over to force extra-time.

We went ahead again at the start of extra-time when Mark blasted home a penalty after Barry Daly was fouled, but they went straight down the field and got a goal in the very next attack. We were a point down at half-time in extra-time and I played a ball out to Paul Coen, who scored a great point to draw us level with only a couple of minutes left.

They got a couple of frees after that and it looked like the game was gone from us when, deep into stoppage time, the most famous goal in Clarinbridge history arrived.

I watched it back again recently and if Mullane or Phelan just looked up, they had the option of passing it short to a spare man instead of lashing it up the field to Jamie Cannon.

I remember Brian Phelan jumping in the air because he thought the game was over.

So many small things made such a difference in the next few seconds. Michael Donoghue got a little flick and when I got the ball I knew I had no option but to go for goal. I decided to let fly with a top-spin shot and hope for the best; the ball spun up in the air off Ian Flynn's hurl and Eanna Murphy ran in to bat the ball into the net.

Even then, when you watch it back on YouTube, keep an eye on all the Clarinbridge lads sprinting back to defend the next ball.

We were just so tuned in and it was all down to coaching and repetition.

The final whistle was the cue for both elation for us and heart-break for them. I had a pint in the Ragg later that evening with Mark and David Forde and a few others. We were absolutely shattered and I turned to the lads and asked, 'Did that match actually happen?'

I'm involved with Westmeath hurlers now and the De La Salle manager in 2011 Michael Ryan was manager there for a few years and I still meet him regularly. The good thing about the aftermath of that game was Micheál Donoghue rang him the next day to commiserate with him and tell him what a privilege it was to be involved in a game like it.

The bottom line was we robbed them twice.

I believe in fate and there is no doubt it was meant to be. We went on to play our best ever half of hurling in the second-half of the club final that year against O'Loughlin Gaels when we came from five points down in the first-half to eventually win by 12. We were always told to concentrate on the next ball and keep driving on, but I had suffered so many disappointments on big days in Croke Park, that when I saw the clock go to 58 minutes, I allowed myself a few seconds to take it all in and enjoy it because I knew in all probability I wouldn't be back.

It was the nicest two or three minutes of my career.

I played on with Clarinbridge for another couple of seasons, but the months after we won the All-Ireland championship left a sour taste when we were forced to play for seven weeks in-a-row before we lost the county final to Gort by two points.

In 2012, which was my final year, we got dragged into the relegation play-offs but thankfully they ended up not being played so we were safe for another year. I won another county football championship with Salthill in 2012 and packed in the football the following season after I got married to Ciara in December.

Ciara is a sister of the Galway footballer Finian Hanley, and our first born child Ruadhán arrived in 2015, but we soon realised something wasn't right and we ended up in Temple Street Hospital for three months, and then two months in Manchester, where he had life-saving surgery.

Ruadhán was diagnosed with a rare form of hyperinsulism, which affects one in 50,000 children. It meant he had dangerous levels of insulin in his body, but thankfully he made a full recovery and is flying it.

We have two more children now, Ben and baby Fiadh, who arrived in 2020. With all that was going on, I decided to merge the charity with Self Help Africa in 2015 and they have taken on all our projects and taken it to a whole new level.

I do a small bit with the GPA now and run my own company called The Inner Winner Institute where I work with company leadership teams. I still find myself referring back to the De La Salle game from time to time.

It was the most enjoyable game I ever played, because of the drama, the fact we won, the fact that I did well and the fact that Mark finally got his All-Ireland medal.

But most of all, it was one game that brought so much joy to others.

FERGAL MOORE

GALWAY 2-21, KILKENNY 2-11
Leinster SHC Final
Croke Park
JULY 8, 2012

Fergal Moore lifts the Bob O'Keeffe Cup after Galway's massive Leinster final win over Kilkenny

★ **GALWAY:** J Skehill; D Collins (0-1), K Hynes, **F Moore**; N Donoghue, T Óg Regan, J Coen; I Tannian, A Smith; D Burke (1-2), N Burke (0-2), C Donnellan (0-5); C Cooney, J Canning (1-10), D Hayes (0-1). Subs: J Glynn for C Cooney, J Regan for Tannian, T Haran for N Burke, J Cooney for Donnellan.

★ **KILKENNY:** D Herity; P Murphy, N Hickey, J Tyrrell; T Walsh, B Hogan, R Doyle; C Buckley, P Hogan; H Shefflin (1-8), TJ Reid, E Larkin; C Fennelly, R Power (0-2), R Hogan 1-0). Subs: A Fogarty for Fennelly, M Rice (0-1) for P Hogan, M Ruth for Reid.

THE ACTION

GALWAY PRODUCED A first-half master class in Croke Park to completely dominate reigning champions Kilkenny and win the Leinster Championship title for the first time. Since Galway joined the province in 2009, Kilkenny have been the dominant force and the Cats were going in search of their eighth Leinster title in-a-row when they ran into a side that finally came of age with a performance of staggering intensity.

Just four minutes in, full-forward Joe Canning had the ball in the Kilkenny net after Niall Burke had opened the scoring. Burke, Canning and wing back David Collins added points to leave Galway 1-6 to 0-0 ahead after 18 minutes, and when David Burke buried a brilliant shot five minutes later it looked like game over.

Cyril Donnellan and Burke again kept the scoreboard moving for Galway as a shell-shocked Kilkenny trailed 2-11 to 0-1 after half an hour, though by half-time a couple of Henry Shefflin frees had the gap back to 2-12 to 0-4.

Nine minutes after the break, Shefflin goaled to breathe new life into the Kilkenny comeback, but there was no stopping Galway, and Joe Canning in particular, as the Portumna man ended up with a personal tally of 1-10. The game was up for Kilkenny long before the end as Anthony Cunningham's men defended like demons and had 10 points to spare by the time referee James McGrath called time on a truly memorable game. Fergal Moore thus became the first Galway player to be presented with the Bob O'Keeffe Cup as the Tribesmen qualified for a first All-Ireland semi-final in seven years.

★ ★ ★ ★ ★

"

I'M THE YOUNGEST of five in our house and my other brothers and sister all played hurling and football growing up. I have vague memories of going to Tuam Stadium to see my older brother Cathal playing with the Galway minor footballers in 1993. Liam Moffatt and Ciaran McDonald were playing underage with Mayo around that time, while Shay Walsh and John Concannon were the big names with Galway.

I played football in St Mary's College until I was 18, mostly because the matches were down in Mayo and Sligo, so it meant getting a full day off school!

I wasn't a great footballer. I was a bit of a 'stopper' but I enjoyed it and being coached by Liam Sammon was a real pleasure. I found there wasn't as much pressure and expectation on you playing football when you were a hurler.

I was lucky enough to have been involved with Galway under-14 and under-16 hurling squads during my time in school and I was on the under-16 team that won the Nenagh Co-Op Tournament when Kevin Brady was our captain. That carried on to minor when John Hardiman was our manager and we won two All-Ireland titles in-a-row in 1999 and 2000.

It was a really brilliant set up with a great management team that also included John Moylan, Mike Murray and Mike Bodkin, and we had a great bunch of players. I wasn't involved as much the second year because I picked up a bad toe injury which robbed me of a summer, but I have two All-Ireland minor medals and had two trips to Croke Park out of it. I look back on those years with very fond memories.

Those lads had a big bearing on how I turned out as a hurler.

John Hardiman was a very progressive young coach who was very intense and very driven in those years as minor manager and before that, Pat Monaghan was in charge of the under-16 team and he was a similar personality who was very detail-orientated and big into the emotional and psychological side of things.

Hardiman was also the first coach I came across who had position specific training and was very tuned in to tactics and team set ups.

The following few years at under-21 level were not as kind and we took a couple of hidings in finals, including one against the Limerick three in-a-row team in 2002. I was captain the following year, which was my final year playing under-21 and we got a good beating from Kilkenny. They had won the senior final the week before and came to Thurles with Tommy Walsh, Aidan Fogarty, Jackie Tyrrell and half the senior team, and beat us by seven points. The under-21 experience wasn't great; John Hardiman had followed us up from minor but it was a different team and we came across a couple of really good sides.

When it comes to being made captain of your county, it really comes down to the management team as regards what they demand of you, but my first experience of being captain was easy. You weren't picked for making a speech, you were picked for what you could do on the field and at training.

That's how I always preferred to lead – let other lads do the talking.

In fairness to John Hardiman and his set up, there wasn't any great need for talking because he had everything pristine and ready to go. I had been involved with the senior panel in 2003 as well but didn't get my first start until the National League the following February against Dublin in Parnell Park.

It was a pretty big deal for me because I had been watching Cathal playing for the previous few years and he was still on the panel, so it was great to train with him for a while. Later on in the summer of 2004, we got an awful hiding from Kilkenny in Thurles in the championship qualifiers. They were a juggernaut that day and we weren't at the races.

In 2005, I was commuting from work in Dublin a few times every week for training and was on and off the team. I wasn't happy with my form and I wasn't happy with how I was being treated so in that instance you have two choices, you can stay and be unhappy and pull the thing down from within, or you can do the right thing and step away if you are not adding anything to a set up.

I chose to step away.

As it turned out, I was transferred from Dublin to Galway with my job as a physio that summer, but I had left the panel and had no regrets.

I got a couple of holidays away that I probably wouldn't have had otherwise and as it happened the senior lads did brilliant and qualified for the All-Ireland final. Mattie Murphy was the minor manager that year and he brought me in as the team physio because I had my degree at that stage.

Frannie Forde was the coach and there were great characters like Mike Haverty, Mike Flanagan and a few other lads involved. Ian O'Connor was the doctor and I was very grateful to Mattie for getting me involved. When the club championship takes a hiatus in the summer, you are at a loose end and as it turned out the minors won the All-Ireland that year and I had a front row view.

I had no regrets seeing the senior lads running out on the field to play Cork afterwards. When you make a big decision like pulling out of a panel you have all that weighed up in your head and you understand that those Galway lads are talented and have the potential to go on and do it. But you have to do what is right for yourself and the squad.

There was the euphoria of the minor dressing-room, but then I immediately became a fan and I couldn't wait for the senior match to start and for Galway to do well.

The lads did really well to get as far as they did and I don't think that Cork team were going to be beaten by anyone that year – they showed how good they were by winning back-to-back titles.

Ger Loughnane took over from Conor Hayes as Galway manager for the 2007 season and I was called back into the squad. I was well rested at that stage and very hungry to get back in. I have to say I thoroughly enjoyed his stewardship and the way he thought about the game.

He had good lads with him like Sean Treacy and Michael Murray from Sarsfields, who was part of those minor and under-21 management teams and knew how to get the best out of me. I was injured a fair bit though and just couldn't take the volume of training back then.

I went off injured against Kilkenny the first year Ger was there and in the second year, a hamstring injury hampered me for the whole summer.

It was only then I realised that my hamstring injuries always seemed to coincide with the club championship starting and I could be training five, six or seven nights a week.

We made massive strides with Ger, especially in that first year, and maybe things went back a small bit in the second year before John McIntyre took over. He brought great professionalism to the role and got John Hardiman and Joe Connolly involved; he brought in Dan Murphy, Tex Callaghan and all of these characters that still endure around Galway hurling today.

John definitely brought things on another step but to win things, everything needs to be right at the right time and while we had a lot of things right, the timing was probably just not there and we hadn't enough players at the stage of their development that was required. We had some qualifier wins but as regards winning a medal in the Leinster or All-Ireland championship, we were close but not quite good enough.

Then in 2010, I got a bad ankle injury in a league game against Dublin in Pearse Stadium and had to get reconstructive surgery. The whole year was written off as a result and after I got back in 2011 we lost to Waterford by 10 points in the All-Ireland quarter-final, and there was another change of manager.

The new man was Anthony Cunningham.

We had a good bit of training done before I was made captain for the year in 2012. Anthony had Tom Helebert and Mattie Kenny with him as selectors, and Kevin Craddock was an outstanding strength and conditioning coach and nutritionist who was also with Connacht rugby at the time. The medical team was excellent as well so we had a serious backroom team in place.

The whole thing felt like it had moved to another level and was all about sharpness and mobility, and was very much match specific.

Still, in comparison to other counties, we wouldn't score too well when it came to facilities and even now, it's way past time Galway had their own Hurling Centre of Excellence. The management set up a gym in a warehouse in Clarinbridge and the first training session we did was in Dangan, followed by a presentation in NUIG.

Anthony was true to his word and everything the management said they would do, they did. One or two of the usual suspects skipped a few training sessions early on when it got a bit tough, but when the rule came in that if you missed a session you had to make it up on your own with a member of management, the attitude changed.

We had a bit of a mixed bag during the league that year and came out the wrong side of a lot of tight games, but the game we learned the most from was on April 1 when we went down to Nowlan Park and got an all-merciful trouncing from Kilkenny. For the older dogs, like myself, it was just another scar but for the younger lads who might have beaten Kilkenny at underage level, it was a real wake-up call.

We eventually beat Dublin in a relegation play-off replay to stay up and we had to work a very good score in the drawn match to earn a replay, which we won well. That set us up nicely for the first game in the Leinster championship against Westmeath in Mullingar, a tricky fixture at the best of times, but on a tight pitch and a big home crowd, it was set up for an ambush.

We had struggled against Westmeath a couple of times in the past, but in 2012 we felt fitter and more in control, so even though they scored 4-12, we never felt like we were in danger and won in the end by 10 points. The same could be said about the Offaly game in the semi-final and it showed that when we were good, we were very good.

But when we switched off, we got punished. It definitely helped to iron out a few things before the provincial final against Kilkenny.

One of the things Anthony had said to us right from start was that we would win Leinster and every time the management team spoke to us, that was the target.

Yet the final that day was more about having another crack at Kilkenny, who were league, Leinster and All-Ireland champions and had given us a trimming a few weeks previously so it was all about measuring us against the best team in the country at that time.

The Thursday before the final we did a bit of hurling at training in Athenry and my dad Pat was there to watch us. I would value his opinion on hurling matters the most, but he saw something that night in the 15 a-side game that made him back Galway to win.

He never bets on GAA matches, but after the final on the Sunday he told me what he had done. I never had that luxury of thinking about winning.

You just have to be so focused when you play Kilkenny, if you switch off for a second they will have scored three or four goals. We got the bus to Dublin on the morning of the match and on the way up I could definitely feel in the atmosphere among the lads that a big performance was coming. Lads were talking to each other but there was no messing and everyone seemed totally focused.

From the first minute of that game, everyone did their job.

The middle diamond, in particular, set the tone. Andy Smith and Iarfhlaith Tannian put in a few great hits, Tony Óg was exceptional that day and after a few minutes we started to see things in Kilkenny that you would not normally see, like Henry Shefflin dropping a free short and missing the next one.

The ball was greasy, and I dropped one in the first-half and Richie Hogan took off on a solo run. I turned to run after him but Joe Canning passed me out and took it off him! I knew then we were on our game.

Damien Hayes came out to midfield as part of our tactical plan and in the end Kilkenny put Aidan Fogarty on him to try and curb his influence. To see our forwards tackling the Kilkenny players so well was very satisfying and ultimately it was work rate that overwhelmed them. We were 14 points up at half-time but the score was never mentioned at the break.

It was just the type of set up we had in charge of us.

They were very driven and wanted us to continue what we were doing. We knew that Kilkenny would come back at some point and have a purple patch, but we always seemed to have a leader who was able to wrestle back the momentum when we needed it most. Cyril Donnellan had a great game that day, Joe kept knocking over the frees and David Burke came up with a few great points to add to his brilliant goal in the first-half.

When you were hurling as long as I had been, and when you had been on the wrong end of the beatings from Kilkenny that I had been, you never felt that the game was won.

The first time that I looked up at the scoreboard was in the final minute as the clock was about to hit 70 minutes, and we were nine points up.

I thought to myself, even for Kilkenny, coming back from this was unlikely. I barely got to celebrate after the final whistle as a Croke Park steward was hauling me off the pitch to go up and get the cup. Isn't it a great complaint to have though because there was nobody hauling the losing captain anywhere.

I had a few seconds to celebrate with the Galway backs that were around me and I shook hands with a few of the Kilkenny boys, who are men to their core and took their beating well, but I knew that we would be meeting them again. I think we earned a bit of respect that day as well and earned it the hard way.

I am a firm believer that you never tempt fate so the acceptance speech was totally off the cuff. I didn't think that it was going to help my performance in any way to have a speech written out for the aftermath of a match whose result had not been determined.

The feeling of being handed over a cup in Croke Park is amazing, but for it to be the first time that we had won a Leinster title was a sweet feeling and something that we only really appreciated much later. I was aware that we had made a bit of history that day so I felt it was very important to thank the people who had helped get us to that point, because you may not get that opportunity again.

As it turned out, I didn't. I was talking about people like Pat McDonagh, our sponsor, who has given so much to Galway hurling and needed to be acknowledged now that we had finally won something. Back in the dressing-room there was euphoria, but nothing wild either because we had been told this was going to happen all year.

It was hugely enjoyable that night when we got back to Galway as well, but nobody went bananas because we knew we had to focus on the next challenge, an All-Ireland semi-final. One of the last things I did before I left Croke Park that day was do an interview on the pitch with Marty Morrissey for RTE News and as I came back in, I saw Brian Cody ahead of me in the tunnel.

There was just the two of us.

I had met Brian on an All Stars tour previously and he is a man I have high regard for. I called him back and after he said well done, I told him we would see them later on in the year.

At the end of the year I picked up an All Star award but if you are going to rank awards, the All-Ireland medal is the one we were really after that year. I was also disappointed for Joe because his form should have been rewarded with Hurler of the Year and while a few other Galway lads got All Stars, a few more were unlucky to lose out.

One of the fondest memories of that year and that performance was the level of commitment that each player showed to one other. You always strive in team sport for everyone to sing off the same hymn sheet and while it doesn't always happen, it did that day.

GEARÓID McINERNEY

GALWAY 0-26, WATERFORD 2-17
All Ireland SHC Final
Croke Park
SEPTEMBER 3, 2017

Gearóid McInerney contests against Austin Gleeson in the 2017 All-Ireland final and raises the Liam MacCarthy Cup high

★ **GALWAY:** C Callanan; A Tuohey, Daithí Burke, J Hanbury; P Mannion, **G McInerney**, A Harte; J Coen (0-1), David Burke (0-4); J Cooney (0-2), J Canning (0-9), J Glynn; C Whelan (0-1), C Cooney (0-3), C Mannion (0-2). Subs: N Burke (0-2) for J Glynn, J Flynn (0-2) for Cathal Mannion, S Maloney for David Burke.

★ **WATERFORD:** S O'Keeffe; S Fives, B Coughlan, N Connors; K Bennett (1-0), T de Búrca, Philip Mahony; J Barron (0-2), K Moran (1-1); D Fives, A Gleeson, Pauric Mahony (0-11); S Bennett, M Walsh (0-1), J Dillon. Subs: M Shanahan for S Bennett, B O'Halloran (0-1) for Dillon, T Ryan (0-1) for Walsh, C Dunford for Jamie Barron, P Curran for Kieran Bennett.

THE ACTION

GALWAY'S 29-YEAR wait for an All-Ireland senior hurling title came to an end as they held off the brave challenge of Waterford to emerge victorious by three points. That they managed to do so without scoring a goal is indicative of the huge points tallies that Micheál Donoghue's side had been putting up all year, including the Leinster final win over Wexford and the heart-stopping semi-final victory over Tipperary.

It looked ominous for Waterford early on as Galway's shooting was impeccable. Four shots at goal in the first four minutes yielded four points. Then came the opening goal of the game when Kevin Moran breathed new life into the Waterford challenge with a score that came against the run of play, but Galway never flinched and got the next two points. Despite having nine points on the board inside the first 14 minutes, Galway were pegged back by Waterford's second goal on 22 minutes when a long range effort from Kieran Bennett went all the way to the net to make it 2-4 to 0-10.

With centre-back Gearoid McInerney and midfielder David Burke lording their respective positions, Galway edged in front by 0-14 to 2-7 by half-time, but Pauric O'Mahony landed five points after the restart to put his side in front by one. Galway subs Niall Burke and Jason Flynn made a huge impact on their introduction and both landed two points apiece, while points from Joe Canning, Conor Cooney and Flynn between the 60th and 63rd minutes ultimately gave the Tribesmen the cushion they needed to hold on and deliver an All-Ireland title that the county had craved for nearly three decades.

★★★★★

＂

THERE ARE FIVE of us in the family, me, my older sister Colleen and younger brother Sean, my mother Ita and father Gerry. We were very young when dad was still playing with Galway but you would still know that he had been part of a very special team in the late 1980s.

I've never looked back at a full run of the 1987 or '88 All-Ireland finals, but as I've got older I have definitely studied the way they played the game those days and watched plenty of clips from different games. It was helter-skelter stuff and they really played on the edge, with incredible passion.

I played a lot of different sports when I was young so it wasn't that I was forced to follow in Gerry's footsteps. The first time I can remember winning a cup was with the Oranmore Boys National School. I was probably the youngest on the team in 3rd class when we played in a schools final in Athenry.

That day the referee got the score wrong and the other team were presented with the cup. Somebody had filmed the game so when the powers-that-be looked back on it they realised we had won and so the cup arrived to our school a few days later!

Pat Burke did a lot of work with us in national school at that time, as did Gerry Fahy in the football, while Brendan Bannon was a big influence with the work he did at underage level in Oranmore. Depending on how various teams were going, I would give more time to either the football or hurling.

Mum told me to take up basketball for a while to try and improve my football skills, but I never really took to it. I'm not sure what level I could have got to playing football, but I was definitely one of the stronger players amongst my group of friends growing up. In my club, Oranmore Maree we have a few dual players, but they are becoming less common and in my own situation, it was after minor that I really concentrated on hurling.

Secondary School in Calasanctius College was very enjoyable and there was always a good balance between education and hurling. Tony Keady was very involved with us as a coach and in my final two years, a City Schools amalgamation team was formed to compete in the Connacht Colleges A championship.

Tony would drive us into training in St Enda's in Galway and we had serious craic in the car. Those years were very important in my development as a hurler and the training that Gerry Spellman did with us brought on a lot of lads like John Hanbury, Tadhg Haran and Dean Higgins as well. We had a good team and were very competitive but couldn't seem to be able to get past Gort Community School, who were a machine in their own right, and also had the advantage of being together in school all the time.

After I finished in Calasanctius, I always planned on taking a year out to help in the sports shop that we have in Oranmore and because I have such a huge interest in all sports, it was a job that came natural to me.

In my final year as a minor in 2008 I didn't make the county panel, but a couple of years later I started training with the county intermediate panel. Dad was training the team, with Noel Turley as manager, and I used my time with the intermediates to get some extra training in. I was playing in the forwards that year and ended up coming on as a sub against Kilkenny and scoring a point, even though we were well beaten.

That was 2010 and I played with the intermediates again the following year, before going in with the under-21s under Anthony Cunningham and Mattie Kenny ahead of the 2011 All-Ireland semi-final against Limerick. I especially remember the build up to that semi-final because, even though I was a sub, I was asked to mark Rory Foy in training to try and mimic what Shane Dowling would be doing in the match itself.

Limerick had won a brilliant Munster final after extra-time against Cork a couple of weeks earlier and they would have been fancied to beat Galway, but we scored 0-22 and won by two points. Niall Burke was on fire that day and scored 0-7 from play and we went on to beat Dublin by 10 points in the final.

Despite playing in the forwards when trying to make the under-21 team in 2011, I was very familiar with playing centre-back all my life for both the school and club. Anthony took over the senior team the following year and it was brilliant to watch them win the Leinster championship and go on a serious run.

They were very unlucky to fall just short in the All-Ireland final, but that was the point where I felt that I could make a difference and decided to do a lot more training on my own and push myself as hard as I could. I made my championship debut for the Galway seniors in the Leinster semi-final in 2014 in Tullamore when I came on at wing forward, and we came from 10 points down with seven minutes to go to draw level.

We lost the replay a week later and then fell apart against Tipperary in the qualifiers when we were six points up and ended up losing by nine. In 2015, I felt I had a good league campaign and then in the opening round of the Leinster championship against Dublin, in what was my first big game, I was marking Danny Sutcliffe.

I've never known a player that runs so deep from the half-forward line to get the ball and I struggled that day to know whether to follow him around the pitch or stay back. Nowadays you would be better equipped with information to deal with a situation like that, so it was a real learning curve, but it was a day that didn't go exactly to plan.

We ended up losing the Leinster and All-Ireland finals to Kilkenny that year, so a year that started out so promisingly faded out and I didn't get on for the latter stages of that championship run.

Micheal Donoghue took over in late 2016 and at that stage I had built up a few years of experience, so I felt I had a lot more to give.

I started to nail down a wing back jersey and we soon got a head of steam up after losing again to Kilkenny in the Leinster final. We beat Clare in the quarter-final and then had yet another epic game against Tipperary which went right down to the wire, before we lost out by a point.

Any game that finishes with one point between the sides at the end leaves the losing team thinking about all the small things and moments that might have cost them a score, but when the massive disappointment of losing died down, we soon realised it was an important platform for 2017.

Tipp hammered Kilkenny in the 2016 final, so we knew we were very close.

We always have the All-Ireland final in the back of our minds at the start of any campaign as the place we want to get to, but Micheál, Frannie, Noel and Lucasz always prepared us then for one game at a time – each match the most important game of the year as we approached it. In the Leinster championship we scored two goals in a pretty comfortable first round win over Dublin and it wasn't like we weren't trying to score goals after that, but we came up against a lot of very defensive formations in Offaly and Wexford.

It is hard to score goals against sweeper systems like Wexford used in the

Leinster final, so we found it a lot easier to take our points and remain patient. All the good teams seem to be able to play a number of different ways, so we worked hard in training in replicating the kind of tactics we would come up against and that included combating the sweeper system.

Aidan Harte was probably the most comfortable player we had for that role, but even my own position at centre-back was evolving and I might find myself playing much deeper for periods of a game as I followed the centre-forward wherever he went. Even since 2017 the game is changing and you could have a scenario where the likes of Dublin play with two centre-forwards, but the most important thing is not to get too bogged down with tactics and just play the game in front of you.

After we won the Leinster final in 2017, we were back in another All-Ireland semi-final against Tipperary for the third year in-a-row.

I don't know why, but I was really calm before that game and was totally convinced we would win. They hit us hard at the start and went three points ahead, but we never panicked and got back to within one at half-time.

The second-half was nip and tuck and could have gone either way, but Joe scored a fantastic point to win the game and it was some way to win an All-Ireland semi-final. It probably meant even more to us given what had happened 12 months earlier. The night after we beat Tipperary, we heard that Tony Keady had taken ill and the few days after that were just crazy. We were knocked right back down after the high of winning an All-Ireland semi-final and the first people I thought of were his family.

Tony was in high spirits on the Monday and is it any wonder?

Nobody would have enjoyed a big championship win over Tipperary more than Tony, but when it was confirmed he had died the whole county was rocked. In fairness to Micheál, he handled the situation very well and all the Galway players, who had held Tony in such high regard, did what they could to pay their respects and support Margaret and the children.

In the weeks that followed there was a quiet determination in everyone that we would go out and perform in the final and honour the memory of one of Galway's greatest ever players.

The fact that it was Waterford we would be playing in the All-Ireland final brought me back to the league quarter-final in Pearse Stadium in April when we came back to beat them by three points, a match that had really kicked off our season.

We knew they would be no soft touch and it would be a really difficult game to win, and I don't know was it actually mentioned in the dressing-room but we were aware that Galway had never beaten Waterford in a championship game – and what better place to change that statistic than in an All-Ireland final.

There was a big difference to me personally coming into Croke Park on All-Ireland final day in 2017 knowing I was playing, compared to 2015 when I was a sub. In that 2015 final, the management had spoken to me about coming on to mark either Walter Walsh or Richie Hogan, so that definitely helped in my preparation even though I didn't come on.

Second time around, I had a similar level of concentration on knowing that I would be marking Austin Gleeson. We drove up on the morning of the final, so we all had a good night's sleep in our own beds.

We got in to see the first-half of the minor final but then we went in to tog out and I forgot about the result until after our match when I heard that Galway had won! We started brilliantly in the 2017 final and the boys up front were on fire, but there was a pattern all year of us starting really well and then letting teams back into it, so I knew that Waterford would come back at us at some stage.

We had a fair bit of video analysis done on Waterford and I knew that Gleeson was the man that made them tick. At training before the final I was marking Paul Flaherty and he got a point off me, so for the rest of the training match I got right up close to him and in his face, almost replicating what I would have to do in the final and it seemed to work.

I knew Austin Gleeson liked to take his own score as well, so if I tracked him there was a pretty good chance I might block him or dispossess him.

I ended up marking him for about 90% of the game, but there were one or two instances where he drifted out to wing forward and you have to trust the other lads to do a job in their positions at that point.

We developed a great resilience under Micheál, so when they got a second goal to draw level after 20 minutes – after we had done all the hurling – it didn't knock us back one bit. The fact that we had edged ahead again by a point at half-time gave us great belief that all we had to do was win the second-half and we would be All-Ireland champions.

I knew that Niall Burke had showed great form going into that All-Ireland final and he would be coming on at some stage. The peculiar thing was, I had seen Niall marking Tadhg De Búrca before and he always did well on him.

It was probably that Niall was really strong in the air and he made a little push off his man before the ball came in that gave him a yard of space. Niall would have really fancied coming on that day and he ended up getting two great points and made a huge difference, but he was also out to make a point because he would have felt he should have been starting that final.

All year though we had subs coming on that made a huge difference and Jason Flynn was another example – his two points were crucial as well.

I tend to look at the clock every now and again to see where we are at – it's important to know if you are two points up and the game is getting late that you drop back and protect the 'D' so you don't concede a goal.

The few seconds before the full-time whistle was a really weird feeling.

We had a sideline ball and the crowd were going nuts because the injury time was up and we were about to be crowned All-Ireland champions. Even after the final whistle, I found it hard to switch off from the absolute focus we had during the game to suddenly the whole thing being over.

It took a while for what was happening to sink in.

After the game, the first man that came up to me was Austin Gleeson and he shook my hand and said a few lovely words about Tony to me that meant an awful lot. He was a real sportsman in that moment of disappointment for his team.

I didn't go too crazy celebrating straight away because I was conscious that the Waterford lads were hurting and I didn't think we should be rubbing it in too much after the great battle we had. I went around and shook the hands of quite a few of them. That reaction was very much the mantra of our manager who always said, 'Don't let your highs be too high... or your lows too low'. That is so important in keeping everyone level headed and was a key reason why we got back to the final the following year.

I didn't really know how well I played, or how well people thought I played, because man marking is a job that can often go unnoticed. The first thing I heard about being in contention for Man of the Match was out in the lobby of the hotel that evening when James Skehill said something to me and I shrugged it off as him messing.

Then I got inside for the meal and I found out he was right. Our captain David Burke got the award and deservedly so, but it was nice to hear people make comparisons with my performance at No. 6 and that of Tony's back in 1988 when he was Man of the Match in Galway's last success. I'd be lying if I said I didn't enjoy the accolades that came my way, including the All Star award the following month, but they seem like the kind of thing I will enjoy more in a few years' time after I retire.

The All Stars trip was another great experience and it is important to get to know the lads from other counties that you come up against every year and not just know them in the context of trying to beat them in a game of hurling.

You have to be able to park the game when it's over and move on.

Even at club training, I would often get into scrapes with Niall Burke, but we would be the best of friends afterwards. 2018 was a bit of a nightmare because of the calf injury that I suffered and never quite got right. I probably spent too much time trying to sort that out and neglected other aspects of my game.

2019 was great for Oranmore Maree as we went on a brilliant run in the club championship and became the first Galway side to win the All-Ireland intermediate championship after we beat Charleville in the final in Croke Park. It was also great to get back up to senior in Galway and hopefully we will be there for many years to come.

But, 2019 was a disappointing year for the county and after being knocked out of the championship on score-difference in Leinster, it was very hard to see Micheál step down. He had taken Galway to the next level and the fear was that we would go backwards again.

You just didn't know who was coming in and for me it was all about maintaining standards. Thankfully we have no worries on that front because Shane O'Neill knows exactly what he is doing and has a great backroom team in place.

In these uncertain times, that is good news for Galway for the future.

99

Printed in Poland
by Amazon Fulfillment
Poland Sp. z o.o., Wrocław

72388608R00134